Praise for *The Afterlife*

"Compassionate, amusing, intelligent, and abs[...] is an engaging and fact-rich new book in w[...] deceased lies easily alongside findings from qu[...] ...ory and truths from Spirit. Science is interwoven with stories, making important new ways of thinking accessible to nonmathematician readers. The book is as full of common sense as it is of vivid, real-life anecdotes and wisdom from the author's lifelong experience. An excellent read!"

— **Nancy Evans Bush, MA**, President Emeritus of
IANDS (International Association for Near-Death Studies)
and author of *The Buddha in Hell and Other Alarms*

"This is an amazing book. *The Afterlife Frequency* bridges ancient wisdom and contemporary science as it illuminates our emerging understanding of what Mark Anthony ... calls the *electromagnetic soul*. It is peppered with enlightening and entertaining professional narratives and personal experiences."

— from the foreword by **Gary E. Schwartz, PhD**,
author of *The Afterlife Experiments*

"Fast paced, emotionally gripping, and well written, this book will appeal to anyone seeking a rational way to understand the mysteries of life, death, and beyond death." — **Dean Radin, PhD**, author of *The Conscious Universe*

"Mark Anthony's *The Afterlife Frequency* is his most comforting and uplifting book yet. Anthony summarizes the compelling evidence of what happens to us after the death of our bodies, spicing his narrative with heartwarming and sometimes hair-raising stories drawn from his personal sensitivity to our spiritual side." — **Bruce Greyson, MD**, cofounder of IANDS
and Carlson Professor Emeritus of Psychiatry and
Neurobehavioral Sciences at University of Virginia

"Can we communicate with our deceased loved ones? This is one of humankind's most enduring questions. *The Afterlife Frequency* brings a new and exciting perspective to this ancient question. With each turn of the page, you will find a treasure trove of insights and inspiration. This outstanding book is expertly written, remarkably easy to read, and enthusiastically recommended." — **Jeffrey Long, MD**, oncologist, founder of NDERF
(Near-Death Experience Research Foundation) and author of the
New York Times bestselling *Evidence of the Afterlife*

"Woven together with fascinating case histories and a well-written narrative are suggested steps for harnessing our own heightened awareness, an understanding of the ongoing role the deceased can play in our lives, and a worldview that may encourage us to become more compassionate, more spiritual, and more loving. I highly recommend it!"

— **Kevin Todeschi**, executive director and CEO of the Edgar Cayce's A.R.E. (Association for Research and Enlightenment) and bestselling author of *Edgar Cayce on Reincarnation and Family Karma*

"The Afterlife Frequency incorporates important information about the history of this topic from both a religious and a scientific perspective. No matter how well read you are concerning life after death, I guarantee you will learn something new. Highly recommended."

— **Col. John Alexander, PhD**, Senior Special Forces US Army Officer (retired) and head of the US military's UFO project, Project Stargate, Los Alamos National Laboratory (retired)

"In this wonderful and instructive book, Mark Anthony provides many impressive examples about the impact of recognizable and verifiable communication with the spirits of deceased loved ones. He explains how spirits are pure energy that never dies, and that spiritual guidance, if properly recognized and accepted, can provide healing for mental, physical, emotional, and spiritual suffering."

— **Pim van Lommel, MD**, cardiologist and author *Consciousness beyond Life*

"This is a well-researched composition of historical documentation and modern references. By weaving together scientific data, psychic messages, and fascinating anecdotes, Mark Anthony provides an evidential case for proof of the afterlife."

— **William Buhlman**, training facilitator for out-of-body experiences (OBE) at the Monroe Institute and author of *Adventures beyond the Body*

"Mark Anthony has done it again. Whether you begin the walk with him from the point of spiritual synchronicity or plug into your new 'spiritual situational awareness' or are captivated by the beautiful stories, you will immediately find yourself in a Q and A with the scientific data, and wonder, 'Are there really *this* many faces of the Light of God?'"

— **Dr. Pat Baccili**, host of *The Dr. Pat Show* and founder of Transformation Talk Radio

"Mark Anthony describes and details the very mysteries of life and death — of electromagnetics, karma, heaven, and hell — in ways no one else does. Utterly fascinating!"

— **Dr. P. M. H. Atwater, LHD**, author of *The Forever Angels*

THE
AFTERLIFE
FREQUENCY

Also by Mark Anthony, JD
Psychic Explorer (aka The Psychic Lawyer)

Evidence of Eternity

Never Letting Go

THE
AFTERLIFE
FREQUENCY

The Scientific Proof
of Spiritual Contact
and How That Awareness
Will Change Your Life

MARK ANTHONY, JD

Foreword by GARY E. SCHWARTZ, PHD

New World Library
Novato, California

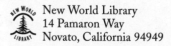 New World Library
14 Pamaron Way
Novato, California 94949

Text design by Tona Pearce Myers

Library of Congress Cataloging-in-Publication Data

Names: Anthony, Mark, date, author.
Title: The afterlife frequency : the scientific proof of spiritual contact and
    how that awareness will change your life / Mark Anthony ; foreword by
    Gary E. Schwartz,
Description: Novato, California : New World Library, [2021] | Includes
    bibliographical references. | Summary: "Drawing upon personal experi-
    ence and scientific theory, a noted spirit medium contends that human
    consciousness survives death and that the living can communicate with
    spirits of the deceased. The author shares personal stories and shows
    readers how they can learn to recognize and interpret messages from the
    spirit world"-- Provided by publisher.
Identifiers: LCCN 2021030128 (print) | LCCN 2021030129 (ebook) |
    ISBN9781608687800 (paperback) | ISBN 9781608687817 (epub)
Subjects: LCSH: Spiritualism. | Future life. | Mediums--Practice.
Classification: LCC BF1272 .A565 2021 (print) | LCC BF1272 (ebook) |
    DDC 133.9/1--dc23
LC record available at https://lccn.loc.gov/2021030128
LC ebook record available at https://lccn.loc.gov/2021030129

First printing, October 2021
ISBN 978-1-60868-780-0
Ebook ISBN 978-1-60868-781-7
Printed in Canada on 100% postconsumer-waste recycled paper

 New World Library is proud to be a Gold Certified Environmen-
tally Responsible Publisher. Publisher certification awarded by
Green Press Initiative.

10   9   8   7   6   5   4   3

This book is dedicated to Shirley MacLaine, a brilliant dancer and Academy Award–winning actress who is down-to-earth yet connected to the cosmos. She is a true spiritual pioneer who went out on a limb by being transparent about her metaphysical beliefs.

Thanks to you, dear Shirley, the genie is out of the bottle!

— Love and light, Mark

CONTENTS

Foreword

THE THIRST FOR TRUTH

by Gary E. Schwartz, PhD

> Eternal Light, Eternal Life.
> — MARK ANTHONY, *The Afterlife Frequency*

> We only have one life, and that life is eternal.
> — RHONDA EKLUND SCHWARTZ, author of *Love Eternal*

TO PUT IT BLUNTLY, this is an amazing book. *The Afterlife Frequency* bridges ancient wisdom and contemporary science as it illuminates our emerging understanding of what Mark Anthony, an Oxford-educated trial attorney licensed to practice law in Florida; in Washington, DC; and before the United States Supreme Court, calls the *electromagnetic soul* (EMS). It is peppered with enlightening and entertaining professional narratives and personal experiences that bring Mark's electromagnetic theory of the eternal soul to light (no pun intended). This book deserves to be enjoyed by millions of readers.

As a university scientist, I agree with Mark's basic theory about the physical underpinnings of the soul. I developed a similar theory in my book *The Living Energy Universe*, published twenty years ago, and illustrated aspects of it in my later books, including *The Afterlife Experiments* and *The Sacred Promise*. My terminology was more academic and unwieldy: I referred to this as "an electromagnetic dynamical info-energy system." Mark's electromagnetic soul terminology is much better, and his creative interweaving of historical explanations with personal illustrations is enlightening, inspiring, and fun.

I have witnessed Mark work as a professional medium in multiple settings, including his participation in mediumship research in my Laboratory for Advances in Consciousness and Health at the University of Arizona. Mark is a genuine psychic medium. His ability to obtain accurate and specific details regarding people's deceased loved ones is stellar. Like the very best mediums I have tested for over twenty years, he regularly gets "dazzle shots" that startle everyone, including himself. If there is anyone who experiences and demonstrates the reality of electromagnetic souls, it is Mark.

The Afterlife Frequency reviews many areas of soul science, from survival of consciousness after physical death and the primacy of consciousness, through spirit involvement in our lives and the controversial topic of hell, to evidence for divine intervention. At every step, Mark interweaves contemporary science with spiritual understanding in an engaging and energizing way. For example, in chapter 1, titled "Spiritual Synchronicity," Mark quotes a Buddhist priest who stated: "As the Western scientist Nikola Tesla said, 'What one man calls God, another calls the laws of physics.'...Life is energy; it is impossible to destroy energy; therefore the energy of life cannot be destroyed."

My inspiration for titling this foreword "The Thirst for Truth" involves an unexpected synchronicity I experienced while I was writing it. The morning I was scheduled to read Mark's book and write the foreword, the idea popped into my head that I should write a follow-up to my book *The Case for Truth: Why and How to Find Truth*, written with my lawyer colleague Alan Bourey, JD, that would focus on the drive to seek truth. The vision for this book was partly inspired by a line in the movie *Denial*, in which the chief British trial attorney explains that understanding the case against Holocaust denial requires an "appetite" for the knowledge. I considered two titles, "The Appetite for Truth" and "The Thirst for Truth," and chose the latter, partly for poetic reasons.

Imagine my surprise when I read the following words in chapter 2 of Mark's book: "Nothing was beyond Leonardo's thirst for knowledge, and the debate over the location of the soul within the human body presented a challenge he couldn't resist."

This is how I think about Mark. He is a genuine truth seeker and is evidence-based to his core. His approach to mediumship is like his approach to the law or science: to seek evidence with an open mind and follow the evidence where it takes him. Mark's thirst for accurate knowledge — for truth — is evident throughout *The Afterlife Frequency*. Furthermore, he reveals the adventure of being a psychic explorer.

This fact leads me to mention another synchronicity I experienced in reading Mark's book and writing this foreword. Originally I was planning to introduce my foreword with a quote from the distinguished fictional English professor Albus Percival Wulfric Brian Dumbledore, headmaster of Hogwarts School of Witchcraft and Wizardry in J.K. Rowling's Harry Potter series. A statement by Professor Dumbledore in the first novel struck me as great wisdom: "To the well-organized mind, death is but the next great adventure."

This profound statement emphasizes that it takes a well-organized mind, which Mark has in spades, to envision the great adventure that follows the death of the physical body. As *The Afterlife Frequency* reveals, Mark revels in adventures.

However, I didn't want to leave the impression that what Mark was writing about was fictional. So despite his connections to London and the University of Oxford as well as the appropriateness of Dumbledore's insight, I decided to delete the quote. Can you imagine my surprise when I read the following dialogue in chapter 3 of Mark's book?

> "Oh, my Gawd! The guests are heah! Be back inna few. Lemme know if yous need anything else."
> Rocky smiled. "Welcome to Harry Potter goes punk rock."
> "My friends in England joke there's no better time to connect with spirits than on a rainy night," I said. "It feels to me that we're definitely in the right place at the right time."

I wondered, was this subtle permission, if not encouragement, to quote Dumbledore's message?

I took a break from writing and decided to turn on the television. As I was flipping through the channels, I noticed that a movie was just starting titled *Harry Potter and the Order of the Phoenix*. After quickly calculating the statistical odds of this occurring by chance alone, I decided to watch the beginning of the movie. To my astonishment, the first scene involves Harry being brought to trial, and who appears to serve as his defense attorney? You guessed it — Professor Dumbledore.

I replayed the scene from my cable box, took screenshots of key images (I do this regularly when I track potentially meaningful synchronicities), and decided to end this foreword with the vision of the next great adventure.

I encourage you to read this book with a discerning, open mind coupled with an appreciative, open heart. The electromagnetic soul, with all of its implications, takes us one step closer to understanding an emerging multidimensional physics of consciousness and spirit. It also takes us another step closer to inventing future technologies that will make soul-to-soul communication — our ability to use technology to communicate with those who have graduated to the greater reality — both possible and practical. Our ten-year research program on what we call the SoulPhone fully supports Mark's theory and experiences.

Will this be another instance of "One small step for a man, one giant leap for humankind"?

The adventure continues.

$\rightharpoonup$

Gary E. Schwartz, PhD, is a professor of psychology, medicine, neurology, psychiatry, and surgery and director of the Laboratory for Advances in Consciousness and Health at the University of Arizona. He received his PhD at Harvard University and was a professor of psychology and psychiatry at Yale University and director of the Yale Psychophysiology Center. His books include *The Afterlife Experiments*, *The G.O.D. Experiments*, *The Energy Healing Experiments*, *The Sacred Promise*, *Super Synchronicity*, and *The Case for Truth* (with Alan Bourey, JD).

INTRODUCTION

I WAS BORN INTO A FAMILY where psychic and mediumistic abilities have spanned generations, so communicating with spirits is in my DNA. I've never viewed spirit contact as weird or something to fear. Unfortunately, many people doubt that spirit contact is possible and even fear it.

As someone who perceives and communicates with spirits regularly, this inspired me to question *how* it happens, *why* it happens, and *where* it happens. My quest for understanding led me to study aspects of the afterlife ranging from the cosmic to the subatomic. This journey has included examining different belief systems, ancient ruins, and unexplained phenomena at mystical hot spots around the globe. Just don't expect a dry read! I trudged through enough dry reads during law school, and I promised myself never to inflict that on anyone.

Many people fail to realize that contact with spirits is actually part of the human experience. For thousands of years people have reported accounts of near-death experiences (NDEs), shared death experiences, deathbed visions, and visitations by the spirits of deceased loved ones. These phenomena have been dubbed supernatural and paranormal. These buzzwords shroud these otherworldly encounters in the mysterious, unknown, and unprovable — and people tend to fear what they don't understand.

The common denominator of these phenomena is they're all forms of what I've termed *interdimensional communication*, which is an interface between our material dimension and the Other Side dimension. This book explains that this happens when the lower vibrational frequency of the human soul aligns with the higher vibration of the afterlife frequency.

The Afterlife Frequency offers scientific explanations for the many facets of interdimensional communication. It also demonstrates how both science and faith often describe the same phenomena through different filters.

The terminology associated with spirit communication has been stuck in the Victorian era for too long. *The Afterlife Frequency* brings the dynamics of spirit communication into the twenty-first century. Each chapter introduces a concept that lays the foundation for the succeeding chapters. To get the most out of this book, make sure to read the chapters in order. Each concept is illustrated by relatable, riveting, emotionally gripping, and uplifting stories — with a dash of humor.

The Afterlife Frequency is not about turning the reader into a medium, because not everyone is a medium. Some people are just more proficient at communicating with spirits than others. Let's face it: we're all good at different things, but no one excels at everything. I can bang around on a piano and I enjoy swimming, but this doesn't mean I'll end up becoming a concert pianist or winning a gold medal for swimming in the Olympics. Even though not everyone is a medium, everyone is capable of having a mediumistic experience and benefiting from it.

One of the key features of this book is the RAFT (recognize, accept, feel, and trust) technique. I developed this four-step process to guide the reader to become more aware of the presence of spirits and spot the signals and messages that we exchange with them. RAFT also provides insight into interpreting messages after the contact.

The Afterlife Frequency breathes new life into understanding the afterlife. It also delves deeply into the pain of grief, including post-traumatic stress disorder (PTSD), while credibly demonstrating how spirits intervene in our lives to help us.

This book also shows readers how to conduct themselves during communication with spirits through a medium. It guides readers to approach a mediumistic session with an open mindset and shows how to remove energetic blocks that can hinder the spirit communication process.

The Afterlife Frequency has been reviewed and endorsed by some of the world's top scientists and researchers in NDEs, consciousness survival, and spirit communication. Be that as it may, naysayers will simply reject the validity of spirit communication. On one end of the naysayer spectrum are those who believe in an afterlife but think spirit communication is somehow evil. Ironically, those who feel this way claim to follow religious texts that are filled with accounts of people who communicate with spiritual entities. On the other end of this spectrum are those who flat-out reject the possibility that life exists beyond physical death. They assert that spirit communication is fantasy and that attempts to prove it are based on pseudoscience. It is interesting to note that in the 1920s the concept of the cellphone was considered fantasy and pseudoscience.

The late subatomic physicist Freeman Dyson stated, "The public has a distorted view of science because children are taught in school that science is a collection of firmly established truths.

In fact, science is not a collection of truths. It is a continuing exploration of mysteries.... Science is the sum total of a great multitude of mysteries. It is an unending argument between a great multitude of voices. It resembles Wikipedia much more than it resembles the *Encyclopedia Britannica*."

During my tenure as a trial lawyer, I often represented people whose beliefs and behaviors I didn't approve of, much less agree with. Yet these people had an absolute right to be represented by an attorney. Similarly, while I may not agree with the opinions of naysayers, they have a right to their opinions. This right is called free speech.

A few years before the demise of the Soviet Union, I was part of a student group studying government in Moscow. The Russian people are amazing, and they live in a beautiful country filled with many natural and architectural wonders. Our hosts welcomed us graciously.

Our guide, however, was another matter entirely. In his late twenties, he was self-confident and often expressed pride in being a member of the Communist Party. He spoke English fluently with a thick Russian accent, and his lack of enthusiasm for keeping watch over a dozen American college kids was more than obvious. His continual lectures about the advantages of living under Marxism-Leninism prompted my classmates to nickname him "The Product of the State."

During one lecture, The Product of the State informed us that Lenin's vision of communism was the highest form of philosophical thought ever achieved by a human mind.

"Are you serious?" I blurted out.

My fellow students were aghast. The Product of the State glared at me as I continued, "You would have us believe that the highest form of philosophical thought ever achieved is — well — boring economic theory?"

"It is not wise to criticize Lenin or Soviet Union," he replied sternly.

"Yeah, but didn't you say earlier that the Soviet Union had the same freedoms as the United States?" The budding law student in me couldn't resist. "And didn't you also show us a copy of the Soviet Union's Constitution, which stated that citizens of the Soviet Union have the right of free speech?"

He walked over to where I was seated, leaned forward just inches from my face, and through clenched teeth said, "American boy — the difference between Soviet Union and United States is not freedom of speech. It is freedom *after* you make the speech."

I learned a lot that day. First, never take freedom for granted. Our freedoms of speech, press, and religion, and the right to vote and peacefully assemble, are both sacred and fragile.

The other lesson I learned was about fear. There are times when fear is justified and times when it isn't. Fear of what would happen to you after making a speech in Moscow's Red Square criticizing the tyranny of the totalitarian regime was absolutely justified.

Other fears aren't justified, because they're based on a primeval fear of the unknown. This is especially true of the many forms of interdimensional communication, which are feared because they're supernatural and paranormal. *The Afterlife Frequency* is about replacing this fear with the light of understanding that the supernatural is part of nature and that the paranormal is actually quite normal.

Chapter 1

SPIRITUAL SYNCHRONICITY

MYSTERIOUS FORCES BEYOND OUR UNDERSTANDING are not only at work in the universe but directly involved in our daily existence.

This may sound ominous, but it shouldn't be frightening. That's because these mysterious forces are energy. Everyone and everything is energy, which is part of an interconnected force. A well-known adage in the realm of quantum physics states that there is no matter, there is just energy, which vibrates at different frequencies. This is not philosophy — this is physics.

It's natural for people to fear the unknown. A mystery is an event or situation that is difficult to understand or explain. One of the greatest mysteries is what happens when we die. Do we cease to exist, or does our existence continue on beyond the material world?

There are logical and rational explanations for everything, even if what is required for them exceeds our current level of science and technology. This includes life after death. As Sir Arthur Conan Doyle, renowned psychic medium and creator of Sherlock

Holmes, wrote, "Once you eliminate the impossible, whatever remains, no matter how improbable, must be the truth."

Terms such as *energy, soul, spirits,* and *synchronicity* have become clichés in the study of life after death, as are statements like, "We're all interconnected," or "Everything happens for a reason." However, flinging around buzzwords and phrases doesn't explain the scientific basis for contact with the higher vibration of the afterlife frequency, which encompasses the existence of the soul, communication with spirits, near-death experiences, and deathbed visions — nor does it explain how we're all interconnected and how synchronicity is possible.

Synchronicity has seeped into our culture as a term used to describe events that seem to neatly fall into place, such as being in the right place at the right time, bumping into someone again and again, or experiencing a series of small coincidences that in hindsight feel destined. Of course, there's also a flip side, like being in the wrong place at the wrong time, taking an unexpected shortcut and ending up in an accident, or simply having a feeling of foreboding.

We experience both positive and negative events in our lives because everything is energy, which carries both positive and negative charges. Dean Radin, PhD, chief scientist at the Institute of Noetic Sciences (IONS) has stated, "The idea of the universe as an interconnected whole is not new; for millennia it's been one of the core assumptions of Eastern philosophies. What is new is that Western science is slowly beginning to realize that some elements of that ancient lore might be correct."

We now know from quantum physics that everything in our material world is composed of the same subatomic particles of electromagnetic energy, known as *quanta*. On the most basic level, all things, from the grains of sand on the beach to your blood cells to the nuclear reactions in the sun, are not only energy but energetically interconnected. All life is energy, and energy never dies.

Spirits are part of this great fabric of energy and of intelligence, which pervades and flows through this energy. Spirits are pure quantum electromagnetic energy and as such can transmit messages and signs to us, acting as a guiding force. This is how we can end up "at the right place at the right time." This is "spiritual synchronicity." The challenge is recognizing, accepting, feeling, and trusting the spirit communication.

It may appear far-fetched to believe that some mysterious spiritual energy could possibly influence our daily lives, but the greatest synchronistic anomaly of all is our very existence.

Everyone familiar with science fiction has heard of antimatter, the energetic opposite of matter, which has the same amount of mass as matter. For every particle of matter, there is a corresponding particle of antimatter. When matter and antimatter particles collide, they cause the most efficient explosion known to science, which results in total annihilation.

According to recent discoveries at CERN (the European Organization for Nuclear Research), the primordial matter-antimatter explosion known as the big bang should have left a total void in its aftermath — meaning that nothing should have been left over to create galaxies, planets, and life-forms. Christian Smorra, the lead scientist at CERN, reported, "All of our observations find a complete symmetry between matter and antimatter, which is why the universe should not actually exist."

This means there are forces beyond our understanding that influence our very existence. If energy never dies and we are all a part of and connected to this immortal composition, then these forces can also influence and be a source of guidance in our daily lives. Understanding this intellectually is one thing — experiencing it up close is quite another.

⌒

My travels have taken me to mystical locations around the globe. In my search for evidence of eternity, I once found myself at a breathtakingly beautiful Buddhist temple in the heart of Thailand's capital, Bangkok. I was there to hear a renowned Buddhist monk. What I didn't realize was how much I was about to learn about spiritual synchronicity.

Spirits, who are pure energy, are around us all constantly. As a psychic medium born with the ability to communicate with spirits, I'm aware of this energy on a daily basis, and this day in Bangkok was no exception. Although I was taking in every word of the speaker, I kept feeling the presence of several spirits around me. Spirits are never alone and tend to come forth in tandem as a collective, but my mind kept drifting to my father's sister Margery. It was an odd comfort, because even though I never met my Aunt Margery before she died, she had been a potent spiritual force in my life since I was a boy. A gifted psychic medium in her own right, she lived in an era when openly discussing the ability to communicate with spirits was considered taboo, if not demonic. But I had a different and special feeling about her. Margery was there with other spirits in force, and this meant I needed to be on my toes.

"Nothing is random," said the priest. "Negative things and positive things happen to everyone because of the chain of karma — the energy of balance, which flows through all of us."

The Buddhist priest paused as his words hung heavily in the humidity of the evening air. He sat on an elevated teakwood dais flanked by pots of colorful orchids in the great sanctuary of Bangkok's Wat Pho Temple. He was a quietly regal figure in an orange robe, his head shaven, his eyes exuding serenity with a hint of humor. A lifetime of yoga made him appear far younger than his seventy-four years.

Wat Pho Temple is home to the 150-foot-tall gold-leafed statue of the reclining Buddha, depicting the great sage during his last hours of earthly life. Fragrant sandalwood smoke wafted gently through the sanctuary as several other large statues of Buddha glittered serenely in the soft candlelight. Vast murals depicting Buddhist teachings decorated the walls, and intricately patterned columns soared upward to the ornate ceiling high above the marble floor. It was a beautiful, peaceful, and inspiring place.

The priest surveyed the scores of students kneeling respectfully before him. Even at night, the intense heat of Thailand permeated every inch of the temple, and sweat poured down my face like a minimonsoon.

There was little I could do to avoid drawing attention to myself. I was the only *farang* in attendance. *Farang* is the Thai word for "foreigner," most often used to describe white Europeans and Americans. Over six feet tall and awash in a sea of perspiration, I was hardly inconspicuous. But I was there to learn, and like the other students who had gathered there, I sat in the uncomfortable Vajrasana position. My legs and feet ached from kneeling for such a long time.

Even with the minor physical discomfort, I felt fortunate to attend this lecture on Buddhism, not only because of the exotic setting, but also because it was presented in English. My fellow students hailed from Thailand, Singapore, Hong Kong, Malaysia, Vietnam, and Japan. Thanks to the British Empire and American technology, English is widely spoken throughout the Far East. The downside for me was that being American doesn't always win popularity contests in Southeast Asia.

Despite Buddhism's firm belief in nonviolence, roughly two dozen Thai police officers were stationed in the temple to maintain order, or, worse, to counter a terrorist attack. Bangkok is a very tolerant and bustling metropolis of over eight million people. The capital of Thailand, it is also home to many diverse ethnic groups, who for the most part live in harmony but sometimes clash. The city is a lively, colorful, exotic, but at times dangerous place. It was difficult to distinguish the police from the military, since both wore camouflage fatigues and carried AK-47 automatic assault rifles. Their presence at the temple made for an odd juxtaposition.

Although my hosts at the temple welcomed me as a friend, the police were another matter. Under their intense scrutiny, I felt it wise to avoid making eye contact. I worried that I might accidentally do something offensive, like pointing the bottom of my bare foot at someone. In Thailand, the bottom of one's foot is considered the filthiest part of the body, and it's supremely insulting to point it at anyone. To do so toward a statue of the Buddha is a crime that can be punishable by imprisonment. With the police glaring at me and statues of Buddha everywhere, my concern was more than a little justified. As an attorney, I knew the last thing I wanted to experience was the Thai criminal justice system up close.

I felt a sense of relief as the priest broke his silence: "Not being subject to death is realizing death is an illusion, because physical death is not the end of the energy of life. Many of you wonder about this, for I can see in your eyes that all of you have suffered the death of a loved one." He looked down and continued in almost a whisper, "No one, including me, is immune from this pain."

The wise man's expression of his own personal grief touched everyone, including the police, whose intense demeanor appeared to lighten.

"The Buddha taught us that the one thing all human beings have in common is suffering," the priest continued. "In a sense we are all united by suffering, and the pain of losing a loved one is great suffering indeed.

"Nothing in this material world is permanent. As humans, we refuse to accept this, and that causes suffering. We grieve for a loved one, because we refuse to accept that no one lives in the material world forever.

"Death is when the life force or energy, which Buddhists and Hindus call *consciousness* and Christians, Jews, and Muslims call *the soul*, leaves the body. Consciousness is energy, and energy is an eternal stream, with neither a beginning nor an end. This is why death does not terminate life.

"As the Western scientist Nikola Tesla said, 'What one man calls God, another calls the laws of physics,'" the priest said, looking in my direction with a slight smile on his lips. "Life is energy; it is impossible to destroy energy; therefore the energy of life cannot be destroyed.

"Our consciousness may be eternal energy, but our existence in a physical body is temporary. We live in a finite state until we are liberated by death and rejoin this eternal energetic state. The body ceases to function and dies — so we have created the illusion of time as a means of measuring our experiences on earth.

"Experiences in life are not random. There is a reason why everything happens, and there are lessons to be learned from all these experiences.

"Bad things can happen to good people — good things can happen to bad people. This is the great teacher we call karma, and the lessons to be learned from our karma are not always immediately revealed. It can take a lifetime, or longer, to fully comprehend the lessons.

"Perhaps the death of someone you love is a lesson that you cannot control everything. There is nothing you can do about the death of a loved one. What you can control is how you react to the death."

He paused, leaped to his feet, clasped his hands in the prayer position, and bowed.

"To see the divine light in others, you have only to look — namaste!"

"Namaste!" the class replied in unison.

"Until next time," he smiled. "Assuming, of course, time exists!"

The priest took his leave, and the students rose. My knees were aching, but I took my time walking slowly toward the entrance of the temple, where our shoes were gathered on small shelves. The police had morphed back into their rigid selves. As much as I wanted to talk with my fellow students, I felt it best to put my shoes on outside the huge front doors and exit quietly.

Emerging from the tranquility of the temple, I reacted just in time to catch a projectile flung at my face.

"O sweaty psychic, drink of the holy water!"

"Thanks, Billy," I said, grateful for the bottle of cold water my best friend tossed at me. He came to meet me after the lecture.

"How did it go with your swami?"

"Swamis are Hindu — he's a Buddhist priest."

"Whatever, dude." Billy knew the difference, having lived in Asia for years.

In life there is the family we're born into, and then there are family members we choose. Billy was my chosen brother. We were eleven years old when we first met, and we went to school and then college together. He'd always been part of my life, and even if we didn't see each other for years, when we reconnected, it seemed like only yesterday.

After college, I went to law school, and Billy ventured to

Asia. He was a linguistic genius and without any formal train-ing learned to speak Japanese, Thai, Indonesian, and even some Cantonese. Being immersed in a language for a few weeks was all he needed to start speaking it. He was teaching English to Japanese executives in Tokyo and decided to take some time off and travel with me to Thailand. I could not have had a better guide.

Like me, Billy had been raised Catholic, but unlike me he was an atheist. Throughout our lives, we debated the existence of God and the afterlife. He felt it was all mythology. Natu-rally, I argued the other side, contending that eventually science would prove the existence of God and the afterlife.

"I still don't understand how you do the psychic thing," Billy said, "and I gotta admit, bro, when you're around, weird things happen. Enough philosophy," he said. "Let's have some fun."

"For me, today was fun."

"That's what you think! Wait till you get a load of what I've got planned," he laughed as he hailed down a tuk tuk.

A tuk tuk is a three-wheeled motorcycle/rickshaw hybrid. The front end looks like a motorcycle, and, like a rickshaw, it has two seats behind the driver. Tuk tuks are fast and maneuver-able and negotiate narrow spaces in a way a taxi can't. They're much cheaper than taxis, making them very popular in South-east Asia.

For Billy and me, traveling by tuk tuk was a great way to experience the sights and sounds of Bangkok. Unfortunately, we also experienced the smells of Bangkok, which meant inhaling thick exhaust fumes from the heavy traffic. My knuckles were white from gripping the bar in front of my seat as the tuk tuk weaved through the tight traffic at high speed.

Bangkok is a city of contrasts, as our new destination made quite clear. After leaving the orderly Buddhist tranquility of

Wat Pho Temple, we arrived at the energetic, hedonistic chaos of Patpong.

Patpong is comprised of two long parallel streets lined by nightclubs. Running straight through the middle of Patpong was a huge median that was an open-air market filled with tables covered by canopies and open for business. Market vendors haggled with customers over every type of merchandise imaginable, such as spices, medications, oriental rugs, jewelry, leather goods, clothing, furniture, and electronics. People from all over the world were there to buy, sell, gawk, and engage in X-rated pleasures.

Lights flashed and music blared from the go-go bars and sex clubs lining Patpong. As we walked through the market, Billy and I kept being approached by men and women holding signs advertising the various acts we could pay to engage in as they exclaimed, "Hey Charlie, special price for you!" "Charlie" was slang for an American male.

I thought the red-light district of Amsterdam was the lewdest place I'd ever seen, but Patpong made it look like Disneyland. The go-go bars offered live sex shows featuring ladies, boys, and "lady boys," as transgendered sex workers are called. Patpong boasts the largest population of lady boys in the world. Pleasure for a price was not only permitted — it was hugely advertised.

In my criminal defense practice, I've represented my share of sex workers, and I've seen how painful this life can be. I've also seen the discrimination endured by trans people. It is repulsive to see anyone enslaved by the sex trade, and Patpong drove that sentiment deep into my heart.

"Uh — Billy — are you serious?"

"About the hookers, no. We're going to the kickboxing match," he said, leading me away from a group trailing us and insisting, "Charlie, Charlie — this show for you!"

We entered a fight club. After haggling with the bouncer

at the door over the cover charge, we were admitted. Waitresses hustled, serving drinks from the bar under the glare of neon lights. A boxing ring was at the center of the club. We were seated at a ringside table.

Apparently it was intermission. A wiry man of about forty or so was in the boxing ring facing off against a large king cobra. The snake stood erect, its hood fully extended. It struck at him repeatedly as he nimbly dashed from side to side, avoiding its bite. The crowd cheered as he eluded the snake, whose bite contains enough venom to kill an elephant.

The cobra struck again, this time hitting its head hard against the mat, throwing it off balance. In a flash, the man grabbed the cobra just below its hood. The snake twisted powerfully in an attempt to wrap itself around his arm, but he quickly thrust it into a large canvas bag and tied the end closed with rope.

A round of beers arrived at our table. Normally, I don't drink, but after seeing that I needed one.

Halftime ended, and two young boxers entered the ring.

My father had been a boxer in the Navy, and we used to enjoy going to the fights, but this match was unlike anything I'd seen before. It was a blood sport. The two fighters went at each other with a vengeance. Punches and kicks flew with lightning speed. The crowd roared as blood and sweat splattered over the ring's ropes into the crowd.

After a few rounds, the loser collapsed and was dragged from the ring. The victor held his boxing gloves high above his sweaty bald head, shiny in the neon light. A bloody toothless grin revealed his years as a kickboxing veteran.

"Billy," I leaned over, "I'm going to call it a night. See you back at the hotel." I had had my fill of "entertainment" for the evening and was exhausted.

"No worries, bro," Billy said, ordering another beer.

Once outside the kickboxing club, I stepped out into Patpong and immediately felt negative energy closing in on me. A tingling sensation ran through my body, meaning the presence of spirits. An image of Aunt Margery flashed in my mind's eye. I was being alerted that something bad was about to happen. An urgent need to leave, and fast, surged through me.

Before I could move, a commotion erupted a few feet in front of me. Two white men — Australians, from their accents — were arguing. Both were in their twenties, very muscular, and towered over the native Thais surrounding them. With their angry, slurred speech, these guys sounded drunk. The situation was escalating in a very bad way.

Crowds of onlookers surrounded the quarrel, and my exit was blocked, as I was suddenly in the middle of curious Thais on one side and argumentative Australians on the other.

"Piss off! She's mine! I paid for her!" one of the Australians yelled at the other.

A young Thai woman stood between them with her arms outstretched.

"Stop, please, do not fight!" she pleaded.

"You bastard!" the other Australian roared as he swung at the other man, who dodged the punch, which instead landed right in the Thai woman's face. She hit the ground, out cold.

"You hit my whore!"

The Thais couldn't care less if two white farang devils fight or even kill each other, but when a farang hits a Thai woman, that's another matter entirely. Rage surged through the crowd as Thai men instantly fell on and attacked the Australians with punches and kicks. The Australians punched back, and another Thai went down — this time a young man.

Women screamed as more Thai men entered the fray and

began jumping on the cursing and screaming Australians, who fought back with everything they had. Within seconds, the violence swept through the crowd, which erupted into a free-for-all. People were fighting in every direction.

I tried to break free of the crowd, but my escape was cut off as the angry crowd closed ranks behind me. Bottles flew from every direction. I was caught in the center of the mayhem. People started punching and throwing bottles at me, assuming I was one of the dirty white farang devils who dared hit a Thai woman.

Whistles blew, meaning the police were now on the scene. Farang started this brawl, and I had no doubt the police were going to arrest every farang there, meaning the two drunken Australians and me.

What I knew of the Thai legal system flooded my head, and it wasn't good. I'd learned from attorneys in Bangkok that innocent until proven guilty didn't exist here! No right to a phone call, no first appearance before a judge, no right to bail, and certainly no right to an attorney. A conviction was practically guaranteed. Being incarcerated anywhere is miserable, but from what I'd heard, Thai prisons are hell on earth. Prisoners in Thailand often starve to death, because jails don't feed them — that's up to their families.

The sea of combatants encircling me was out of control. Dozens of police officers wielding weapons plowed into the crowd, making a beeline toward the Australians. Trapped, I was terrified for my life.

"Dear God," I prayed, "please! I need a miracle, and I need it now."

At that moment, a young boy pushed between the rioters and grabbed my hand, yanking it. I couldn't help noticing how skinny he was and how bony was his grasp.

"Charlie! Charlie! You come with me now!"

Intuition immediately told me this skinny kid was my ticket out of there. He pulled me to the ground, and we crawled toward the tables in the market as people stumbled over us. Blows and kicks hit me until we reached temporary shelter under a table.

"Come, Charlie!" he pointed to a dilapidated tuk tuk parked at the far end of the table. Because of its run-down condition, I wondered if it was even drivable.

We scrambled on hands and knees for about fifty feet beneath the tables. Glass from broken bottles shattered around us as the violence intensified. My hands and knees started bleeding as we crawled over shards of glass.

At the end of the table, the kid sprang to his feet, stood before the tuk tuk, and shouted, "You pay me now!"

I wasn't in the mood to haggle, so I pulled out a $100 bill. "Get me out of here!"

At the time, the average Thai made about $300 per year. I was waving more money than this kid had probably ever seen at one time.

"No problem, Charlie!" He flew into the driver's seat, grabbed the handlebars, and tried to kick-start the tuk tuk. It smoked and backfired. I jumped into the passenger seat as the ignition sputtered and the tuk tuk lurched forward — this pile of junk actually worked!

Revving the engine full throttle, he drove right into the crowd.

People leaped out of the way as bottles continued to fly, many aimed at us. The kid zoomed the tuk tuk over the center median of Patpong.

A cop jumped in front of us and blew his whistle, ordering us to stop. The kid barely missed him as the tuk tuk swerved around the cop at escape velocity. We sped to the main drag off

Patpong, veering to avoid oncoming traffic and leaving the riot in the rearview.

There's an old expression saying that money talks, but that night in Bangkok, it did a lot more than that.

"Charlie — you need me tomorrow?" my driver beamed, dropping me off at my hotel twenty minutes later.

"Uh — we'll see — thank you — so why me — why did you help me?"

"I know you help me," he beamed.

I helped *you?*

"You good man. You not hit lady. *Chock-dee-na*, Charlie!" he said, wishing me good luck in Thai.

"*Chock-dee-na*," I replied as the backfiring tuk tuk sped away.

Once in my hotel room, I washed the blood off and pulled slivers of glass from hands and knees, then collapsed on my bed. I was exhausted but too wound up to sleep. My mind was swirling, trying to process everything.

About an hour later, Billy entered, looking three sheets to the wind, and sat on his bed.

"Bro — there was a huge riot out front of the bar — glad you left before it happened."

"Not exactly," I said and explained how I escaped arrest with the help of a skinny twelve-year-old future Motocross champion.

"Okay, so you're a lawyer, psychic, and now what? Indiana Jones?" Billy laughed.

"According to the priest I saw today, everything is synchronicity — everything happens for a reason."

Billy interjected, "Carl Jung believed in synchronicity, that nothing is random, that there's no such thing as a coincidence, because everything is part of a deeper order."

"You're a creature of contradictions, Billy. I didn't think you believed in a divine order."

"Mark, don't you always say we have to keep an open mind?" He smiled. "Look where you are — in Thailand, having the time of your life, seeing and learning things you've only dreamed about — and tonight, you were in the right place at the right time for Tuk Tuk Kid to save your ass. Of course, I like to take a more practical view of synchronicity, like Ray Kroc."

"Wait — what — the CEO of McDonald's?"

"Ray Kroc said the two most important elements for success are being in the right place at the right time, and second, doing something about it."

"So what's your point?"

Billy beamed, reached for the telephone on the table between our beds, and put the receiver to his ear.

"Who are you calling, Billy?"

"It's Copernicus. He says you're not the center of the universe."

"What?"

"Don't you get it, Mark? Tuk Tuk Kid was in the right place at the right time, saw an opportunity, and grabbed it. You gave him enough money to feed his family for a year. This isn't all about you getting rescued. Sure, that was part of it, but did it occur to you that maybe you were directed there for the kid as much as he was there for you?"

"What about the Australian guys?" I wondered aloud.

"They chose to start a fight — maybe that was their karma. Think about it, dude — right now *you* could be sitting next to them in the same cell."

"I can't stop thinking of that, and but for the grace of God..."

"Goes Tuk Tuk Kid!" Billy interjected. "Synchronicity, bro — nothing is a coincidence, because everything happens for a reason."

Chapter 2

THE LIGHT OF THE ELECTROMAGNETIC SOUL

ARISTOTLE IS CREDITED WITH posing the paradox, "What came first — the chicken or the egg?"

At first blush, this may appear to simply be an exercise in rhetoric — asking a question for which there seems to be no answer. The point of such an exercise is to sharpen one's skills for debate, reasoning, and abstract thought.

Although most rhetorical questions do not require a direct answer, this one does. An egg must be laid by a chicken, and in order for a chicken to lay the egg, a chicken must first exist, which can only happen after it is hatched from an egg. So which one was the cause and which one was the result — the chicken or the egg? Chickens exist, and there is a logical explanation for their genesis, whether we have discovered the answer or not.

What the ancient Greeks were actually asking went far beyond poultry. The real question was, "What came first — consciousness or the brain?"

Consciousness is the term used by philosophers and psychologists to describe the unique sense of self that separates one from everyone and everything else in existence. It gives each of us our individuality and contains the attributes that bestow us with our uniqueness. These attributes include personality, observations, experiences, knowledge, and love for others. In layman's terms, this is known as *mind*. It is called the *soul* or *spirit* by people of faith; the *brain's electrical field* by medical professionals; and the *quantum electromagnetic energy field within the brain* by physicists.

Consciousness encompasses more than mere self-awareness and the ability to perceive and interact with the material world dimension. Nor is it limited by the scope of our five physical senses of sight, hearing, smell, taste, and touch. As pure energy, consciousness is capable of perception beyond the material world to the dimensions of the Other Side. Because the soul/consciousness is energy, it is eternal and lives on even after physical death.

Survival of consciousness beyond physical death is not hocus-pocus or wishful thinking. I know this from firsthand experience, because I'm a psychic medium who was born with the ability to perceive and communicate with spirits. The afterlife is not just a matter of subjective opinion based on my personal experiences communicating with spirits. There is a logical explanation for the existence of the soul, the afterlife, spirit communication, and synchronicity, which can be explained through quantum physics.

Quantum physics! Please resist the urge to put this book down for fear of being assaulted by a barrage of mathematical equations. Spoiler alert! That's not happening here! This chapter may be a tad technical, but it is essential for grasping the stories and concepts that follow it. Instead of climbing the cliffs of complex calculations, we will sail smoothly through history and the concepts that reveal how I developed the term *electromagnetic soul*.

The debate over what came first, the consciousness or the brain, has been going on since long before Aristotle. It brings us further back through the mists of time, four thousand years ago, to India and the world's oldest continuously practiced religion, Hinduism. Hindus refer to the soul as the *atman*. They believe the atman preexists the human body and is eternal. The atman goes through a series of incarnations, a process known as reincarnation, until it no longer needs to return to the material world.

Meanwhile, according to tradition, in the Middle East, the patriarch Abraham was born sometime around 1800 BC, during the Bronze Age, in present-day Iraq. Judaism, Christianity, and Islam all trace their roots to the patriarch Abraham, which is why they're known as the Abrahamic religions. For the most part, the followers of these faiths embrace the belief that the soul preexists the body, comes into the body at birth, and leaves it at physical death.

Twelve centuries after Abraham, around 600 BC, Siddhartha Gautama, better known as the Buddha, emerged on the spiritual scene in India. Although Buddha did not express belief in a soul per se, he referred to the mind as "that which is aware." Buddhists also believe in reincarnation. They hold that each living being has a continuity or stream of consciousness that flows from one life to the next.

Two centuries after the birth of Buddhism, the ancient Greek philosophers posed the paradox of poultry, about whether the body and the consciousness were one or separate.

By the seventh century after the birth of Jesus, Christianity had become the dominant belief system in Europe, while Islam spread throughout North Africa, the Middle East, and eventually as far east as Indonesia. Although these faiths have emphasized the importance of peace, it's a gross understatement to say that their followers have not always coexisted peacefully. Yet despite their differences, Christians and Muslims agree in principle that God exists, and the soul is immortal.

For the next thousand years, during the medieval era in the West, also known as the Age of Faith, the debate over whether the soul and body were separate was apparently settled. In this period, the concept of separation of church and state was unknown. Practically every country on earth was a form of theocracy, meaning that religion and government were tightly intertwined. For people who questioned religious dogma, or who had the ability to perceive and communicate with spirits, this was a dangerous time. As the "Psychic Lawyer," I would be remiss if I didn't briefly digress to explain what happened to these people in that era.

Imagine that it is the tenth century AD in either Christian Paris or Islamic Cairo. (Take your pick, because both were essentially theocracies.) If you walked into the city square and announced that you were an atheist, or, even worse, could see the spirits of dead people, you would immediately be arrested and charged with heresy and/or witchcraft. This would be followed by your complete confession, no doubt exacted through excruciating torture. The formality of a trial came next, in an ecclesiastical court in Paris, or in a sharia law court in Cairo. No matter. In either system of justice, you would be found guilty and sentenced to being the entertainment at an upcoming stoning, burning, beheading, or some other hideous form of public execution.

The legal systems in theocracies may not have been fair by modern-day standards of justice, but they were predictable. Freedoms we take for granted, such as free speech and freedom of belief, simply did not exist in this era.

Fortunately, the material world is constantly changing, and

to paraphrase the Buddha, the only thing that is permanent is impermanence.

Enter the Age of Discovery in the sixteenth century. Cultures around the globe began to trade and interact with one another. An influx of new ideas and concepts flooded into Europe, which experienced huge technological advancement. European kings welcomed the benefits of science with enthusiasm, especially when it came to military technology. Native Americans, on the other hand, were less than thrilled about being "discovered." Sub-Saharan Africans shared this lack of enthusiasm, because millions of them were captured and forced into slavery by Europeans. Thus began the rise of the European colonial empires, which occupied countries around the globe until the empires' demise after the Second World War.

The Age of Discovery coincided with the Renaissance, which was the artistic, political, cultural, philosophical, and economic rebirth of Europe. Advances in science eventually led to the development of the scientific method: the process of identifying a question, developing a hypothesis about it, and then solving it through objective analysis, data collection, and experimentation. This led to a growing class of intellectuals, who began to openly question whether the concepts of a soul and an afterlife were merely mythological or could be proved through the scientific method.

Leonardo da Vinci may have been the first to apply the scientific method to the study of the soul. He was an inventor, painter, sculptor, architect, engineer, and scientist who arguably possessed one of the greatest minds the earth has produced. Leonardo's genius enabled him to conceive of inventions far beyond the technology of his day. Case in point: he drew plans for a helicopter five centuries before one could actually be constructed.

Da Vinci's charming manner enchanted both political and religious leaders, enabling him to maneuver through the rigidity of Italian society, which was still controlled by the Catholic Church. On the other hand, he bent Church rules, ignored the norms of society, and somehow managed to get away with it unscathed. Leaders of the establishment may not have always approved of what he did, but they couldn't deny Leonardo's artistic and scientific genius, so they tended to give him a pass.

In the intellectual circles of Leonardo's day, the question was not whether the soul existed, but where it resided in the human body. Many believed it was in the heart, known as the *cardiocentric soul*, while others believed it was in the brain, the so-called *cephalocentric soul*.

Nothing was beyond Leonardo's thirst for knowledge, and the debate over the location of the soul within the human body presented a challenge he couldn't resist. Unlike his colleagues, who were content to debate this philosophical question while sipping fine wines in the piazzas of Italy, da Vinci was a man of action, who believed the answer to this spiritual quest lay in science.

Although dissecting human corpses was banned and severely punished by the Catholic Church, da Vinci's anatomical search involved quite a bit of dissection. As usual, he avoided Church scrutiny and conducted his research in secret. He spent years collecting data from ancient and contemporary sources and then applying the scientific method to his own observations and studies. Leonardo's research indicated that the heart, while a magnificent organ, is essentially a pump. He concluded that the *sensus communis* (common sense) location of the soul was in the intricate and complex brain. Once again, Leonardo da Vinci was centuries ahead of his time.

In the seventeenth century, French mathematician and

philosopher René Descartes rocked the world of faith with his groundbreaking *Meditations on First Philosophy*. Descartes, like da Vinci before him, used dissection, mostly of animals, in order to study brains. He believed that understanding the structure of brains could lead to discovering the location of the consciousness. His objective was to prove the existence of God and the immortality of the soul. The centerpiece of his work is the statement "I think, therefore I am." His doctrine became known as *Cartesian dualism*, meaning that the sense of self doesn't come from the material body, but from the soul, an energetic entity separate from the body.

The later seventeenth century brought the Age of Enlightenment and scientific superstar Sir Isaac Newton, whose genius influences us to this day. He was one of the early developers of calculus and posited the theory of gravity and the laws of motion, which are basic to the study of physics.

There was another side to Great Britain's Sir Isaac. He was a man of deep faith, who actually spent more time searching for hidden messages in biblical passages than he did studying science. Newton believed in God, but not in an immortal human soul. For Newton, consciousness and thought were a by-product of the brain rather than an immaterial force without physical substance that existed after the death of the human body.

Newton and his followers gave rise to *reductive materialism*: the belief that only the material world is real and that everything in the universe is made of physical matter. All physical matter, when reduced to its most basic level, can be observed as molecules, which are in turn composed of atoms (ergo, "reductive materialism"). According to this school, the buck stopped at atoms and molecules — end of the material world story.

The Enlightenment intensified the divide between faith and science. Walls grew up between the two camps. The faithful saw the scientific community, who rejected God and the afterlife, as heretical and atheistic. The scientific community looked down their academic noses at the faithful as followers of primitive, unsubstantiated, and unprovable mythological beliefs.

By the nineteenth century, science was in its heyday. One of the great leaps forward in physics occurred in 1873 when the Scottish genius James Clerk Maxwell released his book *A Treatise on Electricity and Magnetism*. Through a series of mathematical equations, Maxwell explained how all electromagnetic phenomena, which include visible light, as well as all other, invisible forms of electromagnetic energy, radiate over a broad range of frequencies and wavelengths. To top it off, Maxwell's equations indicated that this invisible energy exists everywhere throughout the universe.

Building on Maxwell's equations, Germany's Heinrich Hertz proved the existence of radio waves in 1886. Italian engineer and inventor Guglielmo Marconi found a practical application for radio waves as a means of transmitting information and in 1901 conducted the first transatlantic radio signal from England to Newfoundland. The era of wireless communication began, and by 1906 human voices and music were broadcast on radio. Within a few decades the form of electromagnetic energy known as radio waves had gone from science fiction to science fact.

The divide between faith and science began to dissolve at the dawn of the twentieth century. A new age of scientific celebrities emerged that included physicists Albert Einstein, Max Planck, Werner Heisenberg, Karl Schwarzschild, Niels Bohr, Louis de Broglie, Erwin Schrödinger, and Richard Feynman, not to mention engineering geniuses Nikola Tesla, Thomas Edison, and George Westinghouse.

In defense of Sir Isaac Newton and his band of reductionist

materialists, they were limited by eighteenth-century technology, whereas the pioneering physicists of the twentieth century were not. Advanced technologies led this new generation of scientific explorers to discover that atoms were not the minutest particles in existence: they are actually composed of even smaller particles, known as *electrons*, *protons*, and *neutrons*. The shocker was the discovery that protons and neutrons are made of even smaller, more basic particles of electromagnetic energy known as *quanta* (*quantum* in the singular) — hence the term *quantum physics*. Electrons, which have a negative electrical charge, are much smaller than protons and neutrons. The mass of an electron is roughly 1/1,800 of the mass of a proton. In other words, electrons are quantum particles. This discovery revealed that everything, at its most basic level, is composed of energy.

In a conversation, parapsychologist Dean Radin, chief scientist of IONS (Institute of Noetic Sciences), explained to me that the energetic reality discovered by physics includes "gravity, nuclear strong, nuclear weak, and electromagnetism. There is also dark energy and dark matter, which are thought to comprise 95 percent of the universe — assuming our current cosmology is correct."

The discussion of these forces can and does fill volumes of books, but it is electromagnetic energy that is the key to understanding life after death, spirit communication, synchronicity, and the afterlife frequency. On a subatomic level, everything in our material world, including us, is, at the most basic level, composed of electromagnetic energy, which also happens to be the same energy that is housed in the human brain.

I have developed the term *electromagnetic soul* because I believe this best describes what we really are — eternal consciousness, which is pure electromagnetic energy. This is my twenty-first-century term, which bridges the divide between the spiritual and the scientific. People of faith believe that the soul/spirit preexists the body and that when the body dies, it lives on. The laws of physics state that energy is neither created nor destroyed, only transferred from one form into another. The soul is electromagnetic energy, which is neither created by the brain nor destroyed at the death of the brain — ergo, the electromagnetic soul, EMS for short.

In this book, I will refer to the electromagnetic soul that has been released from the body as a *spirit*. This is for the sake of brevity, especially during stories involving communication with spirits. However, kindly keep in mind that in this book, the terms *spirit* and *electromagnetic soul* describe the same thing.

The EMS is not some fanciful metaphor. It is an established fact that the brain has an electrical field. For decades brainwave frequencies have been mapped and studied through the EEG (electroencephalogram) and QEEG (quantitative electroencephalogram), which are devices used to measure electrical activity within the brain. However, conventional biomedical research focuses almost entirely on the activity of brain cells, known as *neurons*, which are essentially the wiring of the brain. The mainstream biomedical position is that consciousness is a by-product of the chemical and electrical functions of the brain, although exactly how this happens is unknown.

Nonetheless, since the 1920s, an electromagnetic field theory of consciousness has been advocated by several scientists. Unfortunately, their work has been considered to be fringe elements and therefore outside the scientific mainstream. Fortunately, this line of thinking is changing with a new generation of researchers in the twenty-first century. Discoveries by scientists such as Gary Schwartz, Johnjoe McFadden, Shelli Joye, Stuart Hameroff, and Sir Roger Penrose have reinforced the understanding that electromagnetic energy is the basis for consciousness.

An important question arises: Why don't scientists solve this dilemma once and for all by using technology to tune in to the afterlife frequency and communicate with electromagnetic souls? The answer may be that while EEG and QEEG are extremely useful for medical research and diagnoses, they're not sensitive enough, nor are they designed to identify the electromagnetic soul, much less tune in to the afterlife frequency.

Shelli Renée Joye, PhD, of the California Institute of Integral Studies has theorized that consciousness may operate at much higher frequencies than those currently being examined through EEG waveform studies. Dr. Joye has stated, "It is entirely feasible that there are specific ranges of harmonic frequencies that interact with mind-brain systems through resonance at far higher frequencies than currently supposed."

Not to worry, though! Technology sensitive enough to tune in to the afterlife frequency and communicate with electromagnetic souls is being developed by Dr. Gary Schwartz of the University of Arizona (author of the foreword to this book). He is head of the SoulPhone Project, which will be discussed in much greater detail in chapter 7.

Twenty-first-century advances in science and quantum physics continue to expand at exponential rates. Quantum physics can explain the electromagnetic soul, the afterlife frequency, spirit communication, near-death experiences, our mutual interconnectedness, and synchronicity. One of the originators of string theory, Dr. Michio Kaku, has even said, "Eternal life does not violate the laws of physics." It is common scientific knowledge that the brain and nervous system have electrical fields. The first law of thermodynamics in physics states that energy can neither be created nor destroyed, only transferred from one form to another. This means that the electromagnetic soul preexisted the brain. It also means that when the brain dies, the energy within it does not cease to exist but is transferred, meaning that the electromagnetic soul survives physical death.

Many people may find it difficult to accept the concepts of the electromagnetic soul and life after death. This is because it's easy to deny phenomena one doesn't understand by proclaiming that there is no scientific basis for them or that they're merely fantasy.

However, just because something is outside of one's realm of expertise or understanding doesn't mean it doesn't exist. There is a logical and scientific basis for everything, whether or not our current level of science and technology can explain it. Until science can explain phenomena that people don't understand, these phenomena tend to be dismissed as unbelievable. Nonetheless, as astrophysicist Neil deGrasse Tyson has observed, "The beauty of science is you don't have to believe it for it to be true." The amazing aspect of science is that it isn't static, and through science our understanding of creation expands daily.

IT'S ONE THING TO HAVE A PHILOSOPHICAL DISCUSSION about consciousness and discuss the afterlife in terms of physics, but quite another to witness it firsthand, as Kristen and her brother, Alfred, did when their mother, Ingrid, died. I met them at an afterlife symposium, and they were eager to share with me how they witnessed evidence of the electromagnetic soul.

Kristen started: "Our mother, Ingrid, was born in 1927 in Frankfurt, Germany. She was an only child. Her parents were Andrea and Peter. Like our mom, we called them 'Mutti' and 'Vati,' which in German means 'Mommy' and 'Daddy.'

"Mom grew up in Hitler's Germany," Kristen continued.

"Her family was one of the few lucky ones. They survived the war. Vati — our grandfather — worked in a government office, so he never saw combat. Even so, Frankfurt was a major city and was bombed heavily, so it was pretty much just rubble by the end of the war."

"When Germany surrendered," Alfred interjected, "the US military occupied Frankfurt. Our mom said her family was terrified of the American troops."

"Until she met Edward — our Dad," Kristen added. "Mom said he was so handsome. He was a second lieutenant in the US Army. He treated her with the utmost respect; even Mutti and Vati adored him. They fell in love and were married in early 1946.

"I know this is a long story, Mr. Anthony, but we needed to talk to you."

"Go on." I was curious.

"So Dad," Kristen continued, "was a career Army officer and signed up for twenty years. He was stationed at US bases around the world. Mom loved it — she liked the travel — and well, they had six kids. We're the two youngest."

"Dad should have retired in '65," Alfred said, "but when the Vietnam War started heating up, he reenlisted. Mom wasn't happy about that."

"She was right," Kristen looked down. "Dad was killed in action during the Tet Offensive in 1968."

"I'm sorry to hear that," I said.

"Dad's death crushed our mom. She'd just turned forty, and all of a sudden, she was a widow and a single mother with six kids. Alfred was just a toddler when our dad died."

"Mom was a real trouper," Alfred added. "She was always optimistic. Never let life get her down. She worked two jobs, raised us, and made us go to church every Sunday.

"After we all left home, our mom kept the family house. Kristen and I lived nearby. For years things were fine, but when she was in her mid-eighties, we knew something wasn't right. She started getting very forgetful, so we took her to a neurologist who specialized in geriatrics. Mom had Alzheimer's disease."

"Our mom was tough," Kristen said. "She insisted on living alone, but it got to the point where she couldn't, and we had to place her in a nursing home."

"Then things got bad." A tear rolled down Alfred's cheek. "The Alzheimer's progressed. She was disoriented — didn't even recognize us, thought her grandkids were strangers. Things went from bad to worse, and she was bedridden. Mom was totally nonresponsive — she lapsed into a coma."

"I'm very sorry to hear this," I told Kristen and Alfred, "but I have a feeling Ingrid's story doesn't end there."

"We had a family meeting, and it was decided that since Alfred and I lived closest to the nursing home, we should be in charge of Mom's treatment and care. I was designated as health-care surrogate, but we both checked on her every day."

"Dr. Kathy Rose, Mom's doctor, said her brain was so severely damaged by the Alzheimer's that she was incapable of speech and would never regain consciousness."

I sensed mounting tension between the two siblings.

"Kristen insisted on a feeding tube to keep Mom alive," Alfred explained, "even though the outcome was a foregone conclusion. It was six weeks of hell, waiting for the call. Then it came — the nursing home called, and we were informed our mother was actively dying.

"We hauled butt to the nursing home," Alfred continued. "Dr. Rose was already at Mom's bedside along with a nurse."

"Tell me what happened, step-by-step," I asked.

"Dr. Rose told us her vital signs were slowing. Kristen agreed to have the feeding tube removed, because it wasn't doing any good. The doctor told us she was sorry, and that it wouldn't be long. I'll never forget seeing the nurse pull the feeding tube out of Mom." Alfred sobbed, shielding his eyes with his hands.

Kristen continued, "I know this sounds strange, but for me, her dying almost felt like a formality. She'd been incoherent and then in a coma. It felt like we'd lost her a long time ago; we just wanted her suffering to be over."

"But then ..." Kristen looked up at me.

"But then what?"

"Suddenly Mom opened her eyes."

"It was so weird," Alfred interjected. "She was really frail, but she lifted her head and said 'Alfred, Kristen — you're such delightful children.'"

"We were stunned. All we could say was 'Mom! We love you!'"

"Give me a hug before I go."

"Kristen was on one side of the bed," said Alfred, "I was on the other, so we leaned over and hugged her. It was amazing!"

"This is incredible!" I remarked.

"Yeah, but wait." Alfred was shaking. "Mom looked from side to side at both of us — I mean really looked into our eyes. She knew who we were. Then she looked between us, stared at the foot of her bed, and said, 'Edward! My love! You came!' And I said, 'Mom, Daddy's dead — you're hallucinating.'"

"I knew she wasn't," Kristen cut her brother short and continued. "Mom was still staring toward the foot of the bed, and then she looked a little to the left. He eyes lit up, and she said, '*Mutti! Vati! Danke, dass Sie für mich gekommen sind.*'"

"At first I thought she'd gone incoherent again and was babbling, but she wasn't — she was speaking German!"

"My German is rusty, Kristen," said Alfred, "but sounds like she said something about her parents."

"'Mommy! Daddy! Thank you for coming for me,'" Kristen clarified.

"Alfred and I were shocked. She saw Daddy, then Mutti and Vati — our grandparents — and thanked them for coming to get her! Then her head sank back into her pillow, she closed her eyes, and expired."

"I kinda went off a bit on Dr. Rose," Alfred said. "I wanted to know how this was possible. I mean, Mom had Alzheimer's. She was brain damaged! She was in a coma! Dr. Rose said she'd never talk again! I asked the doctor how Mom could just wake up, recognize us, and speak coherently in English and then in German? How was this possible?"

"What did the doctor say?" I asked.

"The neurologist stood there staring at Mom's body and then said, 'My God. I think we've just witnessed terminal lucidity.'"

MEDICAL SCIENCE IS CURRENTLY AT A LOSS to explain how 10 percent of nonresponsive terminally ill and brain damaged people suddenly regain full consciousness and mental clarity prior to death. This phenomenon has been labeled *terminal lucidity* by German researcher and biologist Michael Nahm.

Dr. Nahm and his colleagues Dr. Bruce Greyson, Emily Kelly, and Erlendur Haraldsson also discovered that terminal lucidity has been observed for thousands of years, from Hippocrates, "the Father of Medicine" in ancient Greece, to classical intellectuals such as Cicero and Plutarch up to the present day. Their research also showed that advances in the study of the human brain over the past 250 years have enabled doctors to more precisely identify mental disorders in patients who experienced terminal lucidity.

These advances have led to an astonishing revelation. For centuries, doctors have observed that terminal lucidity is not limited to one type of mental disorder. It occurs in an extremely wide array of mental impairments, such as Alzheimer's disease, dementia, brain tumors, brain abscesses, meningitis, strokes, schizophrenia, and affective disorders.

As observed by Professor Alexander Batthyány of the University of Vienna, terminal lucidity defies medical science not only because it happens but because it happens in such a broad range of mental disorders, each of which damage the brain in different ways. This can mean everything from brain cancer, brain tumors, meningitis, stroke, dementia, severe mental illness, and many other neurodegenerative disorders. If terminal lucidity occurred in only one type of brain disorder, there would be an obvious biological explanation for how and why it occurs.

Dr. Nahm agrees. "I do have my doubts that it can be explained biochemically. When you see terminal lucidity in the context of all the other end-of-life experiences or near-death phenomena, they all seem to point to the fact that human consciousness is not tied to a one-to-one relation to the brain physiology. I find that very, very interesting. This can tell us many important things about the nature of our consciousness."

One thing all neuroscientists agree on is that the cerebral cortex doesn't suddenly grow billions of new neurons prior to death. Yet terminal lucidity continues to defy medical and scientific explanation — or does it?

Traditionally, science has been split into two main groups: biological and physical. Biological science, which includes medicine, is the study of living organisms. The physical sciences focus on the study of inorganic materials such as chemicals, molecules, atoms, and energy. However, the difference between biology and physics is irrelevant at the subatomic level, since everything is composed of quanta — aka electromagnetic energy.

This indicates that the common denominator in terminal lucidity isn't the type of brain disorder; it is electromagnetic energy. According to the Astrophysics Science Division at NASA, "the electromagnetic spectrum is the range of all types of electromagnetic radiation. Radiation is energy that travels and spreads out as it goes — the visible light that comes from a lamp in your house and the radio waves that come from a radio station are two types of electromagnetic radiation. The other types of radiation that make up the electromagnetic spectrum are microwaves, infrared light, ultraviolet light, X-rays and gamma-rays."

All electromagnetic energy travels at the speed of light, which is 186,282 miles (299,792 kilometers) per second. Nothing can move faster than the speed of light. One unique thing about light is that it is the only form of electromagnetic energy visible to the naked eye.

The importance of light in understanding our electromagnetic soul cannot be underestimated. As Albert Einstein said, "Matter is energy, energy is light, we are all light beings."

In order to understand terminal lucidity, it may help to examine what happens in an incandescent light bulb, which suddenly gets brighter immediately before burning out. This occurs because the tungsten in the light bulb filament has degraded to the point where it can no longer regulate the amount of electricity flowing through it. So in the last moments of the bulb's life, more energy is surging through the bulb than it can handle, which results in a last blast of light before it burns out. The light bulb didn't create the electricity that illuminates the bulb;

it only houses it until the filament can no longer handle that amount of energy.

Terminal lucidity also involves the flow of electromagnetic energy, but through the brain. A healthy brain is capable of regulating the amount of electromagnetic energy that travels through it. However, when the brain begins to degrade, it can no longer control this flow of energy properly. When the electromagnetic soul begins to separate from the body, there is an energy spike, which is more than the impaired brain is capable of regulating. This sudden energy surge creates a brief window of time during which a person regains consciousness and is capable of communication. Terminal lucidity may offer evidence that the electromagnetic soul — who and what we are — is not created by the brain, but rather *housed* in the brain.

In other words, the brain no more creates the electromagnetic soul than a light bulb creates the electricity that flows through it. In both examples, the brain and the bulb temporarily house the energy that flows through them until they're no longer capable of regulating that energy.

Light is the energy of life. If it were not for the light generated by the nuclear fusion reactions within our sun, the Earth would be nothing more than a chunk of ice drifting through space. Through photosynthesis, plants convert the energy of light into nutrients. All forms of food on Earth begin with plants. Animals and humans eat plants and/or animals that consume plants.

Light is also essential to one's spirituality. Since ancient times, belief systems worldwide describe an encounter with the Divine Power known as God in terms of Light. One of the most familiar examples may be found in Exodus 3:2–4, during the spiritual transformation of Moses, when he saw that "though the bush was on fire it did not burn up."

It is believed the Torah was mostly written sometime between the seventh and fifth centuries BC, during the Iron Age. The events described in the Torah occurred sometime around 1300 BC, during the Bronze Age. How would Moses describe in Bronze Age terms this intense concentration of radiant electromagnetic energy that appeared in a bush? Other than the sun or lightning, the most powerful form of radiant energy Moses would be familiar with was fire. Hence, using the vernacular of the day, he would describe this intense radiant light as a fire that burned yet did not burn the bush.

This is merely one example from the sacred texts of all religions worldwide, which describe the Divine Power we call God in terms of a bright white light. Perhaps these are best summarized by the thirteenth-century Persian Islamic poet and scholar Mevlana Jalaluddin Rumi, who wrote, "The lamps are different, / But the Light is the same. / One matter, one energy, one Light, one Light-mind, / Endlessly emanating all things."

Perceiving the Divine as Light corresponds with the scientific study of the afterlife. Since the 1970s, studies of survival of consciousness and NDEs have shown the immense importance of light during spiritual encounters.

An NDE occurs when a person clinically dies and his or her electromagnetic soul temporarily separates from the body and then returns as the person comes back to life. Those who have had a near-death experience describe meeting a collective of spirits who are deceased loved ones — they then encounter the brilliant Light. Many NDE subjects — including me — believe that glimpsing this Light is, if for only an instant, the spiritual energy of God. Yet even the word *God* is too limiting to describe this Light of infinite love and limitless intelligence.

Spiritual development also involves the quest to find the Inner Light within oneself. For centuries, this has been viewed as a personal, spiritual, and philosophical matter, although in recent years it appears there is a scientific basis for the light within.

Recent discoveries have shown that the cells of all living organisms emit a low-intensity flash of light known as *biophotons*. This phenomenon is very different from bioluminescence, which is light produced by a chemical reaction within certain species, such as fireflies and lantern fish. Bioluminescence is highly visible and used for breeding, hunting prey, and defense against predators. Biophotons, on the other hand, are low-level flashes of light that are undetectable by the naked human eye. They are extremely important to all living organisms as a form of internal communication.

Quantum physicist Sergey Mayburov of the Russian Academy of Sciences concluded, "Biophoton streams consist of short quasiperiodic bursts ... similar to those used to send binary data." Professor Fritz-Albert Popp of the International Institute of Biophysics in Germany agrees: "Biophoton emission is a general phenomenon of living systems.... Biophotons originate from a coherent photon field within the living organism, its function being intra and intercellular regulation and communication."

For humans, light as a means of transmitting information is a fact of life. Aside from space agencies using lasers to communicate with spacecraft and satellites, back on planet Earth, we've been using fiber-optic cable for decades. Fiber-optic cable reflects light along a wire and is used for telecommunication and computer networking. Then of course there are all the other forms of electromagnetic energy that we use on a daily basis to transmit and receive information. Remote controls emit infrared energy to open garage doors and turn on televisions. Wi-Fi and Bluetooth use electromagnetic energy so we can text, make calls, and access the internet, not to mention listen to music transmitted to us by radio waves.

However, the discovery of biophotons shows that the cells of all living beings generate and use light to transmit information to other cells. Our bodies and the bodies of all living organisms emit light. This light, which is both external and internal, exists within all of us. In essence, our body is a matrix of light. The Light that is Divine is also the light within. Einstein was definitely onto something when he said we are light beings.

The official position of neuroscience, which is the study of the brain, is that consciousness cannot exist without the physical organ of the brain; memories are formed by chemical reactions and electrical impulses within the brain. But neuroscience still can't explain how consciousness is created. That is because consciousness is not created by the brain but is merely housed in the brain.

This claim may no longer be a philosophical question but a scientific fact. Harvard neurosurgeon Dr. Eben Alexander was an admitted atheist until his near-death experience took his electromagnetic soul out of his body into another dimension. During a lecture at the International Association for Near-Death Studies (IANDS), Dr. Alexander said, "Practically every neurology textbook has hundreds of pages about the functions of the brain, and only a paragraph or two about consciousness. Medical science simply cannot explain consciousness as being created by the brain."

Dr. Alexander's observation that medical science cannot explain consciousness is correct. This is because medical science is seeking the answer strictly in terms of biology, instead of on the subatomic level as energy. Physicist Evan Harris Walker referred to the brain as "the 'hosting hardware' of our consciousness. It is a carbon 12 and salt water resonator. Our consciousness is the electrical current that is constantly beaming in and out of the organ, and our brain is a quantum antenna that resonates like a crystal transceiver."

Dr. Robert Lanza, of Wake Forest University School of Medicine and head of Astellas Global Regenerative Medicine, stated, "Death of consciousness simply does not exist. It only exists as a thought because people identify themselves with their body.... If the body receives consciousness in the same way that a cable box receives satellite signals, then of course consciousness does not end at the death of the physical body."

Consciousness researcher Sir Roger Penrose of Oxford University, in conjunction with his colleague Dr. Stuart Hameroff of the University of Arizona, has stated, "The origin of consciousness reflects our place in the universe, the nature of our existence. Did consciousness evolve from complex computations among brain neurons, as most scientists assert? Or has consciousness, in some sense, been here all along, as spiritual approaches maintain?"

According to the National Academy of Sciences, the human brain may account for only 2 percent of the weight of the body, but consumes over 20 percent of its energy. The brain is a rather hungry organ, consuming energy at ten times the rate of the rest of the body per gram of tissue.

Since energy can neither be created nor destroyed, only transferred from one form to another, the light of the electromagnetic soul is not created by the human brain, nor is it extinguished by the physical death of the brain. So what happens to the brain's energy, the electromagnetic soul, at physical death?

Professor Hans-Peter Dürr of Germany's Max Planck Institute for Nuclear Physics has likened the brain to a computer's hard drive. He uses this comparison to explain that at death, the information on that hard drive/brain isn't lost but is instead transferred onto the spiritual quantum field. Professor Dürr states, "When I die, I do not lose this information, this consciousness. The body dies but the spiritual quantum field continues. In this way, I am immortal."

In my work as a psychic medium, I communicate with spirits on a daily basis. Once separated from the brain, the electromagnetic soul not only remains coherent, but becomes part of something far greater than we may be able to comprehend in our finite human form. To borrow from Professor Dürr's computer analogy, at physical death the electromagnetic soul is uploaded to a higher vibrational frequency, something like a cosmic internet, although I believe a more accurate term is the *collective consciousness*.

To return to Aristotle's question, "What came first — the chicken or the egg?" The answer is the electromagnetic soul.

Chapter 3

COLLECTIVE CONSCIOUSNESS COMMUNICATION

JOHN LENNON ONCE REMARKED, "If I'd lived in Roman times, I'd have lived in Rome. Where else? Today America is the Roman Empire and New York is Rome itself."

Unless the Giants or the Yankees lose, it's a safe bet that most New Yorkers have no desire to throw anyone to the lions. Nevertheless, like ancient Rome in its heyday, New York City, especially its shining gem, Manhattan, is the epicenter of world commerce, art, music, culture, literature, entertainment, industry, and fashion. Its educational institutions boast some of the greatest minds in the world. The city is a diverse and vast collective of millions of people who live and work side by side. The aesthetic appeal of New York City is accentuated by engineering wonders, architectural masterpieces, and beautiful parks.

On a sunny day, there's no better way to take in the sights, sounds, and scents of Manhattan than by foot. The city is a walker's paradise. That is, of course, unless it's February, 30 degrees (-1 Celsius), and raining, as it was the afternoon I'd just finished taping a segment at 30 Rock, NBC's studios at Rockefeller

Center. If New York is the new Rome, then Rockefeller Center, with its majestic Art Deco skyscraper, is the new Forum of Augustus. As my manager, Rocky, and I left the studio and stepped out into the icy rain, I could only imagine that during miserable weather, it was as hard finding a chariot in ancient Rome as it was getting a taxi in New York.

After what seemed like an eternity standing in freezing rain, hailing a taxi with no success, Rocky said, "It's only eight blocks — let's walk it." Having lived in Manhattan for some years, she knew a shortcut to the bookstore where I was scheduled for a spirit communication event.

This event was a bit out of the ordinary. Within hours of my landing in New York, the venue contacted Rocky asking if I would conduct a special spirit communication session limited to twenty-four people. Normally, during my speaking tours every day is fully booked, but as synchronicity would have it, this event fit perfectly between the TV appearance and my speaking engagement at Columbia University the next day.

Accepting our fate that neither taxi nor chariot would rescue us from the rain, we sloshed through the misty streets. Sharing an umbrella and clad in black trench coats, we laughed about how we must have resembled Cold War spies — well, the cold part at least.

After a few blocks I realized we weren't the only ones braving the freezing streets.

"I feel cold chills and tingles."

"No kidding, Mark. It's freezing."

"Rocky, we're not alone."

"It's Manhattan — people are everywhere," she replied.

"It's not that. We're being followed."

Rocky glanced over her shoulder behind us and turned to me. "You mean *you're* being followed, don't you?"

"There's a difference between cold chills from weather and chills from that tingly electrical sensation I get when spirits are around."

"Are you okay?"

"Yes, it's just — I feel the spirits of children all around me."

We rounded the corner onto a small side street and approached the quaint bookshop. After ascending the short set of stairs, we left the bitter outside cold and entered the cozy warmth inside. The shop was illuminated by the soft glow of Himalayan salt lamps. Antique wooden shelves stacked with old books reached to the ceiling, the smell of their ancient pages permeating the air.

"Namaste! You must be Mark and Rocky. I'm Eleanor, the store owner," said an exquisitely coiffed gray-haired woman draped in an aqua and purple caftan, who seemed to glide across the room to greet us. Eleanor was every inch the New Age New Yorker.

"Victoria! Be a dear and show our guests to the sanctuary."

A pale twentysomething woman with a black spiked Mohawk hairstyle emerged from behind a bookshelf. She was sporting the Goth look, being clad in a black lace dress and black leather high-heeled boots. Victoria's shiny black fingernails matched her black eyelid makeup, mascara, and lipstick. Her earrings were tiny silver skulls, which matched her skull necklace and bracelets.

Without uttering a word, Victoria motioned us to follow her toward a darkened hallway at the back of the store. The wooden floor creaked underfoot as we were led through white double French doors into the sanctuary. The large rectangular room was illuminated by dozens of candles, which cast flickering light upon the whitewashed brick walls. An immense Persian rug spanned the length of the sanctuary, which could have easily seated fifty people, although the precise number of twenty-four chairs for this evening's event was already in place.

Victoria turned to us and smiled, revealing her pierced tongue. I wondered if I should have brought a crucifix and a clove of garlic.

"It's a trip to meetcha, Rocky and Mista Ant-nee!" Victoria exclaimed in a thick Brooklyn accent.

"That's kind of you to say," I replied. "I must admit, you're quite the trip yourself."

"Yeah, I get dat a lot." Victoria smiled again. "I love the whole talkin' to the dead thing."

"Thanks. I'm looking forward to tonight."

"Oh, my Gawd! The guests are heah! Be back inna few. Lemme know if yous need anything else."

Rocky smiled. "Welcome to Harry Potter goes punk rock."

"My friends in England joke there's no better time to connect with spirits than on a rainy night," I said. "It feels to me that we're definitely in the right place at the right time."

As Victoria directed the guests to their seats, I wondered if my English friends had a point, because I felt the presence of spirits intensify. Rocky introduced me, and at the conclusion of my introductory explanation, I opened my brain to the afterlife frequency.

"There's a large group of spirits here — children — they all appear under the age of fourteen," I began. "I feel such an intense love being projected by them to all of you."

The crowd stared at me in silence.

"There are spirits of adults connected to all of you, but they're on the periphery of this group of children and are stepping aside so the children can communicate.

"I'm sensing the spirit of a young boy. He was between seven and ten years of age when he passed. There's a thinning sensation — this is a cancer indicator. There was a major issue with his blood. Does this make sense to anyone?"

A man stood and said solemnly, "My nine-year-old son died of leukemia."

"Another spirit is coming through — feels like a girl about six years old — abrupt impact sensation — feels like a traumatic passing. I'm seeing a bicycle — this was a terrible accident."

A woman acknowledged that her daughter died when she was hit by a car while riding her bicycle.

After half a dozen connections, I paused. "So far every spirit that's come through has been a child. How many of you have lost a child?"

Every hand in the room went up.

A gentleman seated at the back of the room stood. "Mark, I put this event together. We're members of a grief support group for parents who have lost children."

"That's why your kids followed me here tonight."

"What do you mean, they *followed* you?"

"On the way here, I felt surrounded by the spirits of children, and now this makes sense. No one is alone on the Other Side — it's a hive mind, a collective consciousness, meaning that spirits are all interconnected. However, spirits can disconnect from the collective. In many instances, groups of spirits with a common bond will come through to communicate with people in the material world who share a common bond."

"How does that apply to us?" another parent asked.

"The common denominator of everyone here tonight is that each one of you has lost a child. I don't have to tell any of you how painful this is. The spirits of your children feel your pain. They love you. They also knew that you and I would be here tonight, so they came through collectively to communicate with you through me."

Suddenly I felt tingles run through my body.

"Several spirits are converging on me," I continued. "A female energy is coming forward from the collective of spirits. She is presenting herself as a ball of white light like a small star — this indicates to me a baby who did not come full-term. This is the spirit of a baby girl."

Terri and Daniel, a couple seated in the third row, raised their hands.

"This is not meant to hurt you. She's transmitting identifiers — facts and evidence to indicate this is your daughter."

Terri cupped her mouth with her hands as Daniel nodded for me to continue.

"Her death wasn't your fault. There was an infection in your uterus. I'm sorry — I don't mean to get so personal, but that's what's being transmitted to me."

"That — that's exactly what happened," Terri sobbed. "She was stillborn because of an infection in my placenta. I've always blamed myself, even though the doctors said it wasn't my fault."

"She's now focusing on you, sir," I said to Daniel. "She indicates you have a problem with your heart."

"No, I don't," Daniel said sharply.

"Are you sure? This is really strong. It keeps getting repeated — a serious issue with your heart."

"Darling," Terri glared at him, "you have an artificial heart valve!"

"Yeah, but my heart's fine!" Daniel glared back at her.

"Daniel, darling, when a surgeon cracks open your chest, cuts out part of your heart, and replaces it with a plastic valve, that *is* an *issue* with your *heart!*"

"Hold on," I interjected. "This is significant because your daughter wants you to know she's around you and is aware of what's happening in your life. Spirits do this by identifying medical, personal, financial, and other pieces of information about you and about what has and is happening in your lives. Things I couldn't possibly know."

"She died in utero — how could she possibly know about Terri's infection? Or about *my* heart?" Daniel asked. "That surgery happened over a year after she was stillborn. How is it possible for her to know these things?"

"The soul preexists the body and lives on after the body ceases to function. Even though your daughter was physically a baby when she died, what she really is is an immortal living spirit perfectly capable of intelligent communication. Spirits are never alone — they're interconnected with other spirits as part of the collective consciousness."

⌇

PEOPLE TEND TO THINK OF SPIRITS as invisible humans, with the same finite mental and physical limitations as people living in the material world. This is natural, because we interpret and classify things on the basis of what we know and what is within our realm of experience.

Traditionally, spirit communication has been perceived as individualized — one spirit at a time communicating with one person at a time. But this is not always the case. In fact, it's far more interesting and complex than that. Spirits will communicate with loved ones in the material world as individuals and in tandem with other spirits. This is *collective consciousness communication.* To understand the complexity of this phenomenon, it's important to realize that spirits are pure energy and therefore are not limited by the confines of a body or the material world.

Wait a nanosecond!

The last chapter stated that *everything* is energy. Why does this book now refer to spirits as pure energy and refer to the human body as material?

Matter and energy are both composed of quanta (particles of electromagnetic energy) on the subatomic level. However, from our human perspective, there is clearly a difference between the material world and the Other Side. That difference is not energy, but the frequency of the energy's vibration.

To simplify, everyone is familiar with AM and FM radio. *FM* stands for *frequency modulation* and *AM* stands for *amplitude modulation*. Frequency is measuring the rate at which something occurs during a given period of time, like radio waves. Amplitude is the measurement of the length and width of these waves as they occur or vibrate.

To illustrate the difference between AM and FM, think of dribbling a basketball. The number of times you dribble a basketball in a minute is the frequency. How high the basketball bounces is amplitude.

Using these basic definitions, let's think of the material world as AM radio and the Other Side as FM. Both are pure energy; it's just that the material world has a lower frequency than the afterlife frequency of the Other Side.

Planck's constant states, "Energy is directly proportional to frequency, so as energy increases so does its frequency." In quantum physics circles, it is acknowledged that there is no matter; there is just energy, which vibrates at different frequencies so as to be perceptible to the senses.

While everything is energy, the difference between the material world and the Other Side is the frequency of energy. That is why I designate the lower vibrational frequency, which we humans can perceive, as the material world, and the afterlife frequency as the higher vibration of spirits.

The electromagnetic soul is housed in the brain the same way data is stored in the hard drive of a computer. During the transitional process we know as death, the frequency of the electromagnetic soul increases as our brain/hard drive ceases to function. Once the vibration of the electromagnetic soul exceeds that of the material confines of the human brain, the electromagnetic soul is uploaded to the higher vibration of the afterlife frequency. By analogy, we could say that when we die, our energy is transferred from AM radio to FM.

AM and FM radio waves, like the material world and the Other Side, are both energy, but they have different frequencies. Energetically they're different dimensions, but they coincide with each other, although sometimes their frequencies overlap.

It's a popular plot device in science fiction TV shows and movies for characters to do a quantum leap and pop back and forth between alternate universes and dimensions. In the sci-fi universe, Captain Kirk alone must have had at least three dozen illicit liaisons on eleven different planets in four alternate dimensions.

Salacious starship captains notwithstanding, the evidence for alternate dimensions and parallel universes is being transported from science fiction to science fact. The theory of parallel universes has been hypothesized in quantum physics circles since 1957, but it was more clearly defined in the 1980s by string theorist Andrei Linde of the Lebedev Physics Institute and later Stanford University, who developed the theory of multiple universes. Multiverse theory claims that our universe is just one of many universes, which exist parallel to each other.

Some of the greatest minds in physics, including Michio Kaku of City College of New York, Sir Roger Penrose of the University of Oxford, Neil Turok of Cambridge University, and Max Tegmark of MIT, endorse multiverse theory and believe evidence to prove it is within our grasp.

Prior to his death in 2018, Stephen Hawking coauthored a paper with Thomas Hertog from the University of Leuven in

Belgium that examined the multiverse theory. They concluded that our universe is just one of many. Like our universe, each of these other universes had their own big bang beginning. Hawking and Hertog predict that we can prove the existence of other universes by detecting the remnants of *their* big bangs in the gravitational waves left over from *our* big bang.

It appears that Hawking and Hertog may be right. Data transmitted from the European Space Agency's Planck space telescope mapped the cosmic microwave background (CMB) of the universe. The CMB is thought to be electromagnetic radiation left over from the big bang. The results were stunning, because they revealed that our universe has several dark recesses, which include holes and extensive gaps.

Theoretical physicist Laura Mersini-Houghton of the University of North Carolina has interpreted these anomalies of the microwave background as evidence that our universe is influenced by other nearby universes and that there could be an infinite number of universes outside of our own.

Within a universe there are dimensions. The ones we are the most familiar with are the three spatial dimensions of length, width, and height and the fourth dimension of time. But wait. Things get even trickier!

According to multiverse theory, the universe contains additional dimensions. The theory is that there are many more dimensions in our universe than we are aware of because humans have not yet developed the technology to detect them. Superstring theory suggests that there must be at least eleven dimensions: ten of space plus one for time. However, this is hotly debated by physicists, many of whom propose there are even more than eleven dimensions of space.

Is it possible to travel between dimensions? From our perspective, we don't give much thought to moving through a three-dimensional space, because we are three-dimensional beings. What about a two-dimensional being, like an amoeba? It lives on planet Earth, so clearly it can exist in a three-dimensional world, but it leads a two-dimensional existence. Professor Thomas Banchoff of Brown University explains, "As we watch through the lenses of a microscope, an amoeba goes about the course of its virtually two-dimensional life, confined to the narrow region between the slide and its coverslip." In other words, an amoeba can't access more than one plane in the third dimension. However, astrophysicist Neil deGrasse Tyson has suggested that if you come from a universe with higher dimensions, then moving between dimensions would be as easy as stepping from one room to another.

Because matter and energy are composed of quanta (electromagnetic energy) on the subatomic level, the difference between the material world and the Other Side is not energy but the frequency of the energy's vibration. We move about the material world because we are three-dimensional beings. Spirits are pure energy and have a much higher vibration rate. They come from a higher energetic frequency, so they are able to travel between the Other Side and our material world at the speed of light. This is also how and why contact between the material world and the Other Side occurs constantly.

This interdimensional communication is like driving on a highway listening to your favorite talk radio show on AM radio when you pass an FM radio station next to the highway. All of a sudden, you simultaneously hear the AM radio show, what's being broadcast from the FM station, and probably some static. Because of your close proximity to the FM station, its energetic frequency has intersected the frequency of the AM station. Meanwhile, your car's radio is receiving all of these radio waves at the same time.

This process is similar to what happens during spirit contact. The frequencies of the material world dimension and the Other Side dimension intersect: ergo, interdimensional communication.

How then can the electromagnetic soul of a loved one know things far beyond what he or she knew while living in the material world? Think of the internet, a global electronic communications network that connects computer networks around the world. An individual hard drive on a computer can store a limited amount of information, but when it connects to the internet, it has virtually unlimited access to information that is far beyond the capacity of a single hard drive.

This is essentially what happens to the electromagnetic soul when it leaves the human body. The Other Side is a collective consciousness, meaning that spirits are interconnected and able to communicate with a vast array of other spirits in the infinite collective, which transcends dimension, frequency, space, and time.

Although the electromagnetic soul is interconnected as part of this collective consciousness, a person never loses his or her individuality. Our greatest attribute is our unique sense of self, which distinguishes us from everyone and everything else in the universe. We each have our own thoughts, memories, feelings, perspectives, and personality, which are enshrined within our immortal electromagnetic souls.

Because everything is energy, spirits and humans remain interconnected, and each life becomes part of a larger whole that comprises the hive mind of the collective consciousness. However, spirits definitely have an edge. They're aware of what is happening in our dimension because once separated from the lower vibration of a material world body, the electromagnetic soul moves at the speed of light. Therefore, by the time you can pour yourself a cup of coffee, a spirit can travel to the moon and back, zip around the world a few times, and then pop in to see what is happening in your life and even transmit a message to you — provided you're open to receiving that message.

The enhanced capabilities of spirits involve more than their speed of motion. As pure energy, they never get tired, sick, or old or die. They also have an expanded capacity for forgiveness and love. This is why they can and will detach from the collective consciousness to communicate with those living in the material world, because they love us and want to help us. The wisdom of the collective consciousness can be tapped into. If it is recognized and trusted, it can provide the living with guidance, warnings, and most importantly, healing.

During interdimensional communication, spirits can contact loved ones in the material world either in an individual capacity or in tandem with other spirits. This is collective consciousness communication. However, spirits are never alone, and while it may appear that a single spirit is reaching out to someone in the material world, that spirit is still part of the collective consciousness. To illustrate this process, think of a chorus singing in unison until a lead singer emerges to sing a solo while supported by the harmony of backup singers. This connection to the collective consciousness accounts for the enhanced wisdom and knowledge a spirit or spirits possess, which far exceed what he, she, or they knew while living in the material world.

The phenomenon of collective consciousness communication has been reported for centuries. Perhaps the most famous accounts in modern history involved Edgar Cayce. Nicknamed the "Sleeping Prophet," Cayce would go into a trancelike state and connect with the collective consciousness. The information he received from the collective consciousness spanned a multitude of subjects ranging from reincarnation to diagnosing and prescribing treatments and cures for various medical conditions.

People from all walks of life, from the obscure to the famous, sought a reading with Edgar Cayce, whose clients included Thomas Edison, composers Irving Berlin and George Gershwin, and even US President Woodrow Wilson. Although he died in 1945, Edgar Cayce remains one of the most controversial figures in the history of psychics. His legacy, however, lives on as the information received through his readings continues to be analyzed to this day.

When spirits adjust their frequency to a lower vibration in order to communicate with people in the material world, they do not just come in one at a time. They come in tandem, which is why collective consciousness communication occurs in personal readings and in group settings.

Collective consciousness communication is quantum entanglement in action, demonstrating how we are all energetically interconnected. Quantum entanglement occurs when subatomic particles move apart from each other, yet they remain entangled, so that a change in one particle instantly creates a change in the other particle. Physicists theorize that this is true even if they're a billion miles apart! Despite distance or dimension, there will be a constant exchange of energy and information between these particles. When we physically die, the electromagnetic soul may vacate the physical vessel of the brain and make a quantum leap to the afterlife frequency of the Other Side dimension, which is the collective consciousness.

Collective consciousness communication can manifest in different ways. Several spirits who share a commonality with a group of people can come through as a group and then disconnect individually from the collective to address their individual loved ones in the material world. This was the case described earlier in this chapter, when several parents who had lost children came together for a spirit communication session. The spirits of their children came through as a collective and then disconnected from the collective to address each individually.

The collective consciousness may communicate several messages simultaneously through a medium to several people at a time. This is typical during spirit communication conducted during a group setting. Spirits understand our finite limitations and realize that a single medium or even a group of mediums in a public setting cannot possibly reach everyone in a large group. In a sense, spirits are making the most efficient and effective use of the limited amount of time and energy finite beings possess, so they attempt to reach as many people as possible with one transmission.

Hence in group mediumship demonstrations, even if you do not receive an individualized reading, you may still have been receiving messages from loved ones in spirit. Every medium, including me, always has people after the group demonstration who will say something to this effect: "When you were doing that reading for that one person, so many of the things that came through for that person also applied to me." Although I may be conducting a reading on one person during a group setting, messages presented will resonate with other people in the audience.

This happened during a spirit communication event in Florida.

I said, "I'm hearing the word 'paisley,' which could be a name, but I'm also getting 'thyroid.' I'm feeling pain in my pancreas, which indicates an issue like diabetes, pancreatitis, or pancreatic cancer. Does this make sense to anyone?"

A woman a few rows from the front raised her hand. "That's for me!"

"In what way?"

"I bought a paisley scarf today, I've got type 2 diabetes, and I was just diagnosed last week with hyperthyroidism."

Two other people raised their hands. I asked them to stand and explain. The first was a gentleman who said, "My father always wore paisley ties. This is weird."

"How so?" I asked.

"My wife and I are thinking of having a garage sale, so last weekend I was going through an old trunk of clothes in the attic, and I found one of my dad's paisley ties. He died from pancreatic cancer."

I turned to the other person who raised her hand. She was seated toward the back of the room.

"My grandmother's last name was Paisley, and she died from complications from hypothyroidism. Lately I've been having some problems, so I went to the doctor yesterday, and she's ordered blood work to test for pancreatitis."

Paisley, thyroid, and pancreatic issues resonated with three different people in three very different ways. This is not a coincidence; this is the nature of frequency transfer during collective consciousness communication. To use me as an example, my finite brain is like a single radio, whereas the afterlife frequency of the collective consciousness is every radio station on the FM radio band from 87.5 to 108.0.

Since my finite human brain can only handle one station at a time, the collective consciousness still got a three-for-one deal by having those three spirits transmit messages simultaneously, starting with "paisley," "pancreas," and "thyroid." Collective consciousness communication makes the most efficient use of humans' finite time and energy by communicating more than one message to more than one person at a time.

This is not far-fetched, because it is the nature of frequency transfer. In fact, humans have their own version of collective consciousness communication. For example, when the Pentagon sends a radio message to Camp Pendleton, it may appear that only one message is being transmitted, although several se-cret, encrypted messages are piggybacked on that signal. While the radio transmission appears to contain only one message, it actually contains multiple messages.

Information of a medical and healing nature is often the subject of collective consciousness communication. How we perceive and interpret the collective consciousness varies de-pending upon the medium. My colleagues who are experienced evidential mediums have noted that when receiving information of a medical nature, they're apparently connected to a higher level of intelligence than just a single spirit.

One of my colleagues indicated that when receiving med-ical information, he sees the image of a doctor in his mind's eye. He interprets this as the collective consciousness creating a point of reference he can relate to, namely a physician, so he knows he's receiving medical information on behalf of the col-lective consciousness.

When I receive information from the collective conscious-ness, particularly of a medical nature, it is very direct and sounds like thousands of voices speaking as one. My finite brain inter-prets this unified focus of intelligence as a brief glimpse into the omnipresence of the collective consciousness.

During my career, I've served as a prosecuting attorney, criminal defense, personal injury, and wrongful death litigator, often handling cases with complex forensic and medical issues. This has required me to understand both the legal and eviden-tiary aspects of the cases, which encompass science, physics, anatomy, and physiology. Spirits know this, which is why they tend to be very direct with me.

That being said, it's as big a surprise to me as it is to the recipient when specific information about medical and physical conditions about which I know nothing comes through me with a high degree of accuracy. Information from the collective consciousness is always accurate. Inaccuracies result from how the information is interpreted by those of us living in the material world.

Collective consciousness communication occurs during private readings with one client or with a small group of clients who are family or close friends. It's typical for several spirits to communicate during a private session, as they did for a client named Jolene. She was one of eleven children, and the spirits of her parents, siblings, and friends couldn't wait to communicate with her. At the end of the session, we counted twenty-four spirits: twenty-one humans, two dogs, and Rusty the horse.

The Other Side uses collective consciousness communication to transfer messages to our material world dimension. It's a powerful spiritual delivery system. If properly recognized and accepted, it can provide guidance and healing for mental, physical, emotional, and spiritual suffering. Collective consciousness communication is always significant, whether the messages are meant for billions of people or a single individual.

IT WAS A BRIGHT SUMMER DAY when I arrived at the bookstore where I was scheduled to conduct an in-person reading. The store owner greeted me cheerfully and let me know that two people were coming for the session. I have a firm policy about anonymity prior to a reading. This is to ensure that what I receive during the interdimensional communication is coming from spirits and not from what I may know ahead of time.

A few minutes later, Chuck and Nicole arrived. They were in their early forties and looked athletic, making me feel a tad guilty for choosing a milkshake over a kale smoothie earlier that day.

Nicole was slender and had an easygoing manner. Chuck wore a baseball cap over his short black hair, sported a five o'clock shadow, and didn't say a word, much less crack a smile. The bookstore had a distinctly New Age look, selling crystals, incense, wind chimes, Indian tapestries, and tie-dyed clothing. Nicole and the store owner chatted and exchanged pleasantries. Chuck stood motionless as his eyes scanned the surroundings.

As I led them to the reading room at the back of the store, Nicole said, "This is for my boyfriend, Chuck. He heard about you and wanted a reading."

We took our seats. I began with my introductory comments about what to expect during an interdimensional communication session and then opened my brain up to the afterlife frequency.

"Three male spirits are coming through in tandem."

Chuck leaned forward intently.

"Very different personalities — one keeps laughing a lot — had a very distinctive laugh — kind of a snorting sound — I keep hearing a name — sounds like Kerry."

"Close enough — his name's Kenny." Chuck half smiled. "He had a weird laugh."

"Kenny is stepping aside for another male — tall blond man projecting the image of a St. Christopher medal — patron saint of travel, but it's also my trigger for the name."

"Christopher! Oh my God!" Chuck beamed.

"Uh — the third guy — he — he — keeps — talking about — uh..."

"About what?"

"Maybe I'm misinterpreting this, Chuck, but — he keeps talking about eating beans and farting in your face."

Chuck rolled his eyes, "Yeah, that's Todd. Beans gave him gas real bad — so he'd eat a big plate of 'em, and when the rest of us were eating, he'd sneak up and cut one right in someone's face, usually mine. It was gross, but it was funny as hell."

We all cracked up, but the levity didn't last long.

"Ahh!" I cringed as an immense shock wave flew through my body.

"You okay?" Nicole asked.

"I'm fine — a jolt to my body indicates an abrupt death."

Chuck and Nicole glanced at each other.

"These guys died traumatically at the same time," I continued. "I hear a loud sound — like walking up to a huge metallic tank, banging on it, and there's a hollow sound. It's loud — like an explosion."

Nicole's hand covered her mouth.

"My unit was on a mission in Afghanistan." Chuck's body tensed. "Our Humvee hit an IED — an improvised explosive device. It exploded. I was the unit commander. All the guys died but me."

"What the fuck!" flew out of my mouth unexpectedly. "I'm sorry — I try to never use that type of language in a reading."

"Don't apologize," said Chuck. "'What the fuck' was the motto of our unit." He paused. "I've always wondered why I survived, and they didn't. I was the commanding officer — I should have died."

"The energy is shifting — I call this collective consciousness communication — all three spirits are speaking as one."

Chuck braced himself.

"You had to live. You're supposed to let others know what happened. You're supposed to help others with loss and guilt."

Chuck stood, clearly shaken. A single tear rolled down his face. "I'm leaving now. I'm going out the back door. I will not allow anyone to see me cry."

Before exiting the room, he paused and turned to me. "Thank you, sir." Within seconds, he vanished through the store's rear entrance.

Nicole gaped. "You have no idea what you did for him!" she exclaimed. "I've never seen him express that much emotion. This is major!"

"That much emotion?" Then it dawned on me. "Nicole, he's special ops, isn't he?"

"Delta Force," she confirmed. "Very highly trained. He was in command of an elite covert antiterrorism operation when their Humvee hit the IED."

"Like the captain who's supposed to go down with his ship," I observed, "Chuck struggles with guilt because as the commander, he feels he should have died, not his men. He's suffering from survivor's guilt."

"Exactly," Nicole replied, "and the counselors at the veterans' hospital asked him to start a support group for veterans racked with guilt."

"Is he going to do it?"

"He's not sure," Nicole explained. "Chuck wants to take the lead to help other veterans, but he knows in a support group you have to express your feelings, and he's worried about that."

"Why's that a problem?"

"Chuck believes he must never appear weak. He says he'd rather die than cry, because to him weeping is weakness."

"Crying isn't weakness; it's healing," I explained. "It's been medically proven that tears of grief differ from regular reflex tears, because grief tears contain the hormones that cause depression and stress. A good cry actually releases these hormones and stimulates endorphins, which can help you feel better. Men need to understand that we have feelings and tear ducts for a reason."

"After hearing from his men today, maybe he will," Nicole replied.

—

MESSAGES RECEIVED THROUGH collective consciousness communication may be subtle or direct, yet they are always powerful. Whether intended for billions of people or just one person, collective consciousness communication can bring change to our world, which may start by transforming a single teardrop into an ocean of healing.

Chapter 4

RAFT

A Four-Step Approach to Recognizing
and Harnessing the Positive Power of
Messages from the Afterlife Frequency

"I WAS THINKING ABOUT HER when the phone rang. It was her!"

"I trusted my gut feeling, and it saved my life. It was a miracle!"

"In a dream, Mom's spirit said to avoid him — then he got arrested for murder!"

Everyone is familiar with "women's intuition," a term used for centuries to describe premonitions and messages experienced by women. Does this mean that women are more psychic and in tune with their spirituality than men? Not necessarily. Successful men, including military and first responders, know the value of trusting their gut instinct.

Whatever label we may assign to premonitions and spirit contact, everyone is capable of experiencing this very real phenomenon. This is because we all have the same basic physiology, which includes the two psychic receptor regions of the body: the pineal gland in the brain and the solar plexus in the abdomen.

The pineal gland is the receptor for messages of a visual,

auditory, and data-based nature. This small endocrine gland, which is about the size of a grain of rice, is located near the center of the brain. It is one of the least understood organs in the body. The pineal gland is our internal clock, because it produces the hormone melatonin, which controls our circadian rhythms. These are the mental, physical, and behavioral patterns that occur during a twenty-four-hour cycle. In short, it tells us when to be alert, active, eat, and sleep.

Circadian rhythms are influenced by light and dark. This indicates that the pineal gland is instrumental in how humans process light, which also happens to be the only form of electromagnetic energy visible to the human eye. Note that from the biophotons in our cells to the sun to perception of the afterlife and the infinite spiritual energy we call God, light is the common denominator.

For thousands of years the Hindus and Buddhists have believed the pineal gland is the location of the third eye. Descartes considered it the seat of the soul.

There's more to the pineal gland than meets the third eye.

Research into it has been going on since the late twentieth century. During that time a British-German study conducted by Professors Serena Roney-Dougal and Gunther Vogl discovered that the pineal gland is affected by electromagnetic fields. Their research indicates that not only does the pineal gland produce melatonin, but electromagnetic energy can trigger it to produce psychoactive hormones that appear connected to psychic and mediumistic activity. According to Professor Vogl, "This could well be related to variations in a psi-conducive state of consciousness, resulting in ostensible psychic occurrences."

In the twenty-first century, the secrets of the pineal gland continue to be revealed. A French-Israeli study conducted by Simon Baconnier, Sidney B. Lang, and René de Seze discovered the presence of calcite and magnetite crystals within the pineal gland. Both of these crystals have piezoelectric properties, which mean they generate an electrical charge when subjected to mechanical force. Although many crystals have such properties, magnetite in particular has an electromagnetic field. It has been well established by the United States National Institutes of Health that the pineal gland is particularly sensitive to electromagnetic energy.

The earliest radios used copper wire to send low levels of electric current through a crystal, which served as an antenna tuning in to radio wave frequencies. The pineal gland may be thought of as a complex biological form of a radio station in our heads. Since the pineal gland controls our circadian rhythms (activity/sleep/wake cycles), it also influences the frequency of our brainwaves.

Brain cells are called *neurons*. *Firing* is the term used to describe what happens when neurons communicate with each other. But this communication encompasses much more than cells talking to each other inside your head.

Molecular geneticist Johnjoe McFadden of the University of Surrey developed CEMI (conscious electromagnetic information) field theory. McFadden proposes that neurons engage in a feedback loop: they both generate electromagnetic fields and are in turn affected by electromagnetic fields outside of the brain. His research incorporates experiments conducted by the California Institute of Technology, which discovered that neurons in the human brain are not only affected by electromagnetic impulses external to the brain but actually fire *synchronously* in resonance with them. According to McFadden, this indicates that the brain can receive signals from external electromagnetic fields and even act in harmony with them.

Thanks to the mysterious pineal gland, we have an extremely

sophisticated communication system in our heads, which enables our brainwave frequency to align with and tune in to the afterlife frequency.

⌒

WHAT ABOUT GUT INSTINCT? Is it more than just a feeling? This brings us to the other psychic receptor located in the abdomen: the enteric nervous system, popularly known as the solar plexus. It's called the solar plexus because the vast numbers of nerve fibers that radiate from it in all directions have been compared to the rays of light radiating from the sun. Evidence suggests that this is where we receive messages of an emotional, sensory, and intuitive nature.

The solar plexus controls the autonomic nervous system, which regulates functions that we don't consciously direct, such as heartbeat, body temperature, breathing, and digestion. The autonomic nervous system includes the sympathetic nervous system, which is responsible for the fight-or-flight reaction. The solar plexus also controls our body's physical response to stress. Intuitive feelings have been referred to as "gut feelings" or "gut instinct" because of the location of the solar plexus in the abdomen and its sensitivity to emotional stress.

The solar plexus is the second most complex bundle of nerves in the human body, outside of the cerebral cortex in the brain. This is one reason Dr. Michael Gershon, professor of anatomy and cellular biology at Columbia-Presbyterian Medical Center in New York, has referred to the solar plexus as the human body's "second brain." Dr. David Wingate, emeritus professor of gastrointestinal science at the University of London, has said, "In evolutionary terms, it makes sense that the body has two brains....Nature seems to have preserved the enteric nervous system (solar plexus) as an independent circuit inside higher animals." Emeran Mayer, professor of physiology, psychiatry, and biobehavioral sciences at UCLA, has observed, "The gut converses with the brain like no other organ. When people talk about going with their gut feelings on an important decision, what they're referring to is an intuitive knowledge based on the close relationship between our emotions and the sensations and feelings in the gastrointestinal (GI) tract.... The system [solar plexus] is way too complicated to have evolved only to make sure things move out of your colon." So when it comes to intuitive feelings, trust your gut!

The two psychic receptors are more than mere parts of the body that are interconnected biologically. They work in tandem. Both are highly sophisticated nerve centers, with electromagnetic energy flowing through them. Not only do they communicate with each other, but they're sensitive to electromagnetic energy external to the human body. The pineal gland enables us to interpret these electromagnetic impulses through visions, auditory messages, and data. The solar plexus interprets these impulses through emotional feelings and physical sensations.

Recognizing the signals received by the pineal gland and the solar plexus is the basis for tuning in to the afterlife frequency. This connection leads to collective consciousness communication, which can and does influence our material world dimension by providing guidance rather than control.

Humans exert control over their behavior in the material world through the exercise of free will. Unfortunately, human behavior is often the result of self-centered, ego-driven impulses, which can result in harming others through anger, bigotry, hatred, and violence.

Guidance and messages from individual spirits or the collective consciousness never advise or direct someone to commit negative acts. You can tell the difference because messages from the collective consciousness lead to physical and emotional healing, inner peace, and conflict resolution. Spiritual guidance can also warn us to avoid potentially dangerous situations.

Messages from spirits can be complex or simple, and signs from spirits may be direct or subtle. It's not always easy to tell the difference between complex and simple messages, especially when a message may initially appear trivial although in fact it is quite significant.

This was underscored for me one afternoon while I was writing this book. I was grappling with the dreaded writer's block. My creative juices dried up, and I couldn't write a single word. For me, creativity can't be forced — it must unfold on its own.

To clear my head, I went outside to go for a walk on the beach. On my way, I felt a jolt to do an about-face and head in the opposite direction, to a bike path near my house.

It was a breezy, sunny day, and the wind gently rustled through the trees. Walking along the path relaxed me. My mental quagmire faded into a daydream state. My mind's eye filled with happy memories of life with my parents when they were living in the material world.

Abruptly I halted. Two shining objects on the ground caught my attention. Two coins, a nickel and a penny, were glowing in the sunlight a few paces ahead of me.

As I went to pick them up, I hesitated when I heard my mother's voice.

"It's bad luck to pick up a coin that isn't heads up!"

"Heads or tails, it's money. Pick 'em up," Dad's voice responded.

Both coins were heads up. I felt my parents were up to something.

"Hmmm, a penny and a nickel — six cents."

"SIXTH SENSE!"

Talk about an aha moment! Both my parents had psychic

and mediumistic abilities, and I grew up in a family where the sixth sense was part of life. Mom taught me everyone has intuitive ability, although many block it. Dad said that people block it because they don't pay attention to the signs.

"No kidding, Mom and Dad," I said aloud, "it's all about the sixth sense, but there's got to be —" cold chills and tingles resonated through my body.

An image from my childhood of Dad standing waist-deep in the ocean flooded my mind's eye. He had been a Navy SEAL, a scuba diver, and a swimming instructor, so we were always in the water. But then in this vision, he held up a blue raft.

Why a raft? That must mean something!

A shock wave resonated through my body as the full impact of the message began to unfold: RECOGNIZE, ACCEPT, FEEL, TRUST. "That's it — RAFT!"

Many people scoff at the thought that a nickel and a penny lying on the ground could be anything more than two random coins. That type of negative mindset blocks messages transmitted from the Other Side.

In this particular situation, a nickel and a penny were not just two coins lying on the ground; they were the focus of a frequency beacon. A frequency beacon is an energetic impulse sent by spirits that directs a human's attention to a particular person, place, or thing.

However, frequency beacons work both ways, because they're also energetic impulses created by our emotions, which are detected by spirits. The frequency beacon I emitted was pondering how to explain a means of recognizing signs from spirits to people who aren't necessarily mediums. The frequency beacon I received was being directed to the exact location of six cents, which meant the sixth sense.

Once I recognized the coins as a sign, I gave myself

permission to accept the reality of the contact experience. I felt the message was about the sixth sense and trusted that it would provide the answer. The glimpse of my Dad holding a raft pointed to an acronym — RAFT — which he knew I'd decipher as "recognize, accept, feel, trust."

Not everyone is a medium, but everyone is capable of perceiving spirits and intuitive messages. The key is learning to recognize the presence of spirits and the signs they present, accepting the reality of the contact, feeling the importance and emotional significance of the message, and trusting your feelings as well as the truth and guidance provided by the message. This is the RAFT technique. Let's examine each step.

Recognize means learning to identify when a spirit or collective of spirits is making his/her/their presence known. It is all the result of a human's electromagnetic field interfacing with the electromagnetic energy of a spirit. Sensing the contact can manifest in different forms, such as a sensation of tingling or cold chills, a glimpse in one's peripheral vision, hearing a familiar person's voice in your mind's ear, or simply knowing. You can also have your attention directed to do something, like turning on a radio and immediately hearing the song that makes you think of a loved one in spirit. You can also be directed to see a specific number combination or even a living being, like a particular type of bird or insect, such as a dragonfly or a butterfly.

Accept the reality of the contact. This will happen when you let down your barriers and give yourself permission to have the contact. This may sound elementary, but people tend to negate or even fear spirit contact, which leads them to dismiss the experience and create an energetic block to it.

The Other Side is a dimension that exists parallel to our material world dimension. Spirits are part of the collective consciousness, and they can and do communicate with us. They don't speak a human language — they speak "frequency." They will transmit signs, images, sounds, and scents and direct our attention to particular things via frequency beacons. This is not hocus-pocus or fantasy. Once you accept the reality of spirit communication and let the spirits (as well as yourself) know that it's okay, they will begin transmitting guidance and information to you.

Feel first; think later! This is where many people hit a dead end with spirit contact (pun intended). Your immediate feeling when you recognize the sign is crucial. It's the first emotional sensation you feel, no matter how outlandish. Spirit communication is an intuitive and emotional process, and it is easy to overanalyze a sensation and rationalize it away.

One of the most common mistakes people make during spirit contact is to overthink or overanalyze the initial imagery or message conveyed. Drawing upon my background as a trial lawyer, I call this "cross-examining the experience." As soon as the imagery or signs from spirits appear, your mind's ego begins the cross-examination to tear the messages apart with questions like, "How can this be true? Isn't this just my imagination? Couldn't this just be a coincidence? Don't you think I'm reading into this? Who would believe me?"

By hyperanalyzing the initial contact, you counteract the positive energy of a spirit with a negative energy barrier, and the spirit will back off. This also happens during a reading when someone immediately shoots down and negates the imagery or message presented by the medium. In short, negative energy blocks the messages transmitted by spirits.

To obtain the maximum benefit from spirit contact, go with your first feeling about the sign. Then, after the experience, analyze why you felt that way and what it meant to you. This is exactly what happened during the "six cents" sign. Once I felt it meant "sixth sense," the full impact of the message began to unfold.

There is a period after the contact that I describe as the "unfolding." At this point, the full impact of the contact will begin to make sense to you. The unfolding can take minutes, hours, days, weeks, and even longer for the full impact of the interdimensional communication to be revealed. More often than not, you will discover it contains multiple meaning messages. I use the term *multiple meaning messages* to describe information received during interdimensional communication that has significance in several ways and on several different levels. There will be more about this in chapter 8: "The Unfolding and Avoiding the No, No, No Syndrome."

Trust ties everything together. This is learning to trust the truth and guidance provided by the spirit contact. It is also about trusting your own feelings. During lectures and public mediumship demonstrations, I often discuss the importance of trusting one's feelings. Then I will ask the audience, "Whenever you have overruled your women's intuition or man's gut instinct, are you happy you did, or did you regret it?" Practically everyone expresses regret for not trusting their feelings.

Spirit communication is transferred to us at lightning speed. It resonates with our body, yet our ego, that pesky creature manufactured in the human brain, wants the last word. This is why fear, rejection, or hyperanalysis can get in the way, thwarting the power of the message.

Spirits know that not everyone is a medium, but they also know that everyone is capable of a mediumistic experience, because everyone possesses the sixth sense to some degree.

The RAFT technique enables you to approach interdimensional communication with an individual spirit or several spirits, aka the collective consciousness. Never underestimate the significance of spirit contact. Perhaps the simplest yet most powerful message from the Other Side is, "I love you."

One of the most common means of interdimensional communication occurs during sleep. This explains the difference between a spiritual visitation and a dream. Unlike the typical surrealism of a dream, a visitation is a coherent experience. It feels different than a dream because it is a lucid conversation with a loved one. The quality of the image of the loved one is generally clearer than in a dream. Visitations have a rational beginning, middle, and end, and the person who had the visitation is convinced of its authenticity.

What a psychic does and what occurs during the dream state involve the same brainwave frequency shift. The pineal gland regulates our activity levels, including when we're awake and when we sleep, so it influences our brainwave frequencies.

There are five known brainwave frequencies: gamma, beta, alpha, theta, and delta. We generate gamma and beta waves while we're awake. Gamma has the most rapid frequency and occurs during intense learning, problem solving, and cognitive processing. The beta state is our normal, everyday set of brainwaves, which enables us to carry on the functions of daily life. As we meditate or drift into a daydream, we enter the alpha state, which is relaxed and comfortable. When we drop to a deeper level of sleep, we enter theta. The delta state occurs during deep, dreamless sleep, when there is a loss of bodily awareness.

The alpha-theta border is the dream state, and it is the frequency where psychic activity occurs. Spirits detect when we're experiencing this brainwave frequency and adjust their frequency in order to obtain a frequency match. When our brainwave frequency and the afterlife frequency are aligned, spirit communication and psychic activity occur.

Normally it takes hours for someone to drift from beta into alpha and then theta. However, for reasons still being studied by neuroscientists, mediums are able to adjust their brainwave frequency from the beta to the alpha-theta state voluntarily and within a few seconds.

The RAFT technique should be applied to spirit contact when we're awake as well as to contact that occurs when we're asleep. I find it fascinating that most people tend to dismiss spirit contact when they are awake, but tend to accept it when asleep. Maybe they feel they aren't responsible for their dreams, so no excuse or explanation is required. In other words, if you tell people that your deceased aunt appeared and spoke to you while you were at work, then they think you're crazy. If the same thing happens in a dream, that's okay — it was just a dream.

Perhaps the RAFT technique comes naturally to humans when it involves contact with spirits during sleep. On these occasions, people are more likely to recognize visitations as spirit contact and accept the experience as real. During the sleep state, emotional barriers come down, as the recipient feels the love and personality of the spirit. People may also trust dreams more than spirit visitations in the conscious state because this is more in keeping with our cultural and religious beliefs. The Bible is loaded with stories of prophetic dreams, frequency beacons, and spiritual signs experienced by people who recognized, accepted, felt, and trusted their positive power. This is particularly true of the two Josephs and the Three Wise Men.

According to the Torah or Old Testament of the Bible, Joseph was a Hebrew who had the ability to interpret dreams. In Genesis 41:1–7, he is summoned by the pharaoh of Egypt, who has experienced two disturbing dreams. In his first dream, Pharaoh saw seven fat, healthy cows emerge from the Nile River, which are followed and devoured by seven skinny cows. In Pharaoh's second dream, seven healthy ears of corn emerge from the Nile, only to be swallowed by seven thin ears of corn.

Using his gift of divination, Joseph prophesizes that Pharaoh's dreams foretell future events that Egypt will experience: seven years of bountiful harvests followed by seven years of famine.

Pharaoh rewards Joseph by appointing him overseer of grain storage and famine preparation. Joseph rises to a position of tremendous power in Egypt, second only to Pharaoh himself. He also becomes the leader of the Hebrew people who fled to Egypt to escape famine. While some verses in scripture condemn prophecy and divination, these passages in Genesis do not, and certainly make a persuasive case for the benefits of recognizing, accepting, feeling, and trusting the significance of dream messages.

In the New Testament, one of the most intriguing concentrations of mystical signs, prophecy, and spirit communication in dreams occurs in Matthew 2:1–23. The Magi, aka the Three Wise Men, were from Persia (modern-day Iran). At the time Persia was part of the Parthian Empire. The Magi were the administrators who ran the bureaucracy of the Parthian Empire, but they were also steeped in mysticism and served as astronomers and astrologers to the royal court.

Astronomy is the observation of stars, constellations, planets, and phenomena such as comets and meteors. Astrology is a form of divination that attempts to determine how the movements and positions of the sun, moon, planets, and stars influence human events. During the Iron Age, most people in the world saw little difference between astronomy and astrology. As far as they were concerned, events on Earth were influenced and foretold by signs from above.

The Magi observed a rare alignment of Saturn, the moon, Jupiter, and the sun that would form in the constellation Aries in mid-April, 6 BC. This was particularly rare because during this alignment there would be a lunar eclipse of Jupiter. We have come to know this alignment, which was observed throughout the world, as the Star of Bethlehem. The Romans even minted a coin to commemorate this astrological event. The existence of this alignment has been verified in recent years by Michael Molnar, professor of astronomy at Rutgers University. Using computer technology to re-create the positions of the planets and the stars in the first century before the birth of Jesus, Molnar confirmed that this particular alignment, which included a lunar eclipse of Jupiter, occurred within the constellation Aries on April 17, 6 BC. These findings were confirmed by a separate study conducted in 2016 by Professor Grant Mathews, director of the department of theoretical astrophysics and cosmology at the University of Notre Dame.

Jupiter was the star of kings, and a lunar eclipse of Jupiter during this rare planetary alignment meant a king of mystical, possibly even divine, origin. Since the alignment occurred within the constellation Aries, which was the astrological symbol for Judea/Israel, the Magi interpreted this as a sign heralding the birth of a great king of the Jewish people. As intellectuals and mystics, they couldn't resist visiting a king whose coming was foretold by signs in the sky, so they assembled a caravan and headed west from Persia to Judea.

This king of course meant Jesus, who, according to Matthew 1:16–17, was descended from King David, ruler of the united kingdoms of Judea and Israel in the tenth century BC. King David was one of the superstars of the Old Testament.

In 6 BC, Judea was ruled by King Herod the Great. Both biblical and historical accounts indicate that Herod was a paranoid megalomaniac who would stop at nothing to stay in power. A clever politician, he used diplomacy for decades to avoid being conquered by the likes of Pompey, Julius Caesar,

Antony and Cleopatra, and eventually Augustus Caesar. Closer to home, anyone whom Herod considered a threat to his throne, including family members, ended up dead.

When a flashy caravan of Magi from Persia arrived, Herod wanted to know why. Since he was making them an offer they couldn't refuse, the Magi accepted Herod's invitation to his court. Despite his homicidal tendencies, Herod could be charming when it suited his purposes. Since Judaism rejected astrology as divination and therefore an abomination, it was banned in Herod's court. As such, Herod's advisors didn't know where to look for, much less how to interpret, the astrological alignment that foretold the coming of this new king of the Jews.

Unlike his advisors, Herod hadn't been raised and educated strictly in the Jewish tradition. He had a Greco-Roman education and, like the Greeks and Romans, took astrological signs seriously. Divine or not, a descendant of the House of David posed a real threat to his throne — and he meant to eliminate that threat.

Despite depictions in art and on Christmas cards, the Star of Bethlehem wasn't a Steven Spielberg–esque, Hollywood-type spotlight beaming directly on the birthplace of Jesus. If it were, Herod could have easily located Jesus without the Magi. This meant that for the time being, Herod needed their assistance to pinpoint the whereabouts of this new king they were so enthusiastic to see. After all, according to Herod, he too wanted to pop by for a visit and pay homage to this divine child.

The Magi were called Wise Men for good reason. Since they were advisors to the court of the Parthian Empire, it's reasonable to assume Herod wasn't the first sociopathic tyrant they had met. The Magi managed to stay in Herod's good graces long enough to part with the understanding that once they discovered the whereabouts of this new king, they'd be sure to let him know.

Once free of Herod, the Magi located Jesus, his mother, Mary, and her husband, Joseph, in the town of Bethlehem. According to Matthew 2:10–11, the Magi presented Jesus with gifts of great mystical and prophetic significance: gold to honor his royal lineage, frankincense to honor his spiritual path, and myrrh to symbolize the sacrifices he would endure.

Just before the Magi prepared to leave, they were warned in a prophetic dream (described in Matthew 2:12) not to return to Herod. The Gospel of Matthew leaves it unclear whether all three Wise Men experienced this dream concurrently. In any event, they took the warning seriously and secretly departed from Judea by an alternate route, thus avoiding King Herod.

Synchronistically, a spiritual entity known as an angel appeared to Joseph in a prophetic dream described in Matthew 2:13, which warned him about Herod. Joseph acted immediately and took Jesus and Mary to safety in Egypt. Joseph recognized the dream as a message, accepted its reality, and clearly felt it was urgent. Trusting his instincts, Joseph sprang into action and swiftly had Jesus and Mary with him on the road to Egypt.

When Herod realized he had been outwitted by the Magi, his psychopathic nature erupted in full force. Since the Magi left Judea from Bethlehem, he concluded that town was the home of this new rival king. To eliminate this threat, Herod immediately ordered his army into Bethlehem to kill all male children up to two years of age.

Many historians cast doubt this ever happened, since there are no official records of the slaughter of these innocent children. On the other hand, this isn't something Herod would have had recorded, and none of his scribes would have been stupid enough to do so without his permission. However, mass murder is not something people forget, so it may have been secretly recorded by sources outside of Herod's court. Throughout his reign,

Herod had over three hundred of his own military commanders executed for treason. He also had his wife, Queen Mariamne, her brother, her mother, and her grandfather executed — not to mention three of his own sons. For a sociopathic personality like Herod, the murder of a few dozen children would have seemed insignificant.

Fortunately, Jesus, Mary, and Joseph escaped the wrath of Herod. As we have seen, the Star of Bethlehem astrological alignment occurred in 6 BC, and historical records indicate Herod died sometime between 4 BC and AD 2. By this reckoning, they would have remained in Egypt for at least two years. Upon the tyrant's death, Matthew 2:19–20 says that Joseph was again visited in a prophetic dream by an angel who told him to take his family back to Judea, because "those who were trying to take the child's life are dead." Joseph felt it was safe then to take Jesus and Mary back to Israel.

If anyone recognized, accepted, felt, and trusted the positive power of signs, frequency beacons, and messages conveyed by spiritual entities to people in the sleep state, it was the Bible's two Josephs and Three Wise Men.

Whether you believe these stories are legendary or literal, they demonstrate how belief systems worldwide embrace dreams as the delivery system for interdimensional communication. These biblical illustrations are not meant to advance one belief system over another, but rather to demonstrate how people throughout history have recognized, accepted, felt, and trusted messages transmitted to them while in the sleep state by spirits and the Eternal Light we call God.

SPIRIT CONTACT IS SELDOM a one-time-only event. Sometimes spirits will contact us in the sleep state, and even though the recipient recognizes, accepts, feels, and trusts the message, the spirit will provide additional validation to underscore the importance of the message.

During a session with Rebecca, the spirit of her son, Jamie, connected with me.

"I'm sensing there were four people present when he died," I said. "Jamie was one of them, but there were two other males and a female. Your son's on the Other Side — the other three people are still here in our world."

"That's correct," Rebecca confirmed.

"It feels like he definitely knew the woman and one of the men, but the other guy, the short guy — he didn't know that one."

"That's right — one of the guys was his roommate, Chad. Jamie didn't know Bart, who was the other guy."

"The woman — Su — Sue — Susan..."

"Susanne! That's Jamie's ex-girlfriend!"

"Jamie says — she thinks with — uh, she — thinks with what's between her legs."

"Jamie would definitely describe her like that — and he's right."

"This was a brutal death."

"It was."

"Jamie's spirit indicates that this was strictly revenge, but it wasn't supposed to be murder."

"That's what I was told by the police." Rebecca paused. "Susanne is a spiteful woman and wanted to get back at him for breaking up with her. She got these two losers to believe Jamie had a lot of money stashed in his bedroom, so the plan was for Chad to let Bart in, then beat and rob Jamie. It was just her way to get Chad and Bart to beat him up."

"It's complicated," I said. "Jamie's spirit is telling me they didn't mean to kill him, but things got out of hand. The little guy, Bart, was like a wild dog. When Jamie hit him, this guy went crazy, and that's when Jamie knew he was going to die, but not like a coward. He was going to die like a man, on his feet, so he fought back."

"My son was a tough guy," Rebecca explained. "After Jamie's roommate, Chad, let them in, they surprised him when he was sleeping. Chad and Bart started roughing him up, but Jamie fought back, punching and kicking in all directions. He hit the shorter guy, Bart, who went berserk — totally crazy."

"I'm seeing a red and black plaid pattern, and it feels like flannel — now I sense he ran for his life, barefoot, naked — then severe impact to the head — I'm tasting blood — does this make sense to you, Rebecca?"

"Yes, it does. Jamie was stark naked when he ran for his life. He ran out the door. They chased him, and he made it to the road near his house, where the short guy, Bart, shot him in the head."

Rebecca paused for a moment. "The police found his red and black flannel pajamas lying by his bed."

"Don't worry about her — she'll either drink herself to death or overdose."

"Oh my God! I'm shocked!" Rebecca exclaimed. "Right after Jamie died — he came to me in a dream and said that exact thing you just said! 'Don't worry about her — she'll either drink herself to death or overdose.'"

"I've seen this phenomenon before. Jamie's spirit is validating that he definitely made contact with you in the sleep state. This is an extremely important message from him."

"I'm so angry. Susanne was involved in his murder, but she wasn't charged, and I want her to be held accountable for her involvement. I want revenge!"

"I can't even begin to imagine how much you must want revenge," I explained, "but revenge isn't the answer. Jamie's spirit has come to you twice, once in a dream and once through me, to tell you, 'Don't worry about her — she'll either drink herself to death or overdose.'"

"There's no way this is a coincidence," Rebecca replied. "Guess I better trust Jamie's message."

"Hold on — one last spirit is coming though — a female — and she's projecting the name — Lizzie? And this is weird — she's holding an ax."

"Seriously?" Rebecca exclaimed.

"Whoa," I paused as the vision intensified. "She's swinging the ax and splitting a jack-o'-lantern in two. She keeps chopping the jack-o'-lantern and repeating, 'He will have a horrible ending in prison.'"

"This is so weird. I was doing a family genealogy and discovered I'm a descendant of Lizzie Borden! Even though she had no children, Lizzie Borden and I have common ancestors."

"Wait — you mean *the* Lizzie Borden — the notorious ax murderer?"

"That's the one, Mark."

"Rebecca, the jack-o'-lantern indicates she's referring to a significant event on or very close to October 31, which is Halloween."

"Oh, my!" Rebecca gasped. "I just received notice yesterday that jury selection in the trial of Bart, the man who shot my son, is scheduled to begin on October 31 — Halloween."

"This vision is intensifying — Lizzie Borden is splitting another pumpkin in two with an ax — her message is 'Justice will be done!'"

"For heaven's sake!" Rebecca exclaimed. "My slogan, every time a reporter confronts me, is, 'Justice for Jamie will be done!'

Mark, I'm a Christian — and I know this is terrible to say — but hearing this from my ancestor's spirit doesn't exactly make me feel bad!"

"I have to confess, Rebecca, I've never had the spirit of a homicidal maniac come through and make someone feel good before."

"Well, Mark, I guess there really is a first time for everything."

Five months later, Rebecca contacted me. Bart's trial did start on October 31. She was happy to report he had been convicted for the premeditated first-degree murder of Jamie and would be spending the remainder of his life in prison.

"I guess Lizzie Borden's spirit was right about Bart getting convicted. I wonder if he'll have a horrible ending in prison, like she said."

"That's very possible, Rebecca."

"Even though Chad didn't kill my son, his trial as an accomplice to murder is still pending. The prosecutors said with the overwhelming evidence against him, a conviction is almost guaranteed."

"What about Jamie's girlfriend, Susanne, who set this whole chain of events in motion?"

"Susanne's public defender made a deal with the prosecution," Rebecca explained. "In exchange for testifying against Bart and Chad, no charges will be filed against her."

"Whoa! How did you feel about her cutting that deal?" I asked.

"Not too good. During the trial, Susanne basked in the attention spotlight of being the prosecution's star witness, although her behavior in court was far from stellar."

"How so?"

"She kept making rude comments to the prosecutors and

the defense attorneys. She would have these angry temper tantrum outbursts. One day she came to court so drunk she couldn't testify. This really irritated the judge, who constantly reprimanded her and even threatened to throw her in jail for contempt of court."

"Must've been hard to watch that."

"It wasn't easy, but despite her antics, Bart was convicted of first-degree murder, and he received a life sentence."

"What about her?"

"I'm glad I trusted my son's message," Rebecca told me.

"Why do you feel that way?"

"The police told me Susanne was the victim of a home invasion. One night, a couple guys bashed in her door, beat her, and took what few things she owned. Word on the street was, she couldn't pay her drug dealer."

"Rather ironic she ended up being a victim of home invasion."

"That's just the beginning, Mark. During Bart's trial, she got arrested several times for burglary and drug possession. When she finally showed up to testify, she had the audacity to smile at me and say, 'Have a nice day.'"

"That must've been difficult for you."

"Since Jamie's murder, Susanne's family and friends have abandoned her," Rebecca continued. "They had it with her stealing from them to support her alcoholism and drug addiction. Last I heard, she got arrested again for drug possession."

Rebecca paused.

"Susanne is one horrible person. She wanted revenge against Jamie for breaking up with her, and what did that do for her? As much as I wanted to get back at her, Jamie wants me to be free of the burden of revenge, because I believe what he said about

Susanne will come to pass: 'Don't worry about her — she'll either drink herself to death or overdose.'"

⌁

MESSAGES FROM SPIRITS are motivated by love and guide people to healing and resolution. They never direct anyone to commit acts of anger, violence, or destruction. There was no way Jamie was going to let revenge destroy his mother's life. That is why spirits like Jamie can be very direct and will even repeat a message to make sure the loved one in the material world will recognize the spirit contact, accept it as real, feel its power, and trust its guidance.

The electromagnetic soul is pure energy and moves at the speed of light. That is how spirits can emit frequency beacons to more than one person at a time. When the multiple recipients of these signs from spirits naturally apply RAFT, this results in synchronicity.

⌁

IT WAS A BEAUTIFUL, sunny November day on the barrier island on the east coast of Florida, where I live. I decided to get up early to fix a sprinkler head in my yard's irrigation system. My neighbor and friend Rob volunteered to help me, and we drove across the causeway to the mainland to go to a hardware store. After purchasing the sprinkler parts, I kept humming the Beatles song "Hey Jude."

"Mark, the Beatles are cool, but uh, what's up with 'Hey Jude' today?"

"Not sure. You know how a song gets in your head. I keep hearing the line 'Take a sad song and make it better.'"

"Yeah, sometimes that happens to me."

"Rob, I feel like taking the north causeway home."

"That's the long way home — ah —" Rob stopped. "Is something up?"

"Not sure, but I feel like taking the scenic route."

The road leading to the causeway back to the barrier island goes through the oldest part of town. Rob and I saw that an art show and a farmer's market were there that morning.

"Rob, I didn't know there was an art show today. Let's check it out!"

"Mark, are you sure? We need to fix your sprinkler."

"Relax. I'm sure the sprinkler will still be broken when we get back."

I pulled over and found a parking spot right away. That in and of itself should have tipped me off that something spiritual was in the works. The art show was in the oldest part of town, which is home to the art museum, civic center, and several art galleries. The artists had their displays set up along the street.

After perusing the art show, Rob wanted to leave when my attention was pulled to a group of people creating sidewalk art with colored chalk. Many of these people were very talented, and several of the murals were striking.

"Wow, these are fantastic!" Rob lit up. "Okay. Fifteen more minutes."

Before I could respond to Rob, I felt drawn to one of the artists, a woman who was lying on her side and drawing a colorful tropical rainforest frog. Her talent was inspiring. She was working under the shade of a tree.

"You're the smart one," I joked. "You've got shade."

"I got here early," she said, continuing her work. "I knew I had to get this spot."

"I've never seen such an incredible drawing of a frog — it is so realistic."

She looked up from her work and our eyes met.

"You're Mark Anthony the psychic, aren't you?"

I knelt down beside her. "Oh my gosh! I remember you! You're Barbara! I did a reading for you at a group event a few years ago!"

She nodded slightly as Rob took a few steps back to give us privacy, doing his best to look as if he wasn't listening.

"I didn't know you were from around here," I said.

"I'm not — I live in Orlando, over an hour drive away."

"The reading I did for you — the spirit of your son came through," I recalled.

"Yes," she paused. "You wrote about it in your book *Never Letting Go*. I appreciated how you honored my son. He was in college when he died, and you told me he was sorry for his death, which was an accidental drug overdose."

"I remember."

"How weird," Barbara said. "I didn't even know about this art show until yesterday, when I saw it in the paper. I just knew I had to be here, and now here you are."

A tingling sensation began to flow through me. "Your son's spirit is coming to me. He has a message for you — is this okay?"

"Absolutely. Mark, what does my son want me to know?"

"He says that you're like a life preserver. Everyone reaches out for you to save them. Sometimes you feel as if you're going under, but you won't — you're a pillar of strength."

"That's how it feels," Barbara replied. "I'm the caretaker for my husband. Because of his severe diabetes, he's just had to have his legs amputated. Sometimes it is just overwhelming, and I don't know if I can cope.

"Today is the ninth anniversary of my son's death," Barbara reflected. "Not a day goes by I don't think of him and feel him around me. I knew he wanted me to be here today, and I feel he orchestrated us meeting today. Thank you so much."

"Your son says he always loved the way you bring color into the world — but — there's more," I continued. "I keep hearing a line from a song: 'Take a sad song and make it better.' It's from the Beatles song 'Hey Jude.'"

She smiled, paused for a moment, and handed me her business card.

Her professional name as an artist was Jude.

Chapter 5

SPIRITUAL SITUATIONAL AWARENESS

"I IGNORED THE SIGNS, and everything that could go wrong did!"

Is everything in life simply a random Las Vegas–style roll of the dice? Not a chance! Everyone experiences synchronicity: a seemingly unplanned sequence that can lead to a life-altering event.

Each experience endured has a cause and a reason for its occurrence. Good things happen to bad people, and bad things happen to good people, not because of a simple stimulus-reaction course of events, but because of the complex chain of intertwining energy and events in the material world.

Even though everyone is not a psychic or a medium, everyone is capable of getting in sync with the afterlife frequency and benefiting from contact with spirits by developing a heightened level of *spiritual situational awareness.* This skill enables you to detect signs transmitted by spirits and know what to do with that information once you receive and process it. The key to developing spiritual situational awareness is to stop blocking the contact, because when you ignore these feelings, it usually ends up in regret — or worse.

Removing this block begins with honing observational skills that are essential to awareness. This means paying attention to information received through the five physical senses. Look, listen, smell, observe, and sense the world around you. Remove distractions that block your perception. This means taking the earbuds out, putting down the cellphone, and most of all, paying attention to your surroundings.

One of the easiest ways to begin developing your basic situational awareness is to simply close your eyes and listen. Make a list of what you hear, no matter what it is. Start at home. You might hear children playing, traffic noises, or the hum of electrical appliances.

Then start to practice this awareness exercise in different places. Take a walk in a park, in the woods, or anywhere outside. Listen and observe. You may begin to hear more than the wind rustling through the trees; you may begin to distinguish between the types of leaves rustling. You will hear more than birds chirping as you realize there are several different types of birds.

If you have difficulty hearing or seeing, you can adapt this exercise to focus on your other senses. If hearing is an issue, be aware of what you see and smell. If vision is an issue, focus on what you hear and smell. Eventually you will get to the point where you begin to appreciate and be aware of the full magnitude of your physical senses. Perhaps you will develop this awareness to the point where you sense your own heartbeat.

This brings us to the next level of observation, which is situational awareness, the perception of what is happening around you in all directions at any given moment. This highly valued skill enables police officers, firefighters, paramedics, and military personnel to make snap judgments in emergency situations. A developed sense of situational awareness warns you what to avoid and guides you to who or what can help during a crisis.

People with a keen sense of situational awareness view the world as spherical rather than two-dimensional. This means having veridical perception, which is developing the ability to observe what is happening around you in all directions: in front, behind, beside, above, and below.

Spiritual situational awareness takes this insight to a higher level. It expands this spherical perception to what is happening around you not just physically but energetically, which includes being open to spirit contact. The challenge is developing this perception, learning to rely on it, and then harnessing its positive power. Spiritual situational awareness can not only alter the course of lives but can save lives.

Developing spiritual situational awareness occurs over time after continued application of the RAFT technique. People progress at different rates in learning to recognize, accept, feel, and trust signs and messages transmitted by spirits. Over time, RAFT can become an ingrained habit, to the point where it seems to be done unconsciously.

Anyone with an ounce of intuition has been in a situation where things just didn't add up, alerting that person to some type of threat or danger. The issue is whether that person reacted quickly and effectively to the signs from spirits. Through RAFT, one will begin to bypass the blocks most people erect against spirit contact. This leads to a heightened sense of spiritual situational awareness, which enables immediate access to the wisdom of the collective consciousness. This can guide you away from harmful behaviors, physical threats, and people who are potentially dangerous.

Successful use of the RAFT technique, and developing a heightened sense of spiritual situational awareness, begins by developing the habit of paying attention to your surroundings.

"BE AWARE!" was my father's motto. He drilled that into my siblings and me for as long as I can remember. Whenever any of us left the house, my father always said two things — first, "I love you," immediately followed by, "be aware."

My father, Earl, had served as a Navy SEAL, and after the service he was a scuba diver and swimming instructor. Thanks to his expertise in scuba, he even dove with the legendary Jacques Cousteau. After marrying my mother, Jeannie, he worked as a NASA engineer and was instrumental to the Apollo program manned missions to the moon. He was part of the team who figured out how to get the ill-fated Apollo 13 safely back to Earth. Needless to say, Dad had an acute sense of situational awareness.

Both of my parents had highly developed psychic and mediumistic abilities. Growing up in a family full of psychics was interesting, to say the least. My parents taught me to respect spirit communication and approach it with reverence. My mother taught me to embrace and trust my feelings in order to use my abilities to their fullest potential.

Not surprisingly, my father taught me the importance of awareness. Whenever my brother, sister, or I made a wisecrack about Dad's "Be aware!" mantra, he'd give us "the look." Aside from getting us to immediately shut up, it also taught us to be aware that teasing a Navy SEAL usually wasn't a good idea.

For my father, "Be aware" wasn't just about walking through a dark parking lot at night. It applied to all situations: the home, classroom, boardroom, traffic, and especially when you were in the water.

I grew up in a small Florida seaside town, so the beach was a fact of life. By the time I was two years old, Dad had taught me to swim. When I was eight, he taught me to snorkel. Snorkeling is like scuba diving in that you wear a mask and propel yourself with swim fins. Unlike scuba diving, which uses tanks for your air supply, snorkeling requires being at the surface to breathe through a tube called a snorkel.

Snorkeling became my passion. Although the ocean at the east coast of Central Florida is beautiful, the water is naturally murky, with low visibility, which doesn't make it ideal for snorkeling. The Bahamas, on the other hand, are known for crystal-clear water. One July when I was thirteen years old, my parents announced they were taking me there on vacation. I couldn't believe we were going to Love Beach on Paradise Island, one of the best snorkeling spots in the Bahamas.

When we arrived at Love Beach, my mother set up camp under a palm-thatched cabana. She was a gifted artist who enjoyed the beauty and serenity of the ocean, but snorkeling definitely wasn't her thing. Mom was a city girl from northern New Jersey, and her idea of adventure involved a shopping trip to Manhattan, fine restaurants, shows, and dancing.

Jeannie was already making friends with other tourists at nearby cabanas as Dad and I prepared for our underwater adventure. Mom said she'd have lunch waiting for us. Although she smiled and wished us well, she looked worried.

We put on our swim fins and walked backward into the water. It's easier than walking forward, flip-flopping over the elongated swim fins like a drunken Daffy Duck.

When we were waist-deep, my father said, "You've always been interested in my work in the space program and about life on other planets."

"Yeah. So?"

"Mark, the ocean is another world. In a sense, it's another dimension. There are things that live there that can't on land, and vice versa. Stay by my side, swim quietly, avoid unnecessary splashing, and always..."

"Be aware. Yeah, I get it," my thirteen-year-old know-it-all self replied.

A mild version of "the look" emerged on Dad's face, immediately suppressing my penchant for sarcasm. He seemed to get a kick out of that as we put on our masks and snorkels. Then together my father and I entered the aquatic world. Since talking isn't practical while underwater, scuba divers and snorkelers use hand signals to communicate. My father made sure I was well versed in this form of communication.

When I reflect back upon that day, I now understand what my father was trying to tell me about parallel dimensions. The ocean truly is another world. We think of other dimensions as distant, inaccessible, and faraway places, when they're actually right next to us. The ocean may be the best way to understand the difference between our world and the Other Side — two systems teeming with energy, very different, yet they coexist and overlap with each other.

Snorkeling is ideal for diving around reefs because the most colorful marine life is found within thirty feet of the surface, where sunlight is brightest. We soon found ourselves in the midst of several schools of colorful tropical fish, which swam by us and around us. The slightest vibration from our motions caused entire schools to instantly react in unison.

The rays of the sun illuminated the spectacular white sand sea bottom, covered by bright-green clumps of seagrass. As we approached the reef, an infinite array of starfish and spiny sea urchins covered the multicolored coral formations. Majestic sea fans swayed gently with the rhythm of the ocean current.

We were swimming side by side about a quarter mile offshore. I was so distracted by the beauty of the reef that I didn't realize I'd separated from Dad until the ocean bottom drastically dropped off into deeper water. The current tugged me away from the shallow waters of the colorful reef.

I was scared and suddenly aware that I was a mere speck floating in the vast deep blue of the ocean. What I wasn't aware of was how much I was splashing while swimming desperately back toward shallower water. Each thrash and splash of my hands and swim fins was a frequency beacon, emitting intense sound wave vibrations in all directions.

Dad silently zoomed to my side and alerted me with a hand signal to surface. When I stuck my head above the water and saw his eyes, I knew it was serious.

"Mark," he whispered, "Get to shore now! Quietly! Don't splash. Don't look back!"

Then I saw it. A massive shark was closing in on us from the open sea. It was roughly two hundred feet away and looked at least twelve feet long. Its dorsal fin skimmed the surface as it shot through the water toward us like a torpedo. From the striped markings on its body, I recognized it as a tiger shark.

The huge predator's mouth was loaded with rows of large sharp teeth, and its black emotionless eyes were locked on us. We were in the shark's domain, where it was superior to us in every way. There was no chance of fighting it off or outswimming it.

Waves of terror shuddered through me. Dad's emphatic hand signals commanded me to follow his orders.

As a SEAL, my father knew how to swim without splashing, and he had taught me this skill. He always said there were times when being able to swim silently in the sea could mean the difference between life and death. This was one of those times.

Sharks are apex predators and extremely sensitive to vibration and frequency. It was bad enough that my earlier splashing attracted the shark to us. Now it was upon us, and if I panicked and started splashing, the shark would immediately identify the rapid frequency of those vibrations as coming from wounded prey, which would trigger its attack response. Mustering all my inner strength, I resisted the urge to panic, grabbed hold of my fear, and started as silently as possible toward the shore, making sure not to splash.

This is all my fault.

I wasn't paying attention and wandered off.

I looked side to side, but didn't see my father.

Dad! Where's Dad?

Defying his order, I looked back. The pit of my stomach collapsed. My father was facing the shark. Dad's body was vertical, head just below the surface, breathing through his snorkel. He was virtually motionless, except for a slight wave of his swim fins to keep him stationary so that his snorkel remained just above the surface. His arms were outstretched. He was trying to look as big as possible without provoking the shark.

The shark was huge. It was separated from my father by barely twenty feet and cruised slowly back and forth, eyeing him. My father was at the mercy of the most merciless of beings.

Dad positioned himself between the shark and me!

He was drawing its attention away from me!

He was going to sacrifice his life for mine!

Abruptly the creature made an erratic maneuver away from my father and zipped away into deeper water. I was astonished at how quickly the shark vanished, but even more so at how fast my Dad could swim underwater toward me without making a sound.

I didn't need any hand signals to tell me to follow him full speed ahead. For all Dad and I knew, the shark was coming back with some friends. A quarter mile is an awfully long way to go when your head is flooded with horrific images of being lunch for an immense carnivorous fish.

We hit the beach, overcome with exhaustion. Huffing and puffing, I threw off my mask and hugged him.

He was ready to die for me. Any man can father a child, but not every man earns the title of Dad. He did.

"I guess it wasn't hungry," Dad panted out a joke.

"I'm sorry, Dad. I totally screwed up."

"The ocean can be your best friend or your worst enemy," Dad said calmly. "Things can change real fast when you're not paying attention. Now do you understand why it's so important to be aware?"

"I do — and I'll never tease you again about telling me that. Dad, I really thought that monster was going to kill you."

"That was scary as hell, Mark, but a shark isn't a monster. It belongs there. We invaded its world. It's a predator, but the most dangerous predators are on land, and they stand on two legs."

FOR MOST PEOPLE, developing spiritual situational awareness takes time and practice. For others, it comes naturally, because they don't block intuitive feelings and subtle signs from spirits. This is true of my business manager, Rocky. She is a woman of many talents. Rocky is a successful businessperson as well as a gifted musician, ballet dancer, and singer. She also has a highly developed sense of spiritual situational awareness.

Our business relationship began when I was in law school. Part of my education was at Oxford University in England, and after that, I finished my degree at Mercer University in Georgia. Rocky heard that I needed a part-time job, and she offered me one at her singing telegram and balloon delivery company in Atlanta as a messenger.

This seemed like a weird job for a law student. On the other hand, since I sang in the school choir as a child, I could carry a tune. As a law student, I was no stranger to public speaking. Yet singing telegram messenger?

"It will build your self-confidence before an audience," Rocky explained.

"How exactly will it do that?"

"Mark, once you get used to wearing a costume to surprise someone in public, hand them balloons, tell jokes, and sing songs, arguing a case in court will be a piece of cake. That, and you'll get paid fifty bucks per telegram. Each gig lasts maybe ten minutes. Do the math. You can do two or three a day and still make it home in time to study. Where else can you make that kind of money without doing anything illegal or immoral?"

"Where do I sign?" I replied.

My first job as a singing telegram messenger was on a Friday afternoon, and my very first telegram was a "gorilla gram" for a lady's birthday party. I took a deep breath, charged into the restaurant in a gorilla costume with a bouquet of Mylar balloons shaped like bananas, beat my hands on my chest, and sang a birthday song to a woman having lunch with her friends.

Apparently it went well, because when I left, the lady and her friends were roaring with laughter. I slipped out the restaurant and headed to the company van.

Rocky was doing the next telegram, so I jumped in the driver's seat. We were under time pressure and facing Atlanta traffic. I only had time to take off the gorilla head part of my costume, while Rocky was in the back of the van doing the final touches on her costume.

Our next stop was for a woman who didn't know she was being promoted to vice president of a bank. Since she was about to become the first female vice president at this branch, the bank executives thought it fitting that she be notified of this by a female superhero.

Although only five feet tall, Rocky was perfect for the role.

She was in peak physical condition. Clad in a form-fitting red leotard with a wide gold belt, a red cape, and arm shields, and crowned with a headband shield, she looked every inch an alpha female superhero.

On the way to the bank, Rocky was practicing her opening lines, "I hereby proclaim you vice president! How's that for the intro, Mark?"

"Try this," I suggested: "On behalf of women superheroes everywhere, I hereby proclaim you vice president!"

The bank was near Underground Atlanta, in the oldest part of the city. Left over from the Civil War, it has great historical significance and is known for shopping, bars, restaurants, and nightclubs. Underground Atlanta can be a lot of fun and attracts a lot of tourists. Unfortunately, it also attracts predators.

The bank building was at the center of a business plaza abutted by a few other tall buildings. The bank's mirrored windows reflected the busy street and plaza, which were packed with people. Finding a parking spot was impossible, so the plan was for me to let Rocky off, circle the area, and pick her up after she finished the job. I pulled the van behind a bus stopped in front of the bank.

Suddenly I felt a sick feeling in the pit of my stomach. Before I could say anything, Rocky abruptly bent over, held her stomach, and said, "I don't like this. Something's wrong!"

Both of us felt our attention drawn to the bank's entrance. One of its many mirrored doors opened. Although the sidewalk was crowded, Rocky pointed to a frail elderly woman who just stepped out of the bank into the middle of the plaza. She must have just made a withdrawal as she was trying to put some money in her purse.

"That lady! She's in danger!" Rocky cried out.

The lady was heading toward the bus in front of us when Rocky zeroed in on a man in his thirties who was at least six feet tall. He wore a dark green sweatshirt, jeans, and a ski hat, which he pulled over his face as he turned directly toward the old woman.

"My God — it's him! I've got to warn her!" Rocky jumped out of the passenger side door.

The man grabbed the woman's purse, wrenched it from her and shoved her to the ground as she screamed, "Help me!"

Onlookers stared doing nothing.

"Hey you! Stop!" Rocky pushed her way through the crowd.

The attacker sprinted away from the plaza on a side street toward an alley that led to Underground Atlanta.

Rocky charged after him.

"Rocky — don't! Are you crazy? He could kill you!" I called out to no avail as she chased after him.

Once the attacker fled the scene, people came to the woman's aid. She was crying and obviously in pain. Cars honked at me to move, so I pulled the van onto the street, which ran parallel to the alley leading to Underground Atlanta. Steering with one hand, I hit 911 on my cellphone with the other.

"Please state the nature of the emergency," the police dispatcher asked.

"I want to report a strong-arm robbery in front of —"

"First National Bank," the dispatcher cut me off. "A bus driver called it in. Units are on scene."

"We're in pursuit of the suspect," I replied.

"What do you mean you're in pursuit? Who are you?"

"Uh — a law student. I don't have time to explain. He's heading toward Underground Atlanta!" I gave the street he was on to the dispatcher.

Meanwhile, the culprit dashed through the crowded sidewalks, shoving people out of his way. He stuffed the stolen cash in his pockets and flung his victim's purse away.

Hot on his heels, Rocky kept yelling, "Stop, thief!"

Underground Atlanta was within sight.

Suddenly, his escape route was cut off by two Atlanta police cars. Officers on foot closed in from all sides on the entrance to Underground Atlanta.

A dozen police officers drew their guns, ready to fire.

"FREEZE!" several yelled, taking aim.

The robber did an about-face to double back but came to a dead stop. His escape was blocked by none other than a female superhero.

"What the hell? I give up!" he shouted, then fell to his knees, raised his hands in the air, and surrendered to a hyperventilating singing telegram messenger half his size.

Rocky caught her breath, stood erect, feet apart, hands on her hips, and felt her cape fluttering in the breeze. During all the commotion, Rocky forgot she was in costume.

The police officers surrounding the scene were perplexed. Guns aimed, they hesitated, looking back and forth over their raised guns at one another and then at the suspect cowering on his knees before what looked like someone out of a superhero comic book.

"This is the guy who robbed that lady!" Rocky pointed to the suspect. "Arrest him!"

Three cops immediately responded and handcuffed him.

A police sergeant stepped forward, holstering his gun. "Who do you think you are, giving my men orders? And who the hell are you anyway?"

"Would you believe — a member of Women Superheroes Everywhere?"

Before he could respond, one of the officers called to him. "Hey, sergeant! There's a guy in a monkey suit over here — says he's with her!"

No matter how you may be dressed at the time, spiritual situational awareness, or psychic ability for that matter, doesn't give you superpowers. They're extensions of your own natural perceptive abilities, which can help you identify dangerous people and situations. How you react to information received this way can be a life-altering event. The challenge is developing this perception, learning to rely on it, and then harnessing its positive power. This includes avoiding dangerous situations, not interjecting yourself into them. When you encounter a dangerous person, it is always best to call the police for help.

IT IS EASY TO BELIEVE in synchronicity when a complex chain of events leads you to being in the right place at the right time. Sometimes synchronicity also means being in the wrong place at the wrong time, which teaches us that no one is insulated from tragedy.

"It will never happen to me." Many people are under the impression that they are somehow immune from being victims of violent crime. This is especially true of those who work in law enforcement and the criminal justice system.

Joy was a criminal defense attorney who served as a public defender in her small hometown. She fought hard for everything she achieved, but it never seemed like enough. In her position as an assistant public defender, she was formidable in the courtroom. Judges and opposing counsel respected her courage and sharp intellect. But where Joy shined the most was during jury selection. Before evidence is presented at trial, a jury must be empaneled. The prosecutor and defense attorney each have the right to ask prospective jurors questions about themselves and their views on various matters in order to select (at least in theory) an unbiased jury.

Joy had an uncanny sense of what prospective jurors felt. She intuitively knew which ones to choose and which to strike from the panel. She always seemed to end up with a jury who identified with her, and this resulted in a strong acquittal rate.

Despite her success in court, back at the office she felt invisible. Since childhood, she always felt that she never stood out in the crowd and just blended into the background. Being one of the few female attorneys in the local male-dominated legal system didn't make things any easier. She was routinely passed over for promotions in favor of her male colleagues.

In her early thirties, she was single, and her personal life was difficult at best. What few relationships she had with men were brief and anything but tender. Suffice it to say there was little happiness in Joy's life.

That was until Rudy was hired by the public defender's office. After law school he'd relocated to the South from Trenton, New Jersey. Seeking experience as a litigator, he believed the public defender's office was a great place to launch his career.

Like Joy, Rudy didn't click with the clique at the office. He was thin and handsome, wore expensive suits, and had a sarcastic sense of humor. His fashion sense and dramatic courtroom style gave rise to assumptions about his sexuality. Coupled with his New Jersey accent, this didn't make him popular with the good old boy hierarchy of the local bar association, much less law enforcement. Behind his back, he was called "Fruity Rudy."

When Rudy was assigned to be her trial partner, Joy was elated. Not only did he respect her professionally, but he also showed actual interest in her as a person. They developed an excellent working relationship. With Joy's intuitive ability and homespun charm, coupled with Rudy's theatrical demeanor, they became a formidable team and won trial after trial. With the highest acquittal rate in the public defender's office, even the higher-ups had to acknowledge their success.

Despite the unsubstantiated rumors about him, Joy developed emotional feelings for Rudy. One August evening, after winning a trial, Rudy wanted to celebrate.

"Let's hit the Clap Trap!" Rudy joked referring to the Sand Trap, a local bar next to a golf course.

Joy giggled anytime he used the bar's nickname Clap Trap, which alluded to its reputation as a singles bar and one where contracting venereal diseases was a very real possibility.

"If you can't score there, you can't score anywhere..." Rudy spoofed Frank Sinatra singing "New York, New York."

Walking to Rudy's car, Joy hesitated when she saw only stars in the night sky.

"New moon. It's one dark night, and humid as hell," Rudy said as he opened the passenger side door of his old clunker mint-green Lincoln Continental for Joy. Normally she was eager to go out for a drink with him, but tonight she felt uneasy.

"Rudy, I think I want to skip tonight."

"What? And break our tradition? No way!"

"I'm nervous. Maybe I should just go home."

"Nervous? C'mon. A drink'll calm ya down."

"I dunno — it's just so dark tonight."

"You're scared of the dark? Ooo! Maybe we'll get abducted by aliens! That's one way to get out of this here hellhole hick town."

"Hey! This here hellhole hick town you is a talkin' about is muh home," Joy jokingly mimicked a heavy drawl. "Okay, you win, but only one drink."

On the short drive to the bar, Rudy rolled down his window and lit up a cigarette. Smoking was the only thing Rudy did that she didn't like. On the other hand, he only smoked when he was anxious. She figured that after the day's trial and her angst about going out, he was feeling some stress. Sensing each other's tension, they chatted about the day's events and their hard-won victory in court.

"Clap Trap's in full swing tonight," Rudy said, looking for a parking spot. "Geez, the lot's full."

Joy's uneasiness intensified. "Maybe we should just call it a night."

"Yankee land yacht cruising through sea of redneck pickup trucks," Rudy joked, trying to lighten the mood in the car. He idled into a spot at the edge of the lot adjoining the golf course. It was pitch-dark and a good two hundred feet from the bar's entrance.

"Rudy, this is eerie. Can you find something closer?"

"You're really scared, aren't you? What's going on, Joy?"

"Ever get that feeling like you're being watched?"

"Yeah, I do, and I've been around you enough to know that when you get a 'feeling,' it's more than a feeling." Rudy looked worried. "Maybe you're right. Let's take a rain check on this."

He extinguished his cigarette and was about to roll up his window when a shadowy figure appeared on his side of the car. A metal object flashed in the dim glow of the car's dashboard lights. These criminal defense lawyers knew the muzzle of a gun when they saw one.

"Don't move! Don't make a sound, and nobody gets hurt," said a raspy voice.

"We'll give you anything — just let us go," Joy said calmly.

"Shut up, or I'll blow Fruity Rudy's head off," the voice hissed.

They immediately realized he knew who they were.

"Don't look at me," the man said as he slowly opened the car door behind Rudy, taking care to press the switch in the car door jamb so the interior dome light didn't come on. He got in and jammed the muzzle of the pistol into the back of Rudy's neck.

"Drive. Head north on the highway." Rudy obeyed and pulled away from the bar and onto the highway.

"I said don't look at me!" the man shouted when he locked eyes with Rudy in the rearview mirror.

As they drove to the highway, the sights of Joy's life — her high school, her church, her office, and the courthouse, the only place she ever felt special — disappeared into the darkness behind her.

After a few miles, the pitch black of the highway was briefly illuminated by the lights from the local no-tell motel. If you scored at the Clap Trap, this was a popular destination for a one-night stand. For a brief second, it brought Joy a glimmer of hope.

"There! Turn there onto that dirt road," the man ordered.

Joy's heart sank as Rudy turned off the highway onto a dirt road. Vaguely familiar with the area, she knew the road led to a large lake about a mile away. Canals that had been used to drain this swampland lined both sides of the bumpy dirt road. They were totally secluded.

"Stop here! Gimme your purse, wallets, cash, jewelry, watches, phones, everything!" he ordered.

Without hesitation they handed over all their valuables.

"Car keys too," he demanded.

Rudy surrendered his keys.

The man shoved his loot in Joy's purse, and then opened the driver's side passenger door. The Lincoln's dome light came on automatically, illuminating his face.

"I said no lights!" he shouted.

But it was too late. Joy immediately recognized the pale,

scrawny, unshaven man with a tattoo of a spiderweb on the left side of his neck as Franklin Kleftis. He was known to law enforcement as a real psycho, with a long and violent criminal record.

"Freaky Frankie!" Joy blurted out his street name, instantly regretting it.

"That's right!" he growled. "And you're that bitch lawyer!" He sprang to Rudy's car door, yanked it open, and aimed his gun at Joy.

With lightning speed, Rudy lunged between Frankie and Joy, shoved her down on the seat, and shielded her body with his. Frankie opened fire at point-blank range.

Gunshots exploded in Joy's ears again and again as Rudy's body convulsed on top of her. A searing wave of fire like a hot poker shot through her left arm and then again. She'd been hit twice.

Click! Click! Click! The gunshots abruptly halted. Frankie cursed at the Colt 2000 semiautomatic pistol he'd bought on the street a few days earlier.

Joy realized his gun jammed. Her best chance of survival was to play possum by keeping her eyes shut and lying perfectly still. Then hopefully this creep would leave, thinking she was dead. She suppressed the urge to scream, even though she was in excruciating pain from being shot and sickened by the warm ooze spreading over her from Rudy's body.

Frankie kept cursing at his gun and then slammed the car door shut, engulfing them in darkness. Joy heard his voice trail off as he stomped away. She lay silent but felt that Freaky Frankie would be back. Rudy had taken three bullets to the head. She knew the warm ooze was blood and brain fragments.

Quietly maneuvering herself out from under his body, Joy whispered, "Rudy! Hang in there. I'll get help."

She gently took his hand, and for a second felt he lightly squeezed hers. Summoning all her energy, she dashed toward the highway. The two bullet holes in her left arm rendered it useless, so she cradled it with her right arm. Joy was losing blood fast and worried she'd pass out. She pressed on her wounds, hoping the pressure would slow the bleeding.

The dirt road was lined with palmettos, and their razor-sharp fronds tore into her. Stumbling in the dark, Joy tripped and tumbled down a canal's embankment. She landed in thick reeds and muck. She knew that swamp water meant snakes and, even worse, alligators. Adrenaline surged through her, and she scrambled up the embankment through thorns and sandspurs, which punctured her skin.

Blood loss was taking its toll. The intense humidity of the night air made it hard to breathe. Joy was in agony and weakening.

Where's the bastard who did this?

If he comes back, I'm dead for sure. Dear God, I'm bleeding to death!

Struggling to keep from panicking, she trudged toward the highway but halted when she saw a fork in the dirt road. It was a small path leading to a cabin about a hundred yards away. A light was on in the cabin! *It's so close! People are there!* She started toward it.

"*No, not there.*" She heard Rudy's voice in her head.

A sense of calm and clarity descended upon her, and for an instant she felt the pit of her stomach tugged slightly in the direction of the highway. A defining moment in a person's life may only last a few seconds, and Joy recognized that this was such a moment. Despite her crippling pain, she trusted the guidance of this unseen presence and turned away from the cabin.

It's a good thing she did, for the cabin was Frankie's hideout.

If she had ignored the contact from Rudy's electromagnetic soul, she would have walked right into the murderer's lair.

At the ramshackle cabin, Frankie worked on unjamming the gun. He was frustrated, since his hands kept shaking. The tremors were getting worse, but he shrugged it off because tonight he felt lucky. His targets just happened to be lawyers whom he loathed. No one saw the carjacking, which meant no one knew they were dead yet. He figured he had time to bury the bodies and get out of town. He planned to sell the Lincoln to a no-questions-asked chop shop he knew that was about twenty miles away. Then he'd move on before anyone knew his victims were reported missing. Frankie patted himself on the back for being so very clever.

That is, until he returned to the Lincoln roughly a half hour later and discovered Joy wasn't there. He went berserk and screamed with anger as he searched for her. Unless she bled to death in the woods, cops would be crawling all over the place. Frankie panicked, dragged Rudy's body from the car, dumped it in the canal, and then sped off in the Lincoln.

Meanwhile these thirty-odd minutes bought Joy enough time to get to the highway. She made for the small roadside hotel about a half mile away. Fearing the killer would be looking for her, she skirted along the edge of the highway, using trees and brush for cover.

In excruciating pain, exhausted, weak, and nauseated from the massive blood loss, Joy had only minutes before she lost consciousness. Through sheer force of willpower, she made the final push toward the motel's orange neon sign, which glowed like a beacon in the dark.

After years as a front desk clerk at a motel with a shady reputation, Hassan thought he'd seen everything until Joy, covered in blood, sweat, mud, and thorns, tumbled through his lobby door. He stared in disbelief as she gasped, "There's been a murder — call the police."

Joy fainted and collapsed to the floor.

Hassan sprang into action and immediately dialed 911 with one hand and grabbed the motel's first aid kit with the other. While paramedics and police were on the way, Hassan stuffed gauze into her wounds to stop the bleeding. He vowed this woman wasn't going to die — not if he could help it.

And he prayed to God with all his might for that help.

Chapter 6

NEAR-DEATH AND SHARED DEATH EXPERIENCES

May the Force Be with You

FOR THOUSANDS OF YEARS, accounts of people who died and then "miraculously" returned to life with tales of their other-worldly encounters have been recorded worldwide. Needless to say, these mysterious incidents of resurrection mystified those who experienced them and baffled religious and medical professionals.

No one even knew what to call these occurrences until the 1970s, when Dr. Raymond Moody applied the scientific method to study this phenomenon. After extensive research, Dr. Moody developed the term *near-death experience* (NDE) to describe the phenomenon involving a person who clinically dies, comes back to life, and recalls what happened while their consciousness was separated from the body. The term for a person who undergoes this phenomenon is *near-death experiencer* (NDEr).

Since the 1970s, survival of consciousness and near-death experience studies have been conducted around the globe. Researchers have found that practically all NDEs have similar characteristics, which include traveling through a tunnel into the light, a floating sensation, enhanced visual perception, and encountering the spirits of deceased loved ones. NDErs return from the experience convinced of the reality of their encounter with the Other Side. They may also exhibit enhanced psychic abilities, loss of a fear of death, and a sense of interconnectedness, feeling that all living beings are part of a greater whole.

Researchers have found that gender, race, ethnicity, religion, or lack of belief in an afterlife are not factors during an NDE. In fact, the most potent element of the NDE is encountering an immensely powerful (yet not blinding) white light of infinite intelligence, understanding, and love. Nancy Evans Bush, president emeritus of IANDS (International Association for Near-Death Studies), has stated, "Most near-death survivors say they don't *think* there is a God. They *know*." NDEr Dr. Eben Alexander has said that "even the word 'God' is too limiting to describe this omnipotent energy."

Skeptics have alleged that NDEs are merely a function of a dying brain. Yet NDE researcher Dr. Kenneth Ring has conducted several studies of NDErs who have been blind since birth, yet return to consciousness and provide a detailed visual account of what they "saw" during the NDE. If an NDE is indeed a function of a dying brain, then why wouldn't the brain draw upon memories and data contained within it instead of suddenly creating something it had never experienced?

Another contention is that NDEs are by-products of anoxia (an oxygen-starved brain) or hypoxia (low levels of oxygen in the brain). But as NDE researcher Jack Hagan III, MD, editor of *Missouri Medicine*, stated, "As our medical and surgical skills increase, we can bring back patients who have traveled further on the path to death than at any other time in history. Their recollections often refute physicians' scientific explanation of how an oxygen-starved brain can produce such intense, vivid, and often corroborated veridical recollections."

NDEs are more common than previously thought. According to Dr. Jeffrey Long, founder of NDERF (Near-Death Experience Research Foundation), it is estimated that 774 NDEs occur daily in the United States alone. Dr. Long has also noted that the number of people who have an NDE is actually much higher, because many people are reluctant to admit their experiences due to social and religious stigma.

Many respected people throughout history have reported what we now know to be near-death experiences. These luminaries include St. Francis of Assisi, Wolfgang Amadeus Mozart, Abraham Lincoln, Queen Victoria, Sir Arthur Conan Doyle, Edgar Cayce, Carl Jung, and Sir Winston Churchill. One of the most intriguing ancient accounts of an NDE was written in the fourth century BC by the Greek philosopher Plato in *The Republic*.

According to Plato, a warrior by the name of Er had been killed in battle. Pursuant to Greek military custom, the bodies of Er and his fallen comrades were gathered so they could be honored as warriors and burned together in a mass funeral pyre. Even though it was over ten days since his death, the body of Er remained intact and had not decomposed. As his body was placed on the funeral pyre and the flames were lit, Er suddenly came back to life.

Aside from the fact Er returned to life just in the nick of time to avoid incineration, he wowed the crowd when describing his ethereal descent into another world. It appears Er had an NDE, particularly given Plato's description of how Er left this world and went into a transcendent reality.

Another ancient account of an NDE was chronicled in the New Testament, written in the first century AD. The apostle Paul writes in 2 Corinthians 12:2–3: "I know a man in Christ who fourteen years ago was caught up to the third heaven. Whether it was in the body or out of the body I do not know — God knows. And I know that this man — whether in the body or apart from the body I do not know, but God knows."

The Bible refers to three heavens. The first is the sky (Genesis 7:11), the second is the realm of stars (Exodus 32:13), and the third is the abode of God (2 Corinthians 12:1–4). This passage about Paul has been generally accepted by theologians as a reference to life after death. In recent years, however, it has been viewed as Paul's description of an NDE, because the man was caught up in the third heaven, which has been widely interpreted as the realm of God. One of the mysteries surrounding this passage is whether Paul was describing someone else's NDE or his own.

The first clinically documented account of an NDE occurred in 1740 with French military physician Pierre-Jean du Monchaux. In his book *Anecdotes de médecine*, Monchaux described the account of a well-respected apothecary (pharmacist) in Paris who fell into an unconscious state. It is unclear whether the apothecary was pronounced dead, but when he did regain consciousness, he told of his encounter with a light so pure and bright that he believed he had entered heaven.

The energy of an electromagnetic soul in the Other Side dimension vibrates at a much higher frequency than the energetic vibration of humans living in the material world. Because the electromagnetic soul moves at the speed of light, travel between dimensions for spirits is as easy as stepping from one room to another. When an electromagnetic soul from the Other Side crosses into the material world dimension, this may be referred to as a visitation. However, when a person physically dies and that person's electromagnetic soul separates from the body and enters the Other Side dimension, and then returns to the person's body, this is a near-death experience (NDE). While it is easy to think of the Other Side dimension as some distant and nebulous alien universe, an NDE reveals it is only a heartbeat away.

≈

By the time I was three and a half years old, my abilities as a medium surfaced, since I had started conversing with my "invisible friends." One advantage of having parents who were also mediums was that they too could see these spirits and knew they weren't a figment of my imagination.

Psychic ability is an inherited, recessive genetic trait, which means that even if it is in the family DNA, not everyone will possess the trait, which sometimes skips a generation. However, both my parents possessed the same recessive trait for psychic ability, which exponentially increased the likelihood that one of their children would have that trait — and that child happened to be me.

Dad was a NASA engineer, and Mom was a commercial illustrator. From outward appearances, my parents, my two older siblings, and I were just the typical American family next door. However, growing up in a home with people who could see spirits was anything but typical.

When I was four years old, my family was living in Orlando, Florida. Being part of the space program often required my father to travel for work. One afternoon in late July, Dad was away on business, leaving my mother home with me, my fourteen-year-old sister, and my ten-year-old brother. An epidemic of impetigo was surging through our community. I contracted this illness and was very sick, running a fever and covered with rashes. Our family doctor instructed my mother to treat the rashes at home by soaking me in the bathtub with a small amount of bleach diluted in the water.

As my mother, Jeannie, put me in the tub, I felt some relief from the itchiness caused by the rashes, but then I took a turn for the worse. My fever soared. In an effort to lower my fever, Jeannie gave me aspirin and added ice to my bath. Despite her efforts, my fever continued to climb. Nothing was working.

What my mother didn't know was that my case of impetigo was much more serious than originally diagnosed, because I had developed septicemia, a potentially lethal bacterial blood infection. My condition rapidly deteriorated, and I began choking and gasping for air.

Jeannie sprang into action, instructing my sister to call an ambulance and my brother to get help from the neighbors.

My sister grabbed the phone as my brother, Earl Joseph, ran outside calling for help. Rory Roule was a fireman and emergency medical technician known in the neighborhood as Fireman Rory. My brother spotted him in his front yard across the street from our house.

Fireman Rory bolted to my mother, who held me in her arms.

"Help me! Mark's dying!"

"Mommy!" my sister called out. "The ambulance is on its way from Orange Memorial!"

"He's barely breathing!" Fireman Rory told Jeannie. "We don't have much time! I have to do CPR!"

Jeannie laid me on the ground as Rory started doing compressions on my chest and performing mouth-to-mouth resuscitation.

"Keep his head back and air passage open!" Rory yelled between breaths.

"He's convulsing!" my mother exclaimed.

"Hang on, Mark!" Fireman Rory shouted as the ambulance sped up to his driveway. A paramedic jumped out of the ambulance, got me on the gurney, and fastened a ventilator mask on me. Mom leaped in the back of the ambulance with him.

"Go, go, go!" Rory shouted to the driver as he slammed the door of the ambulance shut as it sped out of the parking lot, leaving Fireman Rory with my brother and sister behind. No one had seen that the ventilator hose had been caught in the ambulance door. My oxygen supply was cut off, and I went into respiratory failure.

"He's not breathing! We're losing him!" the paramedic yelled.

"The air hose is stuck in the door!" Jeannie shouted, trying to yank it loose.

Suddenly, I shot upward through the roof of the ambulance. It was like jumping up and down on my bed, except I went a lot higher and didn't come back down. As I soared upward, I could see the ambulance shrinking in the distance as it sped away from my house. I thought it was weird that the ambulance had numbers on its roof. Everything looked smaller and smaller as I flew upward.

I was so happy that I didn't feel sick anymore. It was fun and even felt better than swimming underwater, as Dad had taught me.

Then a flash of bright light brought me somewhere else. But where?

Through the light, a large crowd of what looked like people formed around me. The weird thing was, they didn't look like any people I'd seen before. They were shaped like people but were clear like water, and they glowed with light from the inside.

The "light people" came closer, encircling me.

As strange as they were, I wasn't afraid, because I knew some of these spirits were my invisible friends, with whom I'd been communicating for some time. I didn't know the other light people, but they knew me.

Although I liked these people and felt safe with them, I wanted to go back to my family. They seemed to know what I was thinking, as their countless voices spoke to me in unison, "Mark, you will go back. You will see us again. We are always with you."

Back in the ambulance, the paramedic told Jeannie, "He's not breathing, and his heart's stopped. Even if I get his heart beating again, unless we get him oxygen, he's dead!"

Opening an ambulance door at high speed was no small feat.

"I'll do it!" Jeannie exclaimed. "Hold me and wait for the count of three!"

The paramedic grabbed the inside of the ambulance with one hand and tightly held my mom's waist belt by the other.

"ONE — TWO — THREE!" Jeannie pushed with all her might and pried the door open just enough to pull the oxygen hose inside with her foot.

Meanwhile, in the serenity of this other world, the light people faded from my view as the Light surrounding all of us glowed even brighter. A strong but gentle presence spoke to me. It was the voice of the Light itself, which calmly said, "Eternal Light, Eternal Life."

"CLEAR!"

The Light vanished as an electrical shock surged through my body.

Terrified, I opened my eyes and saw a strange man looming over me, holding two large paddles. He dropped them and thrust his fingers onto my throat.

"We got a pulse!" he yelled to my mother over the ambulance's roaring engine and shrieking siren.

I'd just been electrocuted back into physical life and was strapped down, a strange mask tightly covered my face, its large hose flailed over me, my chest was sore from being pounded on, and my skin itched from rashes. I felt horrible, but what hurt most was seeing tears streaming down my mother's face.

"He's breathing!" Mom cried out, "Oh, thank God!"

Even strapped to the gurney, my body thrashed from side to side with every swerve of the speeding ambulance. Mom and the paramedic did their best to keep from falling over and to keep me steady. Moments later, at the hospital, people poured into the ambulance and rushed me into the emergency room.

Several hours later, I roused. With the aid of intravenous antibiotics, the septicemia was brought under control, and my fever started to come down. I saw my father standing next to my mother, brother, and sister. When Dad heard what happened, he had flown back to Orlando.

"Mommy, Daddy, what does *eternal* mean?"

My parents looked at each other.

"Tell us what happened, Mark," Dad asked.

I told my parents what I had seen and what had happened. Somehow they seemed to understand.

Even though I'd already been perceiving spirits, a near-death experience was a lot for a four-year-old to process. At the time of my NDE, I certainly did not comprehend the meaning of "Eternal Light, Eternal Life." Why would the Divine Power we call God present such a concise yet complex message to a child?

⌐

THE MAGNITUDE OF THIS MESSAGE'S MEANING has taken years to unfold and make sense to me. Although many people want immediate answers and gratification from spirit communication, spirits are not on our timetable. This is partly why it can take a lifetime to fully understand a message received through interdimensional communication.

My NDE was the catalyst for recognizing incidents of spiritual synchronicity throughout my life. Years after my NDE, when I was studying quantum physics, my attention was directed to Albert Einstein's statement, "We are all light beings." The light people were electromagnetic souls, and my NDE was my first communication with the collective consciousness. The One Voice, which conveyed the message "Eternal Light, Eternal Life," enabled me to accept the reality of the afterlife and to glimpse that the collective consciousness is interconnected with an infinite energy, which we call God.

People who emerge from an NDE tend to become calmer, less judgmental, less materialistic, more spiritual, more compassionate and loving. In some instances, NDErs develop enhanced psychic ability as well as a sense of interconnectedness with the universe.

The aftereffects of NDEs extend far beyond the life of a single person. They have inspired spiritual leaders, philosophers, artists, writers, musicians, and even modern filmmakers. In fact, an NDE very well may have been the inspiration for George Lucas when he created one of the most successful movie franchises of all time, *Star Wars*. Lucas eloquently described his NDE to journalist Maria Popova:

> When I was eighteen I was in an automobile accident and went through a near-death experience. I was actually taken away from the scene, presumed dead, and it wasn't until I reached the hospital that the doctors revived my heartbeat and brought me back to life. This is the kind of experience that molds people's beliefs.
>
> It is possible that on a spiritual level we are all

connected in a way that continues beyond the comings and goings of various life forms. My best guess is that we share a collective spirit or life force or consciousness that encompasses and goes beyond individual life forms. There's a part of us that connects to other humans, connects to other animals, connects to plants, connects to the planet, connects to the universe. I don't think we can understand it through any kind of verbal, written or intellectual means. But I do believe that we all know this, even if it is on a level beyond our normal conscious thoughts.

If we have a meaningful place in this process, it is to try to fit into a healthy, symbiotic relationship with other life force. Everybody, ultimately, is trying to reach harmony with the other parts of the life force. And in trying to figure out what life is all about, we ultimately come down to expressions of compassion and love, helping the rest of the life force, caring about others without any conditions or expectations, without expecting to get anything in return. This is expressed in every religion, by every prophet.

As Lucas explains, one aftereffect of an NDE is the sense that everyone and everything is interconnected. Anyone who has seen *Star Wars* has heard the expression, "May the Force be with you." According to Lucas, "The Force is an energy field created by all living things. It surrounds us and penetrates us. It binds the galaxy together." The Force appears to be Lucas's description of the awareness, obtained during an NDE, that we are all energetically interconnected. This certainly sounds a lot like quanta, the particles of electromagnetic energy that compose everything in existence. Electromagnetic force carries two types of charges: positive and negative.

The heroes of *Star Wars* are Jedi Knights such as Luke Skywalker, Obi-Wan Kenobi, and of course science fiction's favorite and wisest green extraterrestrial, Yoda. The Jedi embrace the positive or light side of the Force. They appear to symbolize the positive aftereffects of NDEs: they do not fear death; are deeply spiritual, compassionate, loving, and calm; avoid being judgmental; and are not concerned with material wealth. They also possess enhanced psychic ability, including the ability to perceive spirits.

The dark side of the Force is represented by Emperor Palpatine, Kylo Ren, and science fiction's quintessential bad guy, Darth Vader. The dark side of the Force symbolizes the negative, fear-based emotions generated by the human ego, which views the self as center of the universe. Those who embrace the dark side are narcissistic and angry and perpetually desire power, control, and wealth. They don't hesitate to inflict violence and fear to obtain their materialistic desires.

The virtues of the Jedi coincide with the lessons learned from NDEs: that true happiness comes not from materialism, power, and control, but from unconditional love, selflessness, and the understanding that all life is connected and part of a greater whole. Even those submerged in the darkness can find the Light, like the villainous Darth Vader, who in his last moments of physical life reconnects with his own inner light, discovering that redemption and forgiveness are always possible.

The purpose of this example isn't to promote *Star Wars*, but rather to illustrate the influence NDEs have had upon creative minds. It's hard to deny the impact Lucas's work has had upon modern pop culture and moviemaking. His success also shows that an NDE is a life-enriching experience on many levels. In 2012 Lucas sold *Star Wars* to the Walt Disney Company for

$4 billion. Then, in harmony with the virtues of a heroic and selfless Jedi Knight, he donated most of it to charity.

———

WHEN WE WAKE UP IN THE MORNING, most of us probably don't think that today may bring a life-changing event that will alter every tomorrow in a way we could not have conceived of yesterday. It may cross even fewer minds that today may be our last day of living in the material world.

One of the most intriguing elements of an NDE is the life review — the proverbial sense that "my life flashed before my eyes." The life review is a powerful component of many NDEs and can profoundly alter the course of one's life.

———

ONE BREEZY AND SUNNY APRIL AFTERNOON in Central Florida, I was at my law office when I heard a commotion coming from the lobby.

"Please, sir! You can't go back there!" The receptionist sounded scared.

"I WANNA SEE HIM NOW, DAMMIT!"

I know that voice! Oh, no! It can't be!

My office door flew open. In stormed a muscular middle-aged man with long salt-and-pepper hair and beard. His black leather jacket bore the emblems of the Steel Sabers motorcycle gang. When he locked his bloodshot blue eyes on me, I noticed a row of stitches across his forehead. He pointed at me and bellowed:

"YOU! EVERY DAY FOR SEVEN YEARS IN PRISON, I THOUGHT OF YOU!"

"Thor!" I gasped.

My mind warped back in time seven years to when I represented Thor, who was on trial for aggravated battery with serious bodily injury. The trial was going badly for us, since all the eyewitnesses testified how Thor's verbal altercation with a neighbor rapidly escalated into Thor severely beating the man in front of his wife and children.

Things went from bad to worse when the victim took the stand and testified how Thor shattered his cheekbone, knocking out four of his teeth. Then the prosecutor asked, "Were you in fear of sustaining great bodily injury?"

If the victim had simply answered "yes" it would've been a slam-dunk conviction for the prosecution. Instead, overcome with emotion, he bellowed out, "Hell, yes, I was scared of him! I still am! Everyone is! He's a goddamned Steel Saber biker with a rap sheet a mile long! The bastard belongs in prison!"

Within seconds, the prosecution's case crumbled. I immediately objected and moved for a mistrial on the grounds that the victim's statement about Thor's reputation and prior record was inadmissible hearsay, inflammatory, and so prejudicial that my client could not possibly receive a fair trial on the facts of this case alone. The prosecutor cringed as the judge begrudgingly sustained my objection and granted a mistrial.

While the mistrial didn't exonerate Thor, it meant there would have to be a new trial with a new jury, which would be expensive and would take months before the case was back in court. This gave me leverage to negotiate a plea bargain with the prosecutor, who reluctantly agreed to a sentence of two years' probation with no incarceration.

Getting Thor to accept this plea bargain was another matter.

"You kicked their ass! Do it again!" Thor roared.

"They won't make the same mistake twice. Take the deal, Thor!"

Against my advice, and after calling me every expletive imaginable, Thor rejected the deal. Since he wouldn't listen to reason, I quit as his lawyer. He hired another attorney, went to trial three months later, was found guilty, and was sentenced to a maximum-security prison.

Now, seven years later, a visibly older but still lethal Thor was poised before me like a rattlesnake ready to strike.

"Every day for seven years in prison, I thought of you!" he repeated. "And why I should have listened to you!"

"So I take it you're not here to kill me?"

"Kill you? Hell, no. But if I was, you'd be dead already."

"Good to know. So what brings you here today?"

"I need your help. I sorta violated my parole."

"Sort of?"

"I kind of caused a head-on collision, and the cops arrested me for driving under the influence of alcohol, which resulted in serious bodily injury." While Thor had not been college-educated, he was highly intelligent and extremely street-smart. He understood how the criminal justice system worked, having been in it most of his life.

"Don't get angry, but I'm not sure I'm the right lawyer for you."

"I swear to you as a Steel Saber, I will listen to and follow your legal advice."

In Thor's world, there was nothing more solemn than his oath as a Steel Saber.

"Before I agree to anything, Thor, tell me what happened."

"When I got out of prison, I was working in construction. One day the guys and me was downing a few beers, and I was pretty toasted. I pulled out of the site in my pickup truck. I didn't see this car and hit it head-on."

"What happened after the collision?"

"The car had three girls in it. They got banged around a bit but had airbags, so they're okay. Well, one broke her arm — she'll live. But I split my head open. Blood was gushing everywhere, and then everything sorta got really weird."

"What do you mean by 'really weird'?"

"I was above the crash, like thirty feet up, looking down at it and actually saw myself laying there bleeding. Cops were standing around. I heard the sons-a-bitches joking it'd be a good thing if I died cuz it'd save them a ton of work and the taxpayers a lot of money."

"Sounds like you had an out-of-body experience!"

"Whoa! I knew you would understand. Word in jail is, you're kinda spooky. It's cool havin' a lawyer who scares people. You kinda scare me too."

"Seriously? I scare you? That's a first."

"Okay — so I was totally outta my body, watching what's happening at the crash, and then next thing I know, I'm shooting like a bullet through a gun barrel right at this bright light."

"You went into the Light?"

"Not exactly — I'm haulin' ass through this tunnel, and then I see myself, my life — like everything I ever did."

"This was more than an out-of-body experience. You had a near-death experience — that's why you experienced the life review," I explained. "In a sense it's your own soul, reflecting upon and evaluating everything you've done in your life."

"Yeah, well, the review wasn't good. I've done some really wicked shit."

"I'm aware of your prior record."

"You ain't aware of shit. My prior record is just what I've been busted for. You don't know the terrible things I've done — and all of it was paraded before me."

Thor sank into a chair in front of my desk. "So I'm shooting through this tunnel, but then something like a vise grip grabs me. I couldn't move — it felt like being stuck in tar. Then I totally started freaking out when the light at the end of the tunnel started closing like the aperture on a camera. I knew this wasn't good.

"I'm stuck in this — this place. It was dark, not pitch-black, but really dim. I was really worried because now the light looked like a speck a million miles away. Worst part is, I wasn't alone. All these huge 'things' — people, I guess — surrounded me, like nothing I ever seen. They was a lot bigger than me, and they sure as shit didn't seem friendly."

"Where do you think you were, Thor?"

"It sure as hell wasn't heaven."

"Ironic choice of words. Go on."

"Whatever it was let me go and I shot toward the light. I'm seeing the aperture opening up — the light is big and bright. I was totally stoked and feeling really good, and just as I'm about to reach the light someone said, 'You have another chance.'"

"Who said you had another chance?"

"That's just it, Mark. It was this voice — I don't even know how to explain it. I can't even say if it was a man or a woman — what I do know is, it wasn't what I hear in my head when I think — but it wasn't just in my head. It was in every bit of me — it knew me."

"Whoa — what happened next?"

"I freakin' wake up in the hospital. The nurse said I've been in a coma for two days. I told them what I saw, and the doctor said it was a hallucination caused by me losing close to five pints of blood."

"Do you think it was a hallucination, Thor?"

"Not a chance. I've done lots of hallucinogenic drugs — acid, magic mushrooms, peyote. I've hallucinated, and this was no hallucination. It was real."

"Do you feel you've been given another chance?"

"Be nice to think so. I never took the whole God thing seriously. But after this, it got me thinking about a lot of things. I've really screwed up my life, and I've hurt a lot of people." Thor paused a moment, then locked his eyes on mine. "But before I get all holy, we need to talk about keepin' my ass out of prison."

After all the time I'd spent as Thor's attorney, I never saw anything remotely spiritual about him until that day. On the surface he was still an angry, violent, and dangerous man, emotionally damaged from a lifetime of crime and impulsive desires. It took a near-death experience for him to discover he had another chance to change his life. What would he do with that chance? And as his NDE showed him, the only person who could answer that was Thor.

~

WHILE THE VAST MAJORITY of NDEs are pleasant, uplifting, and euphoric, some people, like Thor, have a "hellish" NDE, which has been more appropriately termed a *distressing near-death experience* (DNDE). While these are the least common type of NDEs, they are nonetheless profound. Researchers Dr. Bruce Greyson and Nancy Evans Bush have observed that a common interpretation of a DNDE is that it is a message to turn one's life around.

John Hagan III, MD, has stated,

> In the DNDE the "heavenly and redemptive" themes of most NDEs are replaced by a "hellish and damnation" experience.... Much time and effort is required by these individuals to work through the debilitation and negative residua of the DNDEs. Researchers have noted three types of reactions to the DNDE among those

who report them. The first type of reaction is "I needed that" in which the individual seeks to make amends in their life and become a better person. The second is reductionism in which the DNDE is explained away or repudiated as a hallucination or an adverse drug reaction. The third group struggles for years trying to comprehend why the DNDE happened to them and why they cannot shake off its negative aftereffects. This reaction tends to result in the experiencer engaging in protracted self-reflection and interpreting the DNDE as a message to "turn one's life around."

Having endured a DNDE, Nancy Evans Bush has observed, "The kind of NDE an individual has is not a permanent measure of their character. Beautiful NDEs happen to dreadfully flawed people, and painful NDEs happen to wonderful people. We have to stop accepting blanket negative judgments about people who have a difficult NDE — sometimes it's just a spiritual bad hair day."

One argument against the authenticity of NDEs is that they're a function of a dying brain, which secretes the psychedelic neurochemical dimethyltryptamine (DMT). In other words, an NDE is simply a chemically induced hallucination and therefore a subjective experience, which cannot be objectively verified.

Dr. Michael Potts of Methodist University has found that although DMT can produce similar phenomena to an NDE, "frequent or key NDE phenomena have not, to my knowledge, been reported among DMT experiencers, such as traveling through a tunnel into a transcendent realm or reporting subsequent to the experience that one perceived veridically during it."

One of Dr. Potts's most intriguing findings centers on the aftereffects of the experiences. Permanent changes in one's life and belief system after NDEs are the rule rather than the exception, but after DMT experiences, permanent changes in one's life, beliefs, or behavior are the exception rather than the rule.

Just because some aspects of an NDE can be artificially re-created through drugs like DMT, or even stimulation of certain parts of the brain, doesn't mean NDEs aren't real. If you shock a dead body with electricity and the body convulses, this doesn't mean you've brought the body back to life. All you've done is artificially replicated muscle movement, mimicking how muscles move when alive. Simulating an experience doesn't make it the real experience.

The argument that NDEs are merely subjective and cannot be objectively verified further diminishes in the face of shared death experiences (SDEs). This is because SDEs have an element of objectivity inasmuch as individuals other than the dying person become part of the experience.

In a discussion I had with Dr. Jeffrey Long, the founder of NDERF, he described an SDE as "an event which occurs around the moment of a person's death. At this time, one or more people share the experience of the dying person transitioning to the afterlife. The living people sharing the transitioning experience with the dying person may be near them or far away. Those reporting SDEs may be family, friends, or acquaintances. These experiences are often powerful and detailed experiences, and their content may be similar to what occurs during near-death experiences. Those involved in SDEs often believe that the SDE they participated in is powerful evidence for the reality of an afterlife."

Dr. Raymond Moody has observed:

Bystanders or onlookers at the death of a patient may include physicians, nurses, other medical personnel, and relatives or friends of the dying. All of these types of bystanders report SDEs that are often indistinguishable from NDEs. For example bystanders sometimes say they saw a transparent replica of the dying person leave that person's body at the point of death. Or they describe leaving their own bodies and rising up to accompany their dying loved one part way toward the light. Onlookers at someone else's death also sometimes report that a brilliant light filled the room, they heard indescribably beautiful music and/or they perceived apparitions of the dead person's deceased loved ones. Occasionally, onlookers empathically report that they co-lived the "life review" of the deceased person.

Skeptics have labeled NDEs as subjective, since the account is based on one person's experience. SDEs, on the other hand, are objective, since more than one person is involved during the experience. Most cases of SDEs involve bystanders observing the experience of a dying person transitioning to the Other Side. But what about several people who transition to the Other Side simultaneously and return to tell of their shared death experience?

One of the most compelling examples of this type of SDE occurred in 1989. It involved a crew of firefighters known as "Hotshots." When it comes to firefighters, Hotshots are the equivalent of Special Forces. These elite teams consist of twenty to twenty-two highly trained personnel, who are deployed to the largest, most dangerous, and most difficult fires around the globe.

In 1996 famed NDE researcher Arvin Gibson interviewed Hotshot John Hernandez about the incident. Hernandez's Hotshots unit was attempting to contain a fire in treacherous mountain terrain. Firefighting is a dangerous occupation under any circumstances, but mountain weather is highly volatile and subject to unpredictable and rapid changes. To further complicate matters, the Hotshots were weighed down by nearly sixty pounds of protective gear and equipment.

Everything was going according to procedure until the wind intensified and sharply changed direction. A deafening blast sent a shock wave across the mountain as trees engulfed by the flames exploded. Fueled by wood and wind, the roaring fire raced toward the Hotshots at tremendous speed, incinerating everything in its path. They were trapped.

The Hotshots' highly developed sense of situational awareness kicked in. With only seconds to react or die, each Hotshot instantly hit the ground facedown, pulling protective gear over their bodies as the flames engulfed them. Hernandez knew he was suffocating as the fire sucked all the oxygen from the air.

"This is it. I am going to die," flooded Hernandez's head. Then he realized he was floating above the fire, watching his body lying on the ground. He immediately saw the spirits of his fellow Hotshots also hovering above the fire with him. They could see one another!

Hernandez noticed something amazing about his teammate Jose, who had been born with a deformed foot. "Look, Jose, your foot is straight!" he exclaimed, realizing that his friend was free of his physical disability and that he'd just communicated that fact to Jose and his fellow Hotshots telepathically.

Upon the awareness he was somehow interconnected with the other Hotshots, Hernandez was instantly transported into another realm. "The light — the fantastic light. It was brighter than the sun shining on a field of snow. Yet I could look at it, and it didn't hurt my eyes."

An all-encompassing sensation of peace and serenity flowed through Hernandez as a collective of spirits emerged from the Light and approached him. He saw his great-grandfather at the head of several other spirits, whom he recognized as deceased relatives.

Hernandez described his experience to NDE researcher Arvin Gibson: "When I was there, everything was so perfect, and my spirit body, it ... it was so free. It felt like everything was limitless."

Although he wanted to remain in this blissful harmony, John felt he was being directed to return to the material world. He begged his great-grandfather to let him stay.

In a flash Hernandez returned to his body, choking and gasping the smoky air.

"When I came back, well you know, there's always something plaguing you, like arthritis, or sore muscles, or ... but not there. Getting back into my physical body felt cramped — held back. For example, when I used to play football for a few days after a game or hard practice I was always sore. The same thing was true after coming back into my physical body. I hurt and felt constrained, and it was hard to get used to for some time."

Lying on the charred mountain slope, Hernandez gathered his wits. The fire, which had swept over him, continued to rage in the distance. He could barely believe his eyes when he saw his fellow Hotshots alive.

Exhausted, the beleaguered Hotshots regrouped at the summit. None of them could understand how they could have survived. The heat from the fire was so intense that it melted their metal tools. From their training and experience, they knew that no one there should have been alive.

None of them, though, were prepared for what came next. The Hotshots talked about leaving their bodies, hovering above the fire, then seeing and communicating with the spirits of all the other Hotshots. The descriptions of their otherworldly experiences had uncanny similarities. Many admitted seeing a bright light and encountering the spirits of deceased loved ones. They also recalled seeing Jose's foot appearing normal. Several Hotshots shared how while in the light they'd been given a choice whether to return to this world. They were at a loss about how any of this was possible, much less how to explain this supernatural experience to anyone outside of their elite unit.

⟿

APPARENTLY WHAT HAPPENS during SDEs coincides with what quantum physics teaches us: that everything is energy and energetically interconnected. There is no matter, just energy, which vibrates at different frequencies so as to be perceptible to the senses. During the dying process, as the electromagnetic soul leaves the body, it emits a high intensity of energy and frequency, creating an overlap with the brainwave frequencies of family members, close friends, and even healthcare workers who are close to the dying person. This temporarily entangles the brainwave frequency of the bystanders with the afterlife frequency of the collective consciousness, resulting in a shared death experience.

This frequency overlap was even more obvious during the Hotshots' SDE inasmuch as they were all suffocating at the same time. They not only encountered the collective consciousness, they became part of it, which enabled them to see and communicate with one another when separated from their bodies.

Once free of the finite confines and perceptions of a material world body, the veridical perception of the electromagnetic soul is no longer inhibited by the lower vibration of the material world. This brings the awareness that everything is energy. Energy is eternal and doesn't age, get sick, or die. This is why during the Hotshots' SDE, they all saw Jose's spirit as free of his physical deformity.

During spirit contact, including NDEs and SDEs, spirits often appear as young, healthy, and attractive. They do this because they can — who wouldn't? But there is another reason they do this. It is to let us know that we are more than bodies, that the electromagnetic soul is pure energy and energy is eternal. Energy doesn't get old, doesn't get sick, and cannot die. There is no beginning, nor is there an end to the consciousness that is our electromagnetic soul.

Or, to paraphrase George Lucas, the Force is always with us, because we are part of the Force that is the collective consciousness.

Chapter 7

AFTER-DEATH COMMUNICATION

Alignment with the Afterlife Frequency

AFTER-DEATH COMMUNICATION (ADC) is a form of inter-dimensional communication that occurs during an alignment of the brainwave frequency of people in our material world dimension and the afterlife frequency of spirits who are part of the collective consciousness of the Other Side dimension. This communication between dimensions is based on the transfer of energy, involving frequency and vibration. Traditionally it has been known as *mediumship*.

After-death communication (ADC) involves people who are not mediums but who report contact with the spirits of deceased loved ones. This occurs because everyone is capable of interfacing with the afterlife frequency. In recent years, the stigma attached to "seeing spirits" has declined, which means more people are admitting they've had encounters with spirits. This is why ADC has become a growing branch of NDE and survival of consciousness studies.

In light of technological advances, this field of discovery is rapidly expanding far beyond subjective accounts of people who report communication with deceased loved ones. Since the early twentieth century, it has been theorized that developing technology for communicating with spirits was possible. In 1920 Thomas Edison, one of the world's most prolific inventors, was quoted in *American Magazine*: "I have been at work for some time building an apparatus to see if it is possible for personalities which have left this earth to communicate with us."

Thomas Edison certainly understood the power of publicity, and this interview exploded into a media sensation. Other interviews, particularly in *Scientific American*, soon followed about Edison's invention, which the press nicknamed the "Spirit Phone." Speculation abounded about whether Edison was serious or if this was just another one of his publicity stunts.

Even though Edison died in 1931 and was never able to finish developing this technology, it appears he was serious about the Spirit Phone. In a 1922 interview titled "Edison's Views Upon Vital Human Problems," the great inventor said, "I do hope myself that personality survives and that we persist. If we do persist upon the other side of the grave, then my apparatus, with its extraordinary delicacy, should one day give us the proof of that persistence, and so of our own eternal life."

Edison's research into technology capable of interdimensional communication with spirits was only the beginning. Since Edison's time, interest in investigating the paranormal from a scientific standpoint has become quite popular. Paranormal investigators now employ a wide array of devices, such as EMF (electromagnetic field) and trifield meters that detect fluctuations in electromagnetic energy, which is associated with the presence of spirits. Other devices, like the spirit box scanner and EVP (electronic voice phenomenon) recorder, scan ultra-high radio wave frequencies with the objective of detecting and even recording the "voices" of spirits.

While these devices have produced some fascinating results, they are just part of the evolution toward more sophisticated technology for detecting and communicating with spirits. At the Laboratory for Advances in Consciousness and Health at the University of Arizona, Dr. Gary Schwartz and his team of electrical engineers and software specialists have created the first SoulPhone communication device.

Dr. Schwartz's colleague Mark Pitstick, DC, is the director of the SoulPhone Foundation, of which I am a board member. Pitstick has indicated that part of the SoulPhone technology encompasses the SoulSwitch, which will allow binary communication, that is, yes and no answers from spirits. According to Pitstick, "Dr. Schwartz's scientific research has definitely demonstrated that life continues after bodily death. Further, it has shown that at least some *postmaterial* ('deceased') persons can communicate with those of us living on earth."

Schwartz and Pitstick state that binary yes/no communication is only the first step. As Pitstick explains, "The next anticipated device is the *SoulKeyboard*, an array of switches that should enable typing and texting with those living in another part of life. The other two planned devices are *SoulVoice* for talking, and *SoulVideo* for audio and video contact. These should provide practical and reliable ways to communicate with postmaterial persons [aka electromagnetic souls]."

If this sounds like science fiction, keep in mind that what is considered science fiction today often becomes the science fact of tomorrow. In 1926 *Collier's Magazine* quoted Nikola Tesla: "When wireless is perfectly applied the whole earth will be converted into a huge brain.... We shall be able to communicate with one another instantly, irrespective of distance. Not only this, but through television and telephony we shall see and hear one another as perfectly as though we were face to face, despite intervening distances of thousands of miles; and the instruments through which we shall be able to do this will be amazingly simple compared with our present telephone. A man will be able to carry one in his vest pocket."

Not many people in 1926 could have conceived of the internet or cellphones, but Nikola Tesla did. It appears that during the twenty-first century, technology will evolve to the level where interdimensional technological communication with spirits will be not only possible but readily available.

Until then, the technology that enables interdimensional communication is within our own biology. Although not everyone is a medium voluntarily capable of interdimensional communication, everyone is capable of experiencing after-death communication (ADC) from spirits. This is because all humans have the same basic physiology. As explained previously, the two psychic receptor areas within the human body are the pineal gland and the solar plexus. These glands are the apparatus that makes one sensitive to the presence of spirits.

There are times when a person is more attuned to the afterlife frequency than others. This generally occurs during the intense emotions associated with the dying process and subsequent death of a loved one.

A deathbed vision (DBV) occurs when a dying person perceives spirits of deceased loved ones. During a discussion I had with Dr. Jeffrey Long about his DBV research, he indicated, "Those dying may report seeing or hearing dead family members, religious/spiritual beings and/or beautiful scenery. DBVs are typically pleasant experiences that seem to reassure those dying. Many DBVs may have content similar to what is reported in near-death experiences. DBVs often do not seem explainable as hallucinations, the effect of medications, or resulting from brain dysfunction. Those observing DBVs in the dying often believe the experiences are real, significant and a part of transitioning to the afterlife."

In my capacity as a medium, families have asked me to be present with them while a loved one is actively dying. It appears that during the process of separating from the brain, the energy of the electromagnetic soul increases. This frequency beacon alerts spirits connected to the dying person that he or she is about to leave the material world and enter the Other Side dimension. This creates a frequency alignment between electromagnetic souls and the dying person: ergo, a deathbed vision.

Deathbed visions and shared death experiences have many similarities, particularly when bystanders such as family members, close friends, and healthcare workers perceive the spirits connected to the person actively dying. Sometimes during a DBV, the spirits are perceptible to the dying person, though not necessarily to bystanders. However, a growing field of study has shown how bystanders often see spirits during a dying person's deathbed vision. As the person dies, the deathbed vision then becomes a shared death experience as the bystanders witness the spirit of the dying person transition to the Other Side.

Don't expect spirits to use only one means of communication. There are many forms of interdimensional communication, and spirits may use a combination of these forms in order to make contact with loved ones in the material world. Spirits will make contact through a medium, during the sleep state, or when the recipient is awake and least expects it. Signs from spirits can be subtle or very direct.

RAFT — recognizing the signs from spirits, accepting the contact as real, feeling the meaning of the message, and trusting its guidance — increases receptivity to after-death communication. Applying RAFT also reveals how many different means of communication spirits will use, as Thea and her family discovered.

I was conducting a Light Circle, which is a spirit communication event limited to no more than ten people. At the conclusion of the Light Circle session, I was drawn to Thea.

"The spirit of a woman who was elderly and very ill at her time of passing is transmitting a name like Paula or Pauline," I conveyed.

"My mother's name was Pauline! Just like her to wait for the finale," Thea replied, smiling.

"She was having trouble breathing — I see a ventilator mask — she's pulling it off, and said 'I'm fine! And I don't have to wear these awful shoes anymore either!' Does that make sense, Thea?"

"You have no idea!" Tears flowed down Thea's face. "Before she died, I asked Mom to find a way to let me know that she would be fine — those were my exact words! And yes, she was having trouble breathing and was on a ventilator."

"What about the shoes?"

"Mom always dressed to the nines. She loved shoes, but during the last year of her life, her bones were so weak she had to wear these special sneakers. She said they were ugly, and she hated them. I'm so happy to hear she doesn't have to wear them anymore."

"She wants you to know another female is with her — Ellen — could be Helen."

"Helen!" Thea exclaimed, "This is what I needed to hear! Can I tell you the whole story? It is really incredible, and that's why I came tonight. I wanted to tell you this."

"It's my firm policy not to let clients explain or provide me information during a reading. I want to make sure everything I convey is coming from a spirit, not from what is already in my brain," I explained.

"But we're at the end of the session," the lady seated next to Thea said.

"Yeah, Mark — we want to know," another woman added as the other attendees nodded in agreement.

"Okay. Since the Light Circle session has concluded, I'll let you explain, Thea."

"My family is Italian and very tight-knit. My mother, Pauline, my sister Lori, and I were very close. Our cousins are more like brothers and sisters. My mother and her cousin, our Aunt Helen, were like sisters. They were inseparable.

"Aunt Helen was a drop-dead gorgeous woman. When she was young, the men went crazy over her. The family nicknamed her 'Helen of Troy' because her father was afraid her good looks might start a war, like the queen in Greek mythology."

"That's hilarious, Thea," an attendee added, "keep going."

"Aunt Helen was always so beautiful and healthy, but in her early eighties, she was diagnosed with pancreatic cancer," Thea reflected. "About the same time Helen got sick, my mother developed severe osteoarthritis and spinal stenosis. Neither one of them was strong enough to leave their homes, so Helen and Pauline were on the phone with each other every day, commiserating.

"When Aunt Helen passed, Mom took a turn for the worse. Her bones became so fragile she couldn't be moved. Since my mother lived with me, I was her primary caretaker.

"When the doctors said Mom was nearing the end, my sister Lori stayed with us round the clock. Hospice crisis care was called in to make Mom as comfortable as possible. We knew it was only a matter of days.

"My mother was feisty till the end. Even though she had to wear the ventilator mask to breathe, she could still talk, and mentally she was sharp as a tack.

"One morning after I'd been up all night with Mom, Lori came in all excited and said, 'Thea, you won't believe this. Cousin Ann called me this morning and said she had a dream about her mother, Helen...' Lori stopped. She was staring at the foot of Mom's bed.

"So I look where Lori's looking, and there's this woman standing there!

149

"Before Lori or I could say anything, Mom says 'Helen!'"

"For a few seconds Lori and I saw Aunt Helen too — right there in Mom's room!

"Mom is wide awake, pulls off the ventilator, and says, 'Oh my God! It's Helen! Look at her, just look at her, she's so young! She's beautiful Helen again!'

"Lori says, 'Mom, we saw her too!'

"As if this wasn't weird enough, then Mom said, 'Oh, and girls, I can't believe how many people were at my service. I can't believe Celia came too!'

"Mark, we haven't heard from Celia in years. We didn't even know if she was still alive."

"Let me see if I understand," I interjected. "Are you saying your mother, Pauline, was talking about her funeral in the past tense?"

"Yes, she was, like she'd already been there — but that's not all!"

"Go for it, Thea!"

"Then Lori says, 'Thea, you're not going to believe this, but Cousin Ann called me this morning and said last night her mother, Helen, came to her in a dream. At first Ann said Aunt Helen looked old and sick, like she did before she died. Then Helen says to Ann, "Wait till you see this," and Helen turned into her younger and beautiful self. This is crazy, because Mom just said the same thing. Helen is young and beautiful again!'

"So Lori is telling me this, and then our mother started talking again."

"What did she say?"

"Mom said, 'Not yet, Helen — not quite yet. I'll be there — but not quite yet.' Four days later, my mother passed."

"I'm so sorry, Thea."

"That's not the end of the story, Mark," Thea continued.

"Lori and I made the funeral arrangements, and the service was a few days after Mom died. With just the obituary notice in the paper, we figured no one really knew, and there'd be maybe twenty people there. Get this — over a hundred people showed up — just like Mom said how she couldn't believe how many people were at her service. Lori and I were overwhelmed by the outpouring of love and respect for Mom."

"That's amazing, Thea."

"The service hadn't started yet, and I was so exhausted. I kneeled and started praying. Someone came up to me and said, 'Your mom was just the greatest lady I've ever known. I just had to come when I heard she passed. I loved her so much.'

"It was Celia! Just like Mom said."

THEA, LORI, AND ANN naturally recognized, accepted, felt, and trusted the contact from the spirits of Helen and Pauline. This is why they were able to experience so many different forms of after-death communication. It began with Helen's daughter, Ann, who had a visitation from her mother in a dream, where Helen appeared young and healthy instead of elderly and cancer-ridden. The next day Lori and Thea caught a glimpse of Helen's spirit at the precise moment their mother Pauline had a deathbed vision of Helen. Pauline's DBV coincides with Ann's dream, because Helen appeared young and beautiful in both forms of contact.

The most intriguing aspect of this DBV is how Pauline related details to her daughters about her funeral, which obviously had not yet occurred. Pauline gave specific and verifiable details about this future event, such as the larger-than-expected number of attendees and the surprise appearance of Celia, whom no one had heard from in several years. How was this possible?

For centuries, philosophers have argued that time is an illusion created by humans. At the close of classical antiquity in the fourth century AD, the Christian philosopher St. Augustine said of time, "If no one asks me, I know; if I wish to explain to him who asks, I know not."

In the seventeen centuries since St. Augustine, despite all of our technological advances, time remains elusive. Physics is the branch of science that studies time, and yet time remains one of the least understood concepts in physics, notably in quantum mechanics. Physicists grapple with the distinction between past, present, and future, with why time appears to move in only one direction, and even with whether time is only "a mental construct or other illusion."

While living in the material world, people are born, grow old, and physically die. Therefore it is practical for humans to believe time exists and is linear, meaning that it moves forward in one direction. For humans, time makes sense, because days are reckoned by the period of light and dark caused by the Earth's rotation, and years are calculated by the changes in seasons based on the Earth's orbit around the sun. Everything humans experience is finite, because everything appears to have a beginning, middle, and end. The concept of time enables humans to identify what is perceived as the past, present, and future.

Physics and philosophy may be on the same page when it comes to time. It has been theorized that at the quantum level, time does not exist and that everything that happens — past, present, and future — all occurs simultaneously. This is based on a theory of the "block-universe," which hypothesizes that space and time are interconnected: a concept known as *space-time*. Einstein's theory of relativity holds that space and time are components of a four-dimensional structure, where every event has its particular space-time coordinates. Because every event has its own coordinate in space-time, this means all points are equally real and occurring, indicating the past and the future are as real as the present.

Physicist Max Tegmark of MIT has said:

> We can portray our reality as either a three-dimensional place where stuff happens over time, or as a four-dimensional place where nothing happens and if it really is the second picture, then change really is an illusion, because there's nothing that's changing; it's all just there — past, present, future. So life is like a movie, and space-time is like the DVD. There's nothing about the DVD itself that is changing in any way, even though there's all this drama unfolding in the movie. We have the illusion, at any given moment, that the past already happened and the future doesn't yet exist, and that things are changing. But all I'm ever aware of is my brain state right now. The only reason I feel like I have a past is that my brain contains memories.

This certainly is a lot to grasp, so let's look at space-time like this: Envision you are a baseball player, and your team is up to bat. Naturally both teams have agreed they must play by the traditional rules of the game. It's your turn to bat, and you step up to the plate and view the entire field from the perspective of a baseball player. Because you're playing by the rules of baseball, you believe that after you hit the ball, there is only one direction to go, from first base to second base and then third, until hopefully you score by returning to home base.

Now imagine your spirit is a drone hovering over the baseball field. Let's call the baseball field space-time. From the drone, you see all the locations on the field: first base, second base, third base, home base, shortstop, right field, left field, center field, and the pitcher's mound. Each of these spots on the ball field has its own unique location. Let's call each spot on the field a coordinate. Now think of each coordinate as an event in your life. From the drone, you see all the coordinates of the whole field at once. You see yourself at each coordinate and what you were doing when you were on the coordinate of first base, what you were doing while on the coordinate of second base, and so on. From this enhanced perspective, you realize that you can see yourself doing all of these things at all of these coordinates at the same time.

From the perspective of the drone hovering above the field, you see the entire field and everything happening on it at once. By the way, while you're hovering above the field, you are no longer confined to the artificially created rules of baseball. You can go in any direction you choose. You can go forward from first base to second, backward from third base to first base, or in another direction entirely, such as from shortstop to right field. No matter what your present coordinate is, the other coordinates on the field are just as real.

Likening the drone to your spirit/electromagnetic soul, the ball field to space-time, and the spots on the field to coordinates in space-time, you can see from the drone's perspective that each coordinate is just as real and current as every other coordinate. In other words, coordinates in space-time are constant, and there is no forward, backward, past, present, or future, because all coordinates in space-time exist now as opposed to being a series of past, present, or future events.

The concept of space-time may clarify many things people describe during SDEs, NDEs, and deathbed visions. One main component of NDEs and SDEs is the sense that everyone and everything is interconnected. During NDEs and SDEs, the electromagnetic soul temporarily leaves the finite confines of the human brain and is able to perceive the infinity of pure energy. Since everything on its most basic, subatomic level is a particle

of electromagnetic energy known as a quantum, once the electromagnetic soul returns to its infinite state, it would naturally
recognize that everything is energy and therefore interconnected.

If time doesn't exist on the quantum level, space-time would
also explain how spirits are able to perceive what we call the future. Once free of the lower and slower vibration and confines
of the human brain, spirits perceive space-time, because they
are no longer limited by the finite perception of a human brain,
which views time as only moving in one direction.

What about Pauline's deathbed vision? She related future
events and provided details about her funeral. These could not
be objectively verified by family members until a week later,
when the funeral actually occurred. It appears the electromagnetic soul of the dying Pauline was in the zone between the
material world dimension and the Other Side dimension. She
had a foot in two dimensions, which enabled her to experience
space-time on the Other Side and then explain what she perceived to her daughters in the material world.

Since all forms of electromagnetic energy move at the speed
of light, the electromagnetic soul also moves at light speed.
That enables spirits/electromagnetic souls to travel between
locations and even dimensions in the blink of an eye. That is
why in many cases of after-death communication, someone will
see the spirit of a loved one who has just died at the exact instant
of that person's death, even though they were not in the same
physical location. After-death communication can also occur to
more than one person at the same time, even if the recipients of
the ADC are in different geographic locations.

AS PART OF MY WORK AS A MEDIUM, I conduct interdimensional communication sessions over the telephone, because

telephone readings are just as accurate as in-person readings. Both spirits and telephone calls are based on electromagnetic energy, which travels at light speed.

I'd come to know Denise from conducting readings for her over the telephone. She is an extremely intelligent, open-minded, and spiritual person. Since our contact has been solely by telephone, we've never met or even seen each other in person. Unfortunately, Denise suffers from a debilitating disease and is unable to travel outside her home except for medical treatment. Although her prognosis is not positive, Denise maintains a positive mental attitude. She once said, "I have a disease, but I'm not the disease, and I refuse to be defined by a disease."

While promoting my book *Evidence of Eternity*, I was on tour in Texas and was invited to appear on the popular TV morning show *Great Day Houston*. The show's host, Deborah Duncan, asked if I would conduct readings for audience members. I stood and opened my brain to the afterlife frequency.

"I'm picking up on the spirit of a woman who was elderly when she passed — she's presenting a name that sounds like Karleen."

Patricia, an audience member, raised her hand and stood. "My grandmother's name was Karleen."

"Karleen is showing me the vegetable okra — is that significant?"

"Okra was my grandmother Karleen's favorite vegetable!"

"I'm also sensing a man who feels like a brother, and due to the pain and sensations I'm experiencing, it feels like he died of a heart attack."

"My brother died of a heart attack," Patricia confirmed.

"He's projecting to me images of airplanes — a lot of airplanes, which indicates he worked with or around aircraft — does that make sense to you?"

"Yes, it does. My brother was an air traffic controller."

After the show, I had to leave for another engagement, so I wasn't able to interact or receive feedback from the audience members immediately after the show.

When I returned to my hotel room later that day and checked my messages, I was surprised to see an email from Denise:

Dear Mark,

Guess what! My sister Patricia was in the audience of *Great Day Houston* this morning. I could barely believe it when you gave her a reading. You brought through the spirits of my grandmother Karleen and then my brother Alex, who, as you related, died of a heart attack. While I was watching the show, the second you mentioned my brother and airplanes, I felt a tingling sensation through my body, and then all of a sudden the lamp next to me came on by itself! I know this was a sign from my brother, because he was an air traffic controller. You truly made my day.

I was stunned. I had no idea of the connection between Denise and Patricia. Since I've never met Denise, I don't know what she looks like, much less if she resembles her sister Patricia. The TV show never informs me beforehand about the identities or names of anyone in the audience. There was no way I could have possibly known Denise and Patricia were related.

Then it dawned on me how this event demonstrated the positive power of after-death communication and how the electromagnetic soul travels at the speed of light. Alex had two sisters, Patricia and Denise. As an electromagnetic soul, he was interconnected with them energetically and knew there would be an opportunity to contact both of them simultaneously. Using me as the conduit, he communicated with his sister Patricia during the live broadcast of *Great Day Houston*, which he knew Denise was watching on TV in real time. The instant he sent a message through me to Patricia in the TV studio, he beamed over to Denise's home at light speed. Since electromagnetic souls are pure energy, they are also capable of influencing electrical fields. When Alex's electromagnetic soul touched Denise, she felt a tingling sensation, which was her nervous system's electrically based physiological response to his contact.

Spirits can affect electrical systems other than the human nervous system, so just to make sure Denise knew it was a visitation from Alex, he caused the lamp next to her to light up. Denise immediately recognized the contact, accepted it as real, felt the presence of his electromagnetic soul, and trusted it was him. By naturally applying RAFT, Denise received the maximum benefit from the after-death communication from the spirit of Alex.

The human nervous system uses electrical energy. When the energy of an electromagnetic soul interphases with the energy of the human nervous system, the physiological response is an electrical sensation, which feels like cold chills and tingling. This is the same physical sensation one experiences during the flight-or-fight response. Many people fear spirit contact because a human's physiological response to contact with an electromagnetic soul is the same sensation that is associated with fear. Unfortunately, this causes people inexperienced with interdimensional communication to assume spirit contact is somehow negative. For thousands of years, after-death communication has been misinterpreted as negative when it really isn't.

⌒

NINA AND TED WERE HAPPILY MARRIED for nearly forty years. One day a massive heart attack took Ted's life. Nina contacted me for a telephone reading, and during the interdimensional communication session the spirit of Ted came through,

"I know lots of people like roses, Nina, but Ted's spirit keeps projecting to me images of red and white roses."

"Red roses were my sweet Ted's favorite," Nina explained. "I always put red roses on his grave on his birthday and at Valentine's Day. Every time I visit the cemetery, I also leave a white rose. To me, a white rose symbolizes the pure love and happiness that we shared."

The next day I received this email from Nina:

> I had scheduled an air-conditioning service for this morning. My serviceman is a young man (perhaps 28) that I like very much. He is very spiritual and very loving toward his mother and grandmother. He has been aware of Ted's passing and always offers to help me with anything when he comes to the house. THIS morning, he brought me one red rose and one white rose with greenery for a vase!!! I almost started crying...I never told him anything about the roses and he knew nothing about what roses meant to Ted and me. I told him how much I appreciated them and asked what prompted him to bring them? He said he felt drawn to these roses and hoped that I would like them!

Spiritual synchronicity is a large component of after-death communication. Spiritual synchronicity is the result of contact with electromagnetic souls, which often guide someone in the material world to act as an instrument of healing and even to be in the right place at the right time without that person ever realizing it.

ONE MORNING BEFORE DAWN, my manager, Rocky, called. "My Aunt Marie is in congestive heart failure. I want to see her before she passes. Please go with me."

My mind flew to memories of the elegant and dynamic woman I knew as Marie. She was highly educated as well as a gifted concert pianist, who had performed at Carnegie Hall in New York City. A seasoned world traveler, she could converse in several languages but was especially fluent in Italian. For Marie, Italian was the language of opera, which she loved dearly.

Marie was a widow whose husband, Nicolas, had passed almost ten years earlier. They'd been happily married for over fifty years. About a year after Nicolas's passing, I'd been privileged to facilitate communication between Marie and his spirit. At first, she was skeptical, but after the session she arranged to have me conduct a mediumship demonstration before several hundred people in her affluent retirement community in Naples, Florida.

I loved spending time with Marie. She taught me many things about the fine arts and classical music. She also had quite the sense of humor, which I saw when she invited me to a night at the opera.

Before the first act began, we encountered a group of her fellow senior citizens in the lobby of the Gulf Shore Opera. These sophisticated patrons of the arts scrutinized me intensely.

"This is my Mark — *he's* my date," Marie announced.

Eyebrows raised as Marie took my arm and whisked me away to our seats.

"Thank you, Mark," she giggled.

"For what?"

"By now they're all gossiping how shameless Marie is cavorting with her boy toy."

"I'm hardly a boy, Marie."

"Oh, please. Compared to them, you're practically a teenager. Besides, I'm the only woman my age whose date isn't in a wheelchair or on oxygen."

My humorous memory faded into the stark reality that Marie

was dying. After the four-hour drive from Central Florida southwest to Naples, Rocky and I arrived at the retirement community. We met with Marie's son, Daniel, and her daughters, Sheila and Adriana.

It's never easy when someone is transitioning, but this was especially difficult. The once robust and energetic Marie was now so frail. The hospice team had placed her on a morphine drip to make her comfortable.

Although Marie was heavily sedated, she smiled faintly when she recognized Rocky, whom she loved like a daughter. I leaned over, took her hand, and kissed her on the cheek. For a second, she gently squeezed my hand. In barely a whisper, she said, "Mark, you're here." There was no other place on earth I was supposed to be.

Not long after we arrived, Marie drifted into a nonresponsive state. It was now only a matter of time. For the next twenty hours, Marie's children, Rocky, and I stayed with Marie. The hospice team and staff at the retirement home were very professional and respected the delicacy of the situation. They attended to Marie's and the family's needs but gave us as much privacy as possible.

It is frustrating to be helpless to save someone you love, and I didn't want to intrude on what the immediate family was enduring. I sat in a chair in the corner and closed my eyes to pray.

Suddenly there was a flash of light in my mind's eye. I felt my consciousness teleported into a different frequency, which I recognized as a contact experience with the collective consciousness.

My experience has shown me that humans cannot comprehend or relate to a spirit's infinite energetic state of existence. That's why during contact experiences spirits will often project the image of a place that our finite human brain can comprehend.

In this vision, the place projected to me was a large white room. The purpose of this construct wasn't about the details of the room, but to create a means of communication.

The important detail projected was a large square opening in the wall before me. It was a passage to something much vaster. On the other side of this threshold, I saw clouds wafting by against an intense blue sky. I understood what the collective consciousness was projecting. The room had boundaries, which symbolized the material world, and the limitless blue sky on the other side of the threshold symbolized eternity.

And then Marie appeared.

She was standing on the threshold between two dimensions, the material world and the Other Side. Marie looked her age but wasn't frail or sick. Clad in a flowing royal-blue gown, she was a splash of color against the stark white, which surrounded us.

What concerned me was Marie did not exude a sense of peacefulness. She stepped forward and embraced me, resting her head against my chest.

"I'm afraid, Mark. I'm so afraid," she told me.

A flash of light exploded in my mind's eye, abruptly ending the vision. This high-intensity vision drained me physically. I felt I'd been gone for hours.

"How long was I out?" I asked Rocky.

"Out? You just sat down there like ten seconds ago."

Rocky and Adriana motioned for me to step out into the hallway.

"At the risk of being overly technical," I explained, "spirit communication is possible even though the person communicating is still alive. I've experienced this before with people in a nonresponsive state like a coma or even those with dementia or Alzheimer's. The brain didn't create the spirit — it only houses the spirit. The brain and body may be sick, but the spirit is pure energy, which doesn't get sick or old or die."

"I've heard about things like this," Adriana replied.

"Your mom's spirit is still tethered to her body energetically. Essentially, she's having an out-of-body experience. Marie is in the process of transitioning, but she's still holding on to her physical body."

We stepped back into Marie's room. I shivered as electrical tingles ran through my body.

"What's happening now, Mark?" Adriana asked.

"There are spirits here — a lot of them," I reported.

At this point, Daniel and Sheila weren't quite sure what to make of what I was saying or why I was even there. Rocky knew Marie's spiritual entourage was about to step forward, so she mentally kept track of the spirits who came through.

"Dottie and Dolly — two women — one's a blonde, the other a ginger," I reported.

An awkward silence filled the room.

"Wait," Daniel broke the tension. "Dad's two sisters! Aunt Dot was a redhead and Aunt Dolly was a blonde."

"A woman's spirit just conveyed the name Evelyn."

"Mom's housekeeper was Evelyn, but she died over twenty years ago!" Sheila responded.

"The spirit of an orange tabby cat just jumped in bed next to Marie — Harpo — does that make sense?"

"Mom loved our orange tabby, Harpo!" Adriana exclaimed, "Harpo died forty years ago!"

"Animals have souls and can communicate," Rocky interjected.

"Daddy!" Shelia's eyes filled with tears, "I swear Daddy is right here next to Mom."

"I feel him too!" Adriana added.

"Your father is here," I explained, "and he's driving a red — more like a burgundy-colored Cadillac."

"Dad gave Mom a burgundy Cadillac," Daniel confirmed, "but that was when we were kids!"

"When a spirit gives me a message of an advisory or explanatory nature and then follows that up with an objectively verifiable fact — in this case, the burgundy-colored Cadillac — that is how the spirit is letting you and me know that we have properly received and interpreted the message. In other words, your dad's spirit is validating that you are feeling his presence."

"Two more spirits are here — do the names Etta and Larry make sense?"

"They were our great-aunt and great-uncle on our Mom's side," Sheila confirmed.

For the next several hours, we stood vigil by Marie's bedside. The collective of spirits waiting to greet Marie when she transitioned was gathering in force. From my perspective, they appeared to come in waves. I would perceive an upsurge of spiritual activity, followed by a lull. This didn't mean that spirits weren't always there. Rather, it meant that I had to muster the mental energy to perceive their higher frequency.

Interdimensional communication isn't just talking. It's alignment of brainwave frequency with the ultra-high frequency of a spirit or a collective of spirits. Although exhilarating, it is also mentally and physically exhausting. Like any other mental or physical activity, the ability to communicate with spirits is like a battery which runs down after prolonged use and must be recharged through rest.

Rocky noted that I described twenty-seven spirits. Between Rocky and Marie's children, they conclusively identified twenty-two of them. The other five seemed to be connected to Marie's grandparents and great-grandparents. It would take time to verify who they were.

About 1 p.m., there was a lull in spiritual activity. I closed my eyes to relax. Apparently the collective consciousness had other plans for me, because a flash of light exploded in my mind's eye.

I had returned to the white room.

Marie stood in the threshold, looking self-confident and brave. "I'm ready now."

In a flash the vision ended.

"Rocky," I said, "we have to leave."

"Why?" She looked upset.

"Marie appreciates that we came and everything we've done, but now she needs to be alone with her children. It's time for us to leave."

Rocky understood. We kissed Marie and gave our fare-wells to Daniel, Sheila, and Adriana. Before leaving Naples, we grabbed a fast-food lunch and proceeded north to Orlando along Route 27. It's an older highway, with lighter traffic, which runs up the center of the state through pastures and orange groves.

To pass the time, Rocky took out a pad and made a list of the spirits that had come through to me. She also asked me to tell her every detail about the visions I experienced at Marie's bedside.

Three hours later, while still on Route 27, I felt a tingling sensation.

"Marie's in the back seat!"

Rocky grabbed her pad and pen. "Tell me!"

"Marie's happy — smiling and laughing. She looks great, like maybe twenty-five years old, she's wearing a white bathing suit, has jet-black hair tied back with a royal-blue scarf, and get this — she's wearing these big 1960s Jackie O–style sunglasses."

I saw from the clock on the dashboard that it was 4:45 p.m.

At 5 p.m., I figured we both needed a break, so I pulled over to a convenience store along the highway.

Rocky's cellphone rang. It was Daniel. She put the call on speakerphone so we could both hear him. He was straining to maintain his composure.

"My mother died," he said, "and just before she passed, something strange happened. Mom opened her eyes, raised her arm, and pointed right at *me*. We made eye contact — then she fell back and died."

"Daniel — Mark saw Marie." Rocky was very upset, so I explained to Daniel how Marie appeared to me, looking so young, and what she was wearing.

"What you described," Daniel drew a breath — "we have a picture of my mother wearing that bathing suit with the royal-blue scarf and Jackie O sunglasses — it was taken on her honeymoon in Bermuda, sixty years ago. How could you know that?"

"Daniel, what time did Marie pass?" Rocky asked.

"Fifteen minutes ago, at 4:45 p.m."

Chapter 8

THE UNFOLDING AND AVOIDING THE NO, NO, NO SYNDROME

THERE IS A PERIOD after interdimensional communication with spirits that I call the "unfolding." It can take hours, days, weeks, or even longer for the full impact of a reading to unfold, that is, to make sense to the recipient. The electromagnetic souls (aka spirits) who are part of the collective consciousness do not speak in a human language. They communicate by adjusting their afterlife frequency to align with the medium's brainwave frequency. During this alignment, spirits emit waves of information to the medium, whose brain converts that energetic impulse into recognizable concepts based on the medium's memories, feelings, and cultural associations.

While messages are being transmitted by spirits, the medium may ask the client confirmation questions such as, "Does this make sense?" or, "Do you recognize this?" Generally the client will recognize and understand the messages being transmitted, but often that isn't the case. The information presented by spirits is not always immediately obvious, and those of us here on the receiving end don't always make the connections.

All too often when the information doesn't immediately resonate, the client will go directly to "No." It is important to avoid falling into the "No, No, No syndrome," because it generates a negative energy barrier, which obstructs connection with the afterlife frequency, and spirits will back off. In other words, it blocks the contact. It's better to leave the energetic door and your mind open by saying, "I'm not sure," or, "I don't know at this time," or even, "Let me think about it."

This is why employing the RAFT technique is so important during spirit contact. While it is absolutely normal to want to hear from a particular spirit or spirits, check expectations at the door. Let the communication flow without creating the negative energy of rejection or intense desire. Again, use RAFT: Recognize the signs of spirit contact, accept and give yourself permission to have the contact — so far, so good — but feeling rather than thinking may be the hurdle to cross. When a message is transmitted by a spirit, the very first thing that pops into your mind — or even better, your heart — is the answer. And finally, trust the message.

The information transmitted from spirits may come in one form or in a combination of ways. The medium may see images or receive visions; hear words, complete sentences, or songs; feel physical sensations and emotions; or smell or taste something significant that is associated with the spirit(s) or the recipient of the message. The medium may also receive what I refer to as a "direct feed," where a large amount of information is transferred at once.

It would be convenient if spirit communication were like texting or instant messaging, where the meaning of the messages immediately unfolded and made sense. In some instances, the meaning of a message or piece of information transmitted to the medium may be immediately apparent, or it may take time for the recipient to fully understand it — ergo, the unfolding.

The unfolding is a complex process, which takes time. This is largely why skeptics and cynics reject the idea that communication with spirits is possible. The difference between a skeptic and a cynic is that a skeptic may not believe in an afterlife or interdimensional communication but is open to the possibility if sufficient evidence is presented. A cynic is merely a closed-minded person who outright rejects something outside his or her realm of experience or understanding.

One of the most prevalent criticisms of mediums is that we're "cold reading," which is essentially guessing or saying something most people have in common and want to hear, for example, the proverbial "your grandmother is here, and she loves you." Cold reading also involves observing responses in a person's body language.

Skepticism and cynicism fade when a spirit transmits information the medium could not possibly have known. Reading someone's body language isn't possible when the interdimensional communication is over the phone and the medium can't see the client.

∾

DURING A TELEPHONE READING FOR SHANNON, the spirit of her late husband, Gavin, came through. Shannon was a very bright person, who rapidly understood and recognized Gavin's messages. But midway through the session, I was presented with an intense but unusual visual image, which made me hesitate.

"Octopus. I know this sounds weird, but I'm seeing the image of an octopus."

"You're kidding! Right?"

"Does an octopus make sense to you?"

"Gavin and I used to live in Belize. Our house was on a

canal, and we used to catch lobsters and keep them in a tank overlooking the canal."

"Okay."

"One morning Gavin and I went outside with our cups of coffee — something we'd do every day — and we freaked out because an octopus had slithered up out of the canal and was stealing our lobsters! Do you think that's what he's talking about?"

"Unless you have another octopus story, I'm kind of thinking, yeah."

"That's so Gavin — he was hilarious!"

Since most people don't have an octopus story, and I don't fling out random images of cephalopods hoping to get a hit, this was Gavin's spirit transmitting evidence of a memorable experience he shared with Shannon.

AFTER CONDUCTING THOUSANDS OF READINGS, I've learned to report what I'm receiving, no matter how strange it may seem. In other words, the weirder it is, the better. This is especially true of visions that are like minimovies, which last only a few seconds but are packed with information. For example, during a telephone session for Amelia, I facilitated communication for her with the spirit of her late husband, Beau.

"Amelia — uh — I'm seeing a vision of the Seven Dwarves, and I'm hearing them sing, 'Hi ho, hi ho, it's off to work we go,' from that *Snow White* movie — does that make sense?"

"I'm not sure."

"There's more — one of the dwarves is walking toward me — he just sneezed at me — it's Sneezy."

"Wait a second! Beau and I loved Halloween. The year

before he died, we went to a Halloween costume party with a group of our friends. We all dressed up as the Seven Dwarves."

"And?"

"On top of his asthma, Beau had a lot of allergies and was always sneezing — so naturally we elected him to be Sneezy!"

Sometimes a message unfolds so quickly that the medium doesn't even have time to process it. I experienced this at the conclusion of an evening of spirit communication in Naples, Florida. There were hundreds of attendees, and at the close of the event I welcomed questions from the audience.

A woman stepped up to the microphone and said, "I was hoping you would've picked me tonight. I really needed to hear from my husband."

"Elvis has left the building," flew out of my mouth.

"Oh, my God! We were married in Las Vegas by an Elvis impersonator!"

This message came through me so fast I was as stunned as she was. With gratitude to her husband's spirit, I replied, "Thank ya, thank ya very much!"

Feel, don't think, is the crucial part of RAFT, and this applies to mediums as much as it does to anyone else. During interdimensional communication, it's particularly important for the medium not to jump to conclusions. Mediums may attach a meaning to certain symbols and images projected by a spirit, but the client's interpretation takes precedence. That is because the communication with the spirit isn't about the medium; it's about the client. Spirits transmit messages through the medium to the client for the client's benefit — and if the client is open, the message will be properly received and interpreted.

RAFT is a process, so it's important to let the information resonate with the recipient before imposing a third party's interpretation of the spirit's message onto the recipient.

I was invited by a fellow medium, who hosts a cable TV show in New York. She asked if I would conduct readings for audience members. I was drawn to a young woman.

"A middle-aged man — feels like he's on the parent level — is coming through, and he's presenting me with the image of a police badge."

"My dad was a police officer," she confirmed.

"I'm feeling pains in my chest and I'm hearing the word 'shots.'"

Immediately the show's host blurted out, "I hear shots too! I feel pains in the chest too! Your father was a police officer, and he was shot in the chest in the line of duty!"

Before I could interject, the young woman replied, "No! Daddy was with his friends at a bar, doing shots of tequila, when he had a massive heart attack and died."

Oops!

Mediums are simply the conduit for the messages transmitted through us for the client's benefit. The "F" part of RAFT — feeling, not thinking — is the hard part. What a medium feels about a spirit's message is one thing, and what a client feels it means may be another. This is why the medium should initially defer to the client's interpretation of a message.

I cannot fault my colleague, because it's hard not to draw conclusions based on first impressions. Once my fellow medium knew the spirit had been a police officer, then sensed the pains in his chest and heard the word "shots," her mind immediately filled in the blanks. She assumed that because he was a police officer, he must have been shot in the chest.

The recipient of the message, on the other hand, recognized, accepted, felt, and trusted it. The transmission from the spirit unfolded, revealing this was her father, who died from a massive heart attack when he was drinking tequila from a shot glass.

Spirit communication is not language-dependent, meaning spirits don't speak a human language like English, Mandarin, or Portuguese. They speak frequency. Even if the spirit when alive spoke an entirely different language than the medium, inter-dimensional communication is still possible.

I was in Palm Beach, Florida, when I met Biba. From her accent she sounded as if she came from Eastern Europe, but I didn't know where. That is, until her mother's spirit made her presence known to me.

"I'm hearing a word — it sounds like Ganny or Gania."

The light of realization sparkled in Biba's eyes.

"Do you speak Croatian, Mark?"

"Not a word."

"That's a Croatian word," Biba explained, "it is spelled G-E-N-I-J-E and pronounced *ganny-yay*. It means 'genius.' When I was a child, my mother called me *mali genije* — her little genius."

Interdimensional communication involves spirits transmitting waves of frequency, which convey intelligent concepts and information to the medium. The medium's brain then translates that into recognizable information based on the medium's memories, feelings, knowledge, or cultural associations.

During an interdimensional communication session for Nadia and her family, the spirit of her father came forward. Nadia was the only person in her family who spoke English, so she translated what I presented to her mother and two brothers.

"Nadia, this may sound strange, but I have a background in classical studies, and the image forming in my mind's eye is a famous mosaic of Alexander the Great racing into battle on his horse. Does that make sense to you in any way?"

"It does very much," Nadia smiled, "My father's name was Alejandro, and in Argentina he raced horses."

Building a rapport with a spirit is essential. Spirits can emit a lot more information than the human brain can process, so initially it may seem as if the medium is only picking up on trivial pieces of information. When the medium receives positive confirmation from the client, that creates a receptive environment, which enables the medium and the spirit to establish a frequency lock; then the spirit will be able to transmit deeper and more detailed messages. Should the client begin to block by rejecting or overthinking, this creates a barrier to the afterlife frequency, and the spirit(s) will back off.

If something doesn't immediately make sense to you during interdimensional communication, avoid shooting it down by going directly to "No." Some people fall into a pattern whereby if they don't immediately recognize information, they instantly reject it. The No, No, No syndrome is the most common block to properly receiving and interpreting messages from spirits.

Every medium I know has encountered clients who fall into the No, No, No syndrome. Not only does it hinder the interdimensional communication, it also transforms what should be an uplifting and healing connection with loved ones in spirit into a frustrating experience for the client and the medium. From the perspective of the collective consciousness, the No, No, No syndrome obstructs their attempt to transmit messages of love, healing, resolution, and guidance. Fortunately, because they're spirits, they're infinitely more patient than those of us living in the material world.

The No, No, No syndrome can be caused by immediate rejection of the information; not paying attention; anxiety, which clouds thinking; reluctance and hesitation to acknowledge the information; overthinking and hyperanalysis the instant information is presented; and ironically, from intense desire to have contact with a spirit. I'd like to share some examples from sessions I've conducted, which can help you to recognize and avoid the No, No, No syndrome.

Any being capable of love is capable of interdimensional communication. Our four-legged loved ones may not have human brains, but they do have electromagnetic souls, which can and do communicate with us from the Other Side. One of the fascinating aspects of interdimensional communication with animals is how they are very direct. This is because our relationship with animals tends to be straightforward and is not flooded with the nuances and subtleties that are characteristic of relationships between humans.

Encountering the spirits of animals requires the same approach as communicating with human spirits, and this means applying RAFT. When the recipient recognizes that the spirit is communicating, accepts the contact as real, feels the message, and trusts its guidance, things go smoothly during interdimensional communication. Things become more difficult when the recipient clogs the energetic field with the No, No, No syndrome.

Lawrence booked a session with me. The spirit of his mother, brother, and father came through, and then in the last moments of the session, another spirit came forward.

"Boston — I'm seeing Boston cream pie — images of Boston, does that make sense?"

"No. There's nothing that makes sense about Boston cream pie."

"Be careful about going right to 'no,' Lawrence. This may not be about pie — it may be about Boston the place or something associated with the word or name 'Boston.'"

"No — never been to Boston — makes no sense."

"Ladybugs — now I'm getting images of ladybugs associated with this spirit."

"Nope — nothing about ladybugs makes sense to me."

"Elsie — the image I associate with that name is Elsie, the cow from the milk commercials. It may have nothing to do with cows or milk, but does the name Elsie make sense to you in any way?"

"No."

"The spirits are backing away — they've let me go."

"I'm really happy my family came through, but my dog died recently, and I was really hoping to hear from my Boston terrier, Elsie."

"Boston?"

"Oh, no!"

"Elsie?"

"Oh my gosh — my Boston terrier, Elsie! And ladybugs! My mother gave me the collar Elsie wore, which had little emblems of ladybugs on it! It just didn't connect."

The No, No, No syndrome obstructs the unfolding. Think of messages and images received during interdimensional communication as putting the pieces of a puzzle together. Each piece of information transmitted is a piece of a puzzle. When assembling a puzzle, if you don't immediately understand what the piece means or where it fits into the puzzle, you don't throw that piece away. Assembling the pieces of a puzzle takes time, just as it does to fully understand the pieces of information transmitted by spirits. Once all the pieces are assembled, you understand how each one relates to the others, and together as a whole, they form a much larger picture.

The No, No, No syndrome can also be caused by fear and anxiety. It's normal to be excited or nervous prior to a reading, but there is no reason to be afraid. Spirits reach out to us because they want to bring messages of love, healing, and resolution, not to scare us or control us. However, many times during interdimensional communication, people are so nervous and afraid that it clouds their thinking.

While I was appearing on the TV show *Great Day Houston*, the host, Deborah Duncan, asked if I would conduct readings for audience members. I stood, and immediately the spirit of an older gentleman connected with me. One of the audience members, Paula, recognized the spirit as her husband. She and her daughter stood and approached the microphone.

The number one fear in the United States is standing and talking before a crowd of people. One would think fear of being mugged, attacked by terrorists, or contracting flesh-eating bacteria would seem worse to most people, but it doesn't. Even those of us who regularly speak in public experience jitters before going on stage.

Paula and her daughter were genteel Texas ladies who suddenly realized they were making contact with the spirit of a husband and father while they were surrounded by lights, cameras, TV crew, and a live audience on television before over a million people. They were terrified and trembled as they stood at the microphone.

Meanwhile, from the Other Side, Paula's husband was going to get a message through to his beloved wife and daughter, no matter what. I proceeded to transmit his messages, and despite their nervousness everything was unfolding well, until the word "Chesterfields," coupled with the intense taste of chewing tobacco and the smell of cigarette smoke, overwhelmed me.

"Chesterfields — I don't know what Chesterfields are — was he a smoker?"

"Yes," Paula replied.

"Okay, I'm hearing 'Chesterfields,' and I don't know what they are, if they're a type of cigarette or cigar, but I'm hearing 'Chesterfields' and tasting tobacco. Did he chew tobacco too?"

"No," Paula's daughter shook her head, "but he was a heavy smoker."

"Heavy smoker — well, I'm getting inundated with tobacco."

Paula and her daughter kept shaking their heads, "No."

Months later, I returned to Houston during another speaking tour and was invited back to *Great Day Houston*. The show started. Deborah Duncan introduced me and then said, "This is an example of what happened the last time he was on *Great Day*."

Right on cue, the clip of the reading with Paula and Chesterfields played.

Deborah smiled, "That was an example of how people sometimes say, 'That doesn't make sense.' Then, when they go home and think about it and look around the house, it becomes evidence."

"All right, yes, it does." I nodded in agreement.

"We have Paula on the phone. Good morning, Paula!" Deborah said.

"Good morning!" Paula's voice came through loud and clear.

"So," Deborah continued, "Chesterfields didn't make sense to you, but when you went home, what did you figure out?"

"Well," Paula replied, "as soon as I walked in, I saw this sign that hangs in a little beauty shop that I have."

Just as Paula said that, a huge image of the posters at her hair salon was projected on the monitors and to the TV audience.

"It's a Chesterfields advertisement, and it's an old antique sign," Paula explained. "It's an advertisement with William Bendix when he played in the movie *The Babe Ruth Story*. He's smoking Chesterfield cigarettes, and that's what he's advertising in the big sign with the big package of Chesterfield cigarettes."

The monitors revealed the poster displaying actor William Bendix with a cigarette in his mouth above the word CHESTERFIELDS. Just below it was a smaller poster advertising chewing tobacco.

"And you just didn't realize that at the time?" Deborah asked.

"Uh — No, I didn't. I kept thinking, 'Chesterfields.' I knew all about them, because I'm from that generation. But it didn't dawn on me that — that sign and my husband always would sit there in the beauty shop with me in the morning to drink coffee. And of course, he's looking right at that sign as he's talking to me, because it was right behind me there and we would talk about William Bendix, because we used to watch him in *The Life of Riley*, and he was in our conversation a lot of the time."

"So there you go! Boom!" Deborah smiled. "Paula, thank you for sharing!"

"Thank you for calling!" Paula replied.

When Paula had been on television, she was so nervous she couldn't fit the pieces of the puzzle together. When she got home and saw the Chesterfields and the chewing tobacco posters, the full impact of her husband's message unfolded. To anyone else, they were just old posters, but to Paula they represented the tender moments she and her husband cherished each morning during a lifetime together.

Hesitating or being reluctant to acknowledge information is another form of the No, No, No syndrome. Spirits are very well aware when someone is intentionally obstructing their attempts to communicate. While they may not like this, in the final analysis they have the last word.

During a public spirit communication event, I sensed the spirit of an elderly man. After I described him, Leslie raised her hand. She was with her two sons: Ron, who had a broken leg and needed a cane to walk, and Hugh, a large muscular man who stood well over six and a half feet tall. Hugh's wife, barely half his size, stood behind them.

The spirit of Leslie's father loved her and her sons dearly. I also detected a mischievous sense of humor. Suddenly the spirit focused on Hugh.

"Bat — I'm seeing an image of the creature a bat — your grandfather keeps referring to bats — do bats make sense to you?"

"No!" Hugh frowned and clenched his fists. I was in a bit of a quandary. I knew the information was relevant, but I didn't exactly want to antagonize this wall of muscle who towered over me.

"Your grandfather keeps projecting to me images of bats. Are you sure there isn't something about you and bats?"

"I SAID NO!" Everyone in the audience suddenly sat up straight in their seats.

"Okay — no worries," I replied, "I'll leave that with you."

The next day I received this email:

We were at your show last night. I was the big fella that stood up with my mom and brother who had the cane. You mentioned that you saw a bat. You said it twice to me. Anyway, when I got home last night, I BS you not, there was a bat flying around my bedroom. I ran downstairs because I have a phobia about bats. But my wife and her girlfriend caught it in a paper sack. Never have had a bat in my house. Just thought I'd let you know. — Hugh

Spirits have an uncanny way of getting their messages through to loved ones in the material world. The spirit of Hugh's grandfather wasn't about to be dismissed by the grandson he loved. Perhaps he was trying to warn Hugh a bat was flying around his bedroom. Or maybe the spirit directed this creature there as a way to say, "Hey! I'm around you!"

In any event, I reassured Hugh I'm just a conduit for the

information. I don't have the ability to inflict biblical plagues of locusts, frogs, or, in this case, bats on anyone.

Once a message is transmitted by a spirit, the very first thing you feel or associate with it is the answer. If you don't immediately understand the message, just note it and let the next round of messages come forward.

After the session, the unfolding begins. This is when to analyze the information and reflect upon it. The unfolding can take hours, days, weeks, or even longer to understand the full impact of the messages and how many different levels of significance there are to the messages presented.

During the internet era, with a few strokes on a keyboard we have immediate access to information and answers to questions. While many people expect the same instant unfolding of messages received during interdimensional communication, that is not always what happens. Nevertheless, no matter how long it takes, when the time is right the unfolding occurs.

During a session for Roni, the spirit of her son Tyler came through. He was sixteen years old when he died from brain cancer. Tyler's spirit transmitted several detailed messages until we hit a barrier.

"Napoleon — he keeps repeating the name Napoleon," I conveyed.

"That doesn't make any sense," Roni replied.

"I'm a history buff," I explained. "My interpretation could be that maybe he admired Napoleon Bonaparte. I also like desserts so it could mean he liked Napoleon dessert pastries. But my interpretation doesn't matter, it's what it means to you that is important."

"I'm sorry, Mark. I can't think of anything about my son that relates to Napoleon."

Five years later I received this email:

Hi Mark, you probably don't remember but years ago you did a reading for me and connected with the spirit of my son Tyler. During the reading "Napoleon" kept coming up. At the time it didn't make sense to me.

This morning I was thinking about Tyler and I was really depressed. Suddenly it hit me. Tyler's favorite all-time movie was this comedy *Napoleon Dynamite*. He quoted lines from it all the time. It never dawned on me during the reading, but now it does and realizing this makes me feel so happy. Thank you.

I've never seen the film *Napoleon Dynamite*, so that reference did not occur to me. But the message was not meant for me — it was for Roni. While the unfolding can take days, weeks, and even years, for Roni it happened at just the right moment.

Another form of the No, No, No syndrome is hyperanalyzing and overthinking a message the instant it arrives. Doing so will halt the energetic flow of information from a spirit.

"Feel, don't think" is a difficult hurdle for many people to cross during interdimensional communication. Many people are analytical by nature or work in fields where analytical ability is required. As an attorney, I know how important it is to be meticulous, detail-oriented, and analytical in the practice of law. However, hyperanalysis can work against you during interdimensional communication. When a message is transmitted directly to you or through a medium, you must feel first and think later.

When you hyperanalyze every message the second it comes in by subjecting it to intense scrutiny, this overthinking creates a block. Interdimensional communication involves metaphorical images, visions, and concepts, which, like the pieces of a puzzle, must be assembled gradually. Refrain from interrupting or subjecting the medium to a barrage of questions during spirit contact. You can't cross-examine spirits as if they're on the witness stand in a courtroom. (Personally, I wish we could, but all that will do is create a barrier and obstruct the communication.)

Although we all want to hear specific things from our loved ones in spirit, going into a reading with a set agenda of what you want to know can create a mindset which causes you to overlook a subtle message as a result of hyperanalyzing. This is what happened during a session with Melanie.

"The spirit of your brother is showing me pickles," I said. "Does that make sense?"

"No," Melanie replied.

"Are you sure? He keeps showing me jars and jars of pickles. He won't let this go."

"No, pickles make no sense!"

"Are you sure? He keeps projecting jars of pickles, barrels of pickles — lots of pickles."

"Well" — her pause for a few moments confirmed that I was receiving good information — "after my brother died, I moved, and I bought a small house just down the street from a factory where they bottle pickles and ship them all over the world."

"So the answer is yes," I replied.

"No, it isn't! He didn't know that! We moved there after he died. Why would he bring up pickles? Pickles don't make any sense! How are pickles important? I just don't understand why of all things he would bring up pickles! So, no, pickles don't make sense."

"Ma'am, if I say, 'pickles,' and you live across the street from a pickle factory, the answer is yes."

"No, it isn't. How does that pertain to him? I can't figure out why pickles make sense."

"Remember what I said prior to the reading — that spirits are not limited by whom or what they knew when they were alive?"

"But why pickles? That's so trivial."

"I don't mean to be flippant, but I don't fling out random condiments hoping to get a hit."

"Oh — OH! I get it! He's telling me he knows I moved near a pickle factory after he died! That means he *is* around me!"

Once the barrier she unintentionally projected by hyper-analyzing came down, the reading flowed beautifully, and deeper messages came through from her brother.

When spirits are aligning their frequency with that of the medium, a lot of information is conveyed and must be sorted out by the medium's brain. It is similar to receiving the entire FM band of radio frequency, so it may appear that the medium is initially detecting trivial pieces of information. By receiving confirmation on seemingly trivial details, the medium and the spirit are building rapport and tuning in to each other's frequency. Once they achieve a frequency match, then deeper and more complex messages will start coming through.

⚊

MANY PEOPLE WONDER WHY they never experience after-death communication in the wake of a loved one's death.

"I want to see her spirit!"

"I want him to be alive again!"

"I want her to come to me in my dreams, and she hasn't!"

"I want, I want, I want" is another form of the No, No, No syndrome, because a bereaved person overcome with angst and desire is unintentionally generating the same mindset, which blocks interdimensional communication.

This is not a criticism of anyone grieving the loss of a loved one. This is devastating emotionally, physically, spiritually, and often financially. While you are mired in the pit of despair and sadness, it is absolutely normal to want to see, hear, and hold your loved one again. Death completely changes the lives of the survivors. While there is nothing we can change about the fact a loved one has died, what we can do is change our reaction to the death. This takes time, and everyone grieves at his or her own pace.

One of the main objectives in the journey through grief is acceptance, not only of the person's death, but of the fact that your relationship has transformed from one of a physical nature to one of a spiritual nature. Spirits will reach out to you. The question, then, is whether you are open to recognizing, accepting, feeling, and trusting the contact (the RAFT technique). Everyone is different and grieves in their individual way, so for some, it may take more time to be open to the contact and not engage in behaviors or a mindset which blocks the contact.

Although one may not intend to do so, an intense state of grief can obstruct after-death communication from a spirit. Emotions emit a lot of energy that creates a barrier to the afterlife frequency. Think of your emotions as deflector shields on starships in the science fiction series *Star Trek* and *Star Wars*. Deflector shields envelop a starship with an energy barrier that repels asteroids, debris, and enemy attacks.

In fact, generating an energy barrier that thwarts other forms of energy isn't just science fiction anymore. NASA and other space agencies are developing deflector shield technology. This will generate an electromagnetic barrier to protect deep spacecraft with human crews by deflecting lethal radioactive energy and preventing collisions with solid objects in space. According to the European Space Agency, when a spacecraft is traveling at extreme velocity, collision with debris only a few centimeters in diameter could destroy it.

Back on planet Earth, both the United States and the United

Kingdom are developing deflector shields for tanks and other combat vehicles. Professor Bryn James of the British Defence Science and Technology Laboratory has explained that super-capacitors capable of generating an intense electromagnetic field to repel small rockets and shrapnel are being developed. Boeing Corporation has even secured a patent for a "method and system for shockwave attenuation via electromagnetic arc," which is essentially an electromagnetic energy shield to deflect shock waves caused by explosions.

How does this apply to after-death communication? Emotions are energetic impulses generated by your brain. The energy you emit can either be receptive or obstructive to spirit contact. When you are overcome with the pain and sadness caused by the loss of a loved one, coupled with the intense desire to have contact with that person's spirit, you can obstruct after-death communication. Without intending to do so, your emotions become deflector shields against the afterlife frequency. What you really want to do is lower these deflector shields and be receptive to the afterlife frequency. The RAFT technique is the process which will enable you to lower the shields. However, the "F" (feeling) is once again the hurdle to cross.

Interdimensional communication isn't an aggressive act; it's an assertive act. Intense desire for and demanding contact from spirits, and then becoming frustrated and angry when it doesn't happen, are aggressive behaviors. This raises the deflector shields. By contrast, being assertive means that you seek the contact but do so without angst, frustration, or intense desire. This lowers your deflector shields. But how do you train yourself to do that?

Start by taking a deep breath through your nose and exhaling from your mouth. As you exhale, envision your breath as a cloud leaving your body, carrying away your stress and expectations. Do this a few times, and then mentally or verbally reframe your request for the contact. Instead of "I *want* you to come to me in my dreams," say, "I welcome you into my dreams" or, "I invite your presence."

This will begin the process of shifting your attitude from aggressive to assertive by replacing your intense demand with a welcoming, open invitation. Do not expect immediate results. It takes practice and patience, and you must avoid reverting to the mindset of demanding. Besides, trying to force a spirit to adhere to your timetable will only generate angst, which will raise your deflector shields.

Now that your deflectors are down and you're receptive to messages from the collective consciousness of spirits, the unfolding begins. It may be immediate, or it may occur over a period of time. Sometimes the unfolding reveals things you didn't know or expect.

~

AVA SCHEDULED A TELEPHONE SESSION, and the spirits of her parents and a few other close relatives came through. She verified their identities and explained how most of them had died decades earlier, so she was at peace with their passing. I wasn't sure if she was engaging in interdimensional communication just out of curiosity or for some other reason. Then, suddenly, everything changed.

"The spirit of a young man is coming through," I relayed. "He's depicting himself in uniform — looks military, and he appears to have been in his mid to late twenties when he died."

"What else?"

"Loud swooshing sound. I've been on helicopters — this sounds like a helicopter."

"That's who I was hoping to hear from!" Ava exclaimed.

"Another spirit is with him — another guy in uniform. I'm receiving a vision, and I'm seeing these guys in the helicopter — but your guy isn't the pilot."

"That's right — he was the copilot."

"The spirit of the pilot keeps saying, 'It wasn't my fault — fuel line — fuel line — fuel line jammed.'"

"What else are you getting, Mark?"

"I feel a slamming sensation to my body. This indicates a quick, abrupt, and unexpected passing. Shock wave flying through me — feels like an explosion!"

"Yes, they died in a helicopter crash," Ava responded, "but I don't know all the details."

"That's okay, Ava, those might unfold for you later — but the message about how it wasn't the pilot's fault is really strong and keeps getting repeated: 'Not my fault, fuel line jammed.'"

"I can't confirm any details other than that the chopper crashed."

"Hold on. Your guy's back and wants you to give Owen a message. Who's Owen?"

"Owen's his brother. What does he want me to tell Owen?"

"'Suck it up and be a bulldog.' Does that make any sense to you?"

"Not yet."

"That's it — they let me go." Exhausted, I took a deep breath.

"Let me explain, Mark. I was in the Navy for almost thirty years. I scheduled an appointment with you to hear from the young lieutenant who died in the helicopter crash. His name was Calvin — but he went by Cal."

"He must've been very important to you."

"I never met Cal."

"Not sure I'm following you, Ava."

"My job in the Navy was to make arrangements to ship the remains of servicemen and -women to their families for burial. Cal was the first one I ever did. I never knew him when he was alive, but I've always felt a connection to him."

Ava was clearly touched by the messages from Cal and the other pilot. I explained to her that even though she couldn't confirm the other details transmitted through me, she shouldn't worry, since the unfolding takes time.

As I've already stressed, in order to avoid the No, No, No syndrome during interdimensional communication, the best approach is not to hyperanalyze or overthink messages the moment they are presented. However, that doesn't apply after the session. That's when to meticulously review and analyze the messages. This process will aid in the unfolding and help you understand the full impact of the messages.

Ava called me a couple months later to discuss the results of her investigation.

"Mark, it's been almost twenty years since this crash, but I think I know why Cal's spirit has been with me."

"What'd you find out?"

"Cal and the other pilot were the best of the best. This wasn't a combat mission. It was a routine training exercise, and conditions that day were ideal. The weather was clear, and everything checked out in the preflight inspection. This chopper should not have gone down."

"But it did."

"Yes, and the *official* story was the crash was caused by pilot error."

"The pilot's spirit said, 'Fuel line jammed.' Then why did the initial report say pilot error?"

"You're a lawyer, so you know about Navy JAG — the Judge Advocate General, right?"

"The JAG Corps — they're the Navy's lawyers."

"They are, but Navy JAG also investigates accidents and crashes, so I started digging and found the results of the JAG investigation, which clearly stated from all accounts the crash was *not* pilot error but *mechanical* failure."

"Then why wasn't that in the official report?"

"I found out that not just the Navy, but the Marines and the Army used this same model of helicopter. And this wasn't the only crash with this chopper model that shouldn't have happened."

"Were the other crashes caused by mechanical failure?"

"They were, and after a few more crashes this model helicopter was grounded. The JAG must have discovered something in this wreckage. But I don't believe it was a cover-up, because there's no way the military would commission a helicopter with a *known* mechanical defect. My feeling is that the crash of Cal's helicopter put into motion a chain of events that led the military to discover a design defect."

"That means finding this defect ultimately saved lives."

"Somehow, I think Cal wanted me and his family to know this. I contacted his brother, Owen."

"Was Owen open to receiving messages from Cal's spirit?"

"Remember during the reading Cal told Owen to 'suck it up'?"

"Vaguely — why?"

"Let me read you Owen's email: 'I know firsthand that Mark was speaking directly to my brother, Cal. I went to the Citadel, and there's a term we used at home in reference to the Citadel, and my mom uses it to this day: "Suck it up and be a bulldog," because the Citadel's mascot is a bulldog, and bulldogs are tough and very determined. We're a military family, and my mother raised us with that saying after our father died. So there you have it.'"

Information received from spirits unfolds at its own pace and may take time. Many people find this exasperating, because they want answers and messages which make sense instantly. Sometimes that is the case — other times it isn't. The beauty of spiritual synchronicity is that the unfolding always occurs at just the right time.

No LOSS IS MORE DEVASTATING than the death of a child. It doesn't matter if the child was a baby or an adult — the death of a child is crippling to a parent. The emotional bond between parent and child is like no other. While intense emotions and pain may initially block one's receptivity to messages from a spirit, they're also frequency beacons which draw a spirit to the bereaved loved ones in the material world.

Hunter was eighteen years old when he was killed in a single-vehicle accident one night when he fell asleep behind the wheel of his car, which hit a tree. His parents, Allan and Tracy, were crushed by the loss of their only child. They came to me for an in-person reading, and as soon as I opened up to frequency, Hunter's spirit made contact.

During the hour-long session, Hunter conveyed several messages and many pieces of verifiable evidence to his parents. Nothing is more rewarding than to see how facilitating contact between parents and the spirit of their child helps to lighten the burden of their grief.

"Hunter's spirit is beginning to recede."

"Thank you, Mark," Tracy said, "this has been very helpful."

"Wait — he's not finished. There's one last message."

I hesitated for a moment, and then took a deep breath.

"'I met Michael Jackson.'"

Hunter's parents clasped hands and fell back into their seats.

"Our son loved Michael Jackson's music," Tracy said. "We even played a Michael Jackson song at his funeral — but..."

"But," Allan continued, "on the way home from Hunter's service, Tracy and I were alone in the car. And we've never mentioned a word of this to anyone — seriously, no one knows this. Tracy said, 'I wonder if he'll meet Michael Jackson in heaven.'"

Chapter 9

SPIRIT INTERVENTION

Nikola Tesla once remarked, "What one man calls God, another calls the laws of physics." Everything in our material world — matter and energy, spiritual and corporeal — is interconnected, because everything on the subatomic level is composed of the same basic units of electromagnetic energy known as quanta. Applying this understanding to a spiritual level explains the "delivery system" for miracles, premonitions, synchronistic events, and psychic activity, including the technical aspects of communication with a spirit, a collective of spirits, and the infinite intelligence known as God.

Spirit intervention explains how spirits affect our lives through premonitions, feelings, influences on chains of events (synchronicity), and even the manipulation of matter and energy. Nothing in our lives is random, and everything falls into place as part of a larger plan, which some call fate, others, synchronicity, and some, the will of God.

MY LIFELONG INTEREST IN SPIRITUALITY and how different cultures perceive God has taken me to mystical and sacred sites across the globe. One of the most alluring is the fabled lost city of Machu Picchu in the Andes Mountains of Peru. Perched above the Urubamba River, one of the headwaters of the Amazon, Machu Picchu overlooks the Sacred Valley, one of the most fertile places on earth. It was a shining jewel of the Incan Empire.

In 1532, Spanish conquistador Francisco Pizarro invaded the Incan Empire with the objective of capturing its capital city, Cusco, located high in the Andes. Driven by the desire to seize Cusco's legendary treasures of gold, silver, and precious jewels, Pizarro's small army of less than two hundred was heavily armed with the latest European military technology, including gunpowder, rifles, cannons, and cavalry.

Despite the small size of his army, Pizarro was confident of success. Just over a decade earlier, the treasure-laden Aztec Empire of Mexico had fallen to conquistador Hernán Cortés. The Aztec emperor, Moctezuma II, made a fatal mistake when he believed the white Spaniards to be gods and welcomed them into his kingdom. By the time the Aztecs realized the Spaniards were merely men lusting for treasure, it was too late. Moctezuma's army was no match for the Spanish military.

The Inca emperor, Atahualpa, was not so gullible and readied an army of eighty thousand warriors to repel the invaders. Unfortunately, smallpox introduced by the Spaniards during the Aztec conquest years earlier had swept southward into Peru, decimating the population. By the time Pizarro's army arrived, much of the Incan army was dead or too sick to fight. Those capable of fighting were armed only with bows and spears and had never been exposed to the explosive force of gunpowder. The Spaniards opened with a barrage of rifle and cannon fire, followed by a cavalry charge.

Incas had never seen troops mounted on horses and were terrified by these "monsters." The Incan army was annihilated and their emperor captured. The greatest civilization of the New World was crushed under the heel of the Spanish invaders. The enormous amount of gold, silver, and precious gems looted from Inca cities was beyond the wildest dreams of the conquerors.

One by one, the cities of the vast Inca Empire, which stretched from modern-day Colombia to Argentina, met with the same fate. Except, of course, Machu Picchu. Perhaps it was never conquered because the Spaniards never heard of this remote and isolated mountaintop city. Mysteriously, four decades after the Spanish invasion, the population of Machu Picchu abandoned the city. It was consumed by dense jungle growth and disappeared from sight. Although the local native people knew something was there, it wasn't officially "discovered" until 1911, when Hiram Bingham of Yale University stumbled upon it with the help of local farmers. Thus the lost city of Machu Picchu emerged as one of the greatest archaeological discoveries of the twentieth century.

Machu Picchu remains shrouded in mystery. For over a century, archaeologists have tried to understand the full purpose of this strange city. It clearly had agricultural and commercial importance as well as deep religious and ceremonial significance. Archaeologists suggest that human sacrifice may have been conducted there to honor the gods.

Machu Picchu was also an observatory for studying the cosmos. Towering above the city is the great mountain of Huayna Picchu, where UFO sightings have been reported for decades.

Intact ancient ruins of a mysterious and mystical lost city abandoned atop a mountain jungle, with evidence of human sacrifice and UFOs! How could I resist?

The sheer beauty of this city in the sky is breathtaking — literally. My home on a barrier island of Florida's east coast is a whopping 9 feet (3 meters) above sea level. This is a stark contrast to Machu Picchu's altitude of 8,000 feet (2,400 meters), which caused my lungs to keep seeking the rare commodity called air.

Despite the difficulty breathing, I was in archaeological paradise. The lush green jungle is a bright contrast to the deep brown hue of the mountains. Masterfully carved by the engineering skill and architectural genius of the Incas, Machu Picchu appears to be a natural extension of the mountains themselves. Immense stone blocks hauled from nearby quarries were used to construct the elaborate system of terraces for agriculture, temples, housing, storage centers, and observatories for studying the stars.

After a few days of hiking and photographing the majesty of Machu Picchu, I felt drawn to the Intihuatana Stone at the Temple of the Sun. This massive stone, shaped like a chair, is believed to have been a royal throne for the Inca rulers so they could observe the position of the sun throughout the year. The four edges of the throne point precisely to the compass directions of north, south, east, and west. The sun god was the chief deity of the Incan pantheon, as is common for societies dependent upon agriculture. This throne enhanced the Inca emperor's connection to the sun god, since knowing when to plant and harvest crops gave him mystical power over life and death.

Looking down from the Intihuatana Stone, I noticed the crowds of visitors leaving, since it would be dark in roughly two hours. It dawned on me I was there alone. I hopped onto the royal throne of the Incas to take in one of the most fantastic views on earth.

Suddenly from behind I heard a sultry female voice, "Is this throne taken?"

I turned and locked eyes with a striking woman clad in

native Andean attire, complete with a white head covering and multicolored poncho woven from alpaca wool. I wasn't sure if it was her infectious laugh or the oxygen deprivation, but I burst into laughter too.

"My empress," I chuckled, yielding the throne to her.

"I am Esmeralda." She looked so natural sitting on the throne. Her beauty was regal and ageless. Her deep green eyes, accentuated by her deep olive complexion, briefly surveyed me and then shifted to gaze at Machu Picchu basking in the soft dusk sunlight.

I discovered she was visiting from Brazil and had been in Peru for several months, living among the Quechua people, who are descendants of the Incas.

"The Temple of the Sun is sacred," Esmeralda told me. "I've come to honor the Eternal Light of Olodumare."

Eternal Light!

"Olodumare? Is that the name of your God?"

"My God? The Eternal Light has many names. The energy you call God and I call Olodumare connects everyone and everything. Both people and spirits serve the will of the Eternal Light."

"How so?" My curiosity was piqued.

"Nothing in life is — how you say — coincidence. Look here." She pointed to a large black ant crawling by the base of the throne. "This ant came from the hole on the east side of the Intihuatana Stone, and its journey is to the hole on the west side of the stone. Think of the east hole as the day you were born, and the west hole as the day you will die. Nothing can change those days."

"Esmeralda, many religions, including Christianity, embrace the belief in a life plan and predestination. But they also believe in free will."

"The free will of this ant is what it chooses to do on the journey between the holes."

She stepped off the throne and bent down on her knees next to the ant. "See how this ant has strayed from its destination." She placed her hand in the ant's path, and it immediately changed course, toward the west hole. "Everyone has a destiny and a purpose, and when you stray too far from your path, the hand of the Eternal Light will guide you back to it. All beings — animals, people, and spirits — are instruments of the Eternal Light."

"If I may ask, what faith do you follow?"

"The Quechua call me a shaman. In Brazil, I'm called a Voodoo high priestess."

"Cool — it's not every day I meet a Voodoo high priestess sitting on a royal throne at Machu Picchu's Temple of the Sun."

"Nor is it every day at Machu Picchu do I meet a lawyer who sees dead people."

"Guess the only things missing," I chuckled, "are aliens from outer space!"

"Perhaps the star people will come." She grinned as we both eyed the peak of Huayna Picchu, where sightings of UFOs are common.

Shadows engulfed us as the sun slipped behind the mountains.

"Mark, we must go, for soon it will be dark, and everywhere there will be *vipro.*"

Vipro? In English that mean vipers, which are poisonous snakes! It was definitely time to leave. Besides, I wasn't about to argue with a Voodoo high priestess seated on a throne as my mind filled with images of negotiating treacherous paths along sheer mountain cliffs slithering with poisonous snakes at night.

WHAT ESMERALDA REFERRED TO as the hand of the Eternal Light and what I call spirit intervention is echoed in belief systems across the globe. Spirit intervention occurs when the collective consciousness intervenes to guide a person to make a decision or engage in a course of action that can be life-altering and even lifesaving. Since spirits are pure energy and are not tied to a material world construct of time, they are able to alert us to what we may perceive to be a future event and can intervene for our benefit.

While spirits are a potent force in our lives, they are not here to control us or override free will. However, they can guide us in the right direction to make the best use of free will. Spirits are persistent and will get their message through one way or another.

This underscores the importance of enhancing one's spiritual situational awareness. When you employ the RAFT technique, the benefits of spirit intervention will become second nature and manifest within seconds. Recognize the presence of a spirit, accept the contact as real, feel the message instead of overthinking it, and then trust the spirit's guidance. It can help you make important life decisions and, in the more immediate sense, help you avoid a potentially dangerous person, place, thing, or behavior.

Spirit intervention may manifest in many ways. It may be transmitted directly to the recipient through a feeling or premonition, or during the sleep state, when the recipient is at rest and the deflector shields are down. It may also be communicated to the recipient via interdimensional communication through a medium.

VALERIE AND DARYL LOST THEIR OLDEST SON to a drug overdose. They came to see me with their surviving son, Carter, for a reading.

"Matthew — does that name resonate with you?"

"His name was Matthew!" His parents and brother smiled.

Matthew's spirit drew my focus to Carter: "Your brother's spirit is insistent that under no circumstances are you to go hang gliding!"

"Oh my gosh!" Carter was stunned. "I'm supposed to go hang gliding in the Florida Keys next week."

His mother glared at him. "Like hell you are!"

"No worries, Mom!" Carter looked startled. "No way am I gonna do that now — I swear!"

"Matthew is switching tracks now," I continued. "'Clean your storm drains, clean the rain gutters.'"

"Why?" Daryl asked.

"Not sure, but he keeps repeating this."

Six months later Daryl, Valerie, and Carter returned for another session. After they took their seats, Daryl asked, "Remember the message about cleaning the storm drains and the rain gutters?"

"I do."

"We followed our son's advice, and we're glad we did," Daryl explained. "We got hit hard by the hurricane last summer, and our neighborhood flooded. Our house was one of the few on our street that didn't flood or have extensive water damage. That's because we had proper drainage, since we'd cleared our rain gutters and cleared the storm drains on the street in front of the house. The ironic thing is the hurricane was named Matthew — our son's name."

~

HEADING OFF A PROBLEM at the pass is a key component of spirit intervention. This is especially true when it comes to messages concerning medical issues. For spirits, healing doesn't always mean treating a condition after it occurs; sometimes it's a matter of intervening to prevent a condition before it happens.

I conducted an interdimensional communication session for Sharon, who is a renowned psychiatrist. The spirit of her mother came through, and I kept hearing in my mind's ear the name "Corinna."

"Corinna was my mother's best friend — they were elementary school teachers together."

"Sharon, do you know if Corinna is having eye issues? Your mom's spirit is transmitting to me physical sensations about Corinna and I'm feeling pain and pressure around my eyes."

"Mark, I haven't spoken to Corinna since Mom died, and that was well over a year ago."

"Sharon, this is really strong," I explained. "Your mother's spirit wants you to contact Corinna and tell her to get her eyes checked — and soon."

About a month after the reading, Sharon contacted me.

"After the reading, I pondered for several days about whether to share the information. I was hesitant because, unlike me and my family, Corinna had been reared in a small town which is religiously fundamentalist. Corinna might completely reject any otherworldly message that did not conform to her beliefs. My even telling her might ruin our friendship, because she might also reject this as an abomination."

"What did you do, Sharon?"

"I finally decided I couldn't ethically withhold messages that might make a difference to Corinna, regardless of the consequences to me."

"So you did call Corinna?"

"To my surprise, Mark, she said she was skeptical but open-minded about mediums. As soon as I told her you'd felt pressure around the eyes, she gasped and confirmed that she'd been feeling eye pressure for the past week or so."

"You trusted the truth of the message from your mom's spirit!"

"I did, but I still wasn't sure what Corinna would do with that information. Two days later, Corinna called me and said after hearing the message, she immediately made an appointment with her ophthalmologist, even though she had just had her annual eye exam a month before. She thought her doctor would wonder why she was coming in again so soon when everything had been clear."

"What did her doctor say?"

"She had the beginning of a subtle condition, which would not have shown up on standard tests until it was much worse, by which time inevitable vision loss would have occurred. Instead, she could take some vitamins and make dietary changes that should arrest the problem now and prevent her from going blind."

"Sharon, this is definitely a case of spirit intervention."

"Corinna told her doctor that she *needed* to come in based on a message from her best friend's spirit that came through a psychic medium."

"How did her doctor respond?"

"Corinna said her physician was Latino and that his mother was known in her community as a healer. He didn't blink an eye, no pun intended, when he heard this message had a spiritual basis. Corinna was extremely grateful and believes she has successfully averted a problem, thanks to my calling, thanks to my mother's contacting her, and thanks to you."

"I'm just the conduit for the information. The thanks must go to God for setting in motion this chain of events that led to saving Corinna's eyesight."

THE ROLE OF A MEDIUM is to convey what is being transmitted from a spirit as accurately and objectively as possible. Many times the information transferred is just as much of a surprise to me as to the client. Unfortunately, on the flip side of the cosmic coin, just because spirits may warn someone of a potentially dangerous situation does not mean that person will listen, much less recognize, accept, feel, or trust the spirit's guidance.

At a public evening of spirit communication, I was connecting random audience members with loved ones in spirit. I was drawn to Amy and Ian, a married couple who appeared to be in their late thirties.

The spirit of Amy's brother Shawn connected with me.

"There is a sense of urgency from Shawn about your husband, Ian."

Ian's eyebrows rose.

"Shawn is concerned about your health," I conveyed.

"I'm fine," Ian replied.

"I'm feeling pain in my stomach, my lower intestines, and colon. This sensation of pain is how Shawn is transmitting to me the parts of your body where there may be a potential problem."

Both Amy and Ian shook their heads.

"I'm not trying to alarm you, but this is serious. Shawn's spirit doesn't want to let this go."

"Ian doesn't have any health issues," Amy interjected.

"Shawn's spirit is also referencing an elevated white blood cell count. Based on what I'm feeling and what he's conveying, I suggest you make a doctor's appointment to get a checkup. Make sure you get a blood test to screen for infection."

"Nothing's wrong with me," Ian insisted.

"My obligation is to convey what I'm being given," I explained. "Therefore my advice is to go for a checkup. If you're fine and there's no health issue, that's great, but if not...This is what I refer to as spirit intervention. This means Shawn's spirit is trying to intervene on your behalf for your own good by alerting you to a potential health problem. With this advance notice, you can prevent it."

Shawn's spirit had delivered his message, and the communication ended.

Amy and Ian smiled politely and returned to their seats.

A few weeks later I received an email from Amy, which read:

> Hi, Mark. My husband, Ian, and I just saw you last month at your spirit communication event. You actually did a reading for us where my brother, Shawn, came through. You said Shawn's spirit was very concerned with my husband and his health and his abdomen. I just wanted to let you know Ian had a massive infection in his intestines. This led to an emergency appendectomy with serious complications. He is in the hospital now and will be there for a week due to the ongoing infection. The surgeons had to remove part of his colon and part of his small intestine. I guess that's what you saw.

I took absolutely no pleasure about being right in this situation.

Amy and Ian disregarded the messages from Shawn's spirit because at the time Ian didn't feel ill. However, a simple blood test would have indicated an elevated white blood cell count, which is an indicator of appendicitis and intestinal infection.

Fortunately, the surgeons were able to save Ian's life. Unfortunately, he had to undergo major surgery and must face the rest of his life without part of his colon and small intestine.

This underscores how important it is to avoid the No, No,

No syndrome. The period of time after the reading, which I refer to as the unfolding, often involves future events. This is because spirits transcend space-time, so they can perceive what we call the future.

My mother, Jeannie, who was a psychic medium, once told me, "Just because we see something, Mark, doesn't mean we can change it. You can lead a horse to water, but you can't make him drink."

Recognize, accept, feel, and trust messages from spirits. This applies whether the message is conveyed by a legitimate psychic or to you directly in a premonition or an after-death communication, such as in a dream. Please take these premonitions seriously, for they are a blessing, and they just may save your life, or the life of someone you love.

~

WE CAN ONLY WONDER how much spirits care about the material world. While I'm certainly open to receiving winning lottery numbers, the spirits' concern for our world goes much deeper than material possessions.

Each piece of information transmitted during interdimensional communication is like a piece of a puzzle. But it's not that simple. The pieces may be presented through subtle signs and thoughts transmitted to the recipient. This information can influence the decisions and behaviors of the recipient.

It's easy to accept the positive power of spirit intervention when all the pieces of the puzzle fall into the right place at the right time. It is much more difficult to acknowledge this when the pieces of the puzzle fall into the wrong place at the wrong time. As difficult as it may be to accept, even the most horrible tragedy, such as the loss of a child, may be part of the spirit intervention puzzle.

There are no words to describe the devastation and excruciating pain caused by the death of a child. As discussed in the previous chapter, the emotional bond between parent and child is unparalleled. Regardless of whether the child was an infant or an adult, for parents who've lost a child, the pain is beyond measure. All too often, even though parents were in no way responsible for their child's death, parents can be overcome with regrets, remorse, and the inability to find inner peace, much less any semblance of joy. Bereaved parents can spend the rest of their lives trying to make sense of the death of their child.

Full understanding of spirit intervention requires seeing the puzzle once all the pieces are assembled. From the human perspective, this can be extremely painful and can take a very long time.

GUILLERMO AND LILY were happily married and lived in Chicago. One night, their world fell to pieces when they received a call that their son, a popular junior high school teacher in his twenties, died unexpectedly under suspicious circumstances.

In the devastating wake of their son's death, Guillermo and Lily both felt the presence of their son's spirit. Unfortunately, some family and friends dismissed their spiritual encounters as wishful thinking or grief-induced hallucinations.

Nevertheless, Guillermo and Lily believed the contact from their son's spirit was real. Their quest to learn more about spirit communication led them to my book *Never Letting Go*, which in turn led them to schedule a telephone session with me.

I began: "A male spirit who appears to have been in his mid-twenties at the time of his passing is coming through. He was strong and physically fit. Does that make sense?"

"Yes," they said in unison.

"His passing was abrupt and unexpected. Sudden heart failure — not from a medical condition, but caused by drugs — does that make sense?"

"Yes, it does," Guillermo replied.

"Your son wants you to know he did not take his own life. Some type of interaction between two different prescription drugs caused cardiac failure."

"This confirms what we believe," Lily explained. "The coroner's report indicated the only drugs in his system were the two prescribed by his doctor. There weren't excessive amounts of either, so it *wasn't* an overdose."

"We hired a medical malpractice firm and are filing a lawsuit." Pain resonated through Guillermo's words. "From what the law firm's toxicology experts have indicated, these two medications should *never* be taken together. If we don't file this lawsuit to stop the negligent practice of prescribing these two medications in combination, then more people like our son will die."

At the conclusion of the reading, Lily said, "Mark, per the instructions on your website, we didn't tell you anything about ourselves."

"I appreciate that," I replied. "The reason for that is to make sure that everything transmitted to me during the reading comes from spirits, not from what I may know ahead of time."

"My husband is an Illinois state senator. We're well known in Chicago, and that's why we wanted to make sure you didn't know anything about us."

"If there is anything I can ever do for you," Guillermo said, "and I mean *anything*, my door is *always* open."

Over a year after the reading for Guillermo and Lily, I was contacted by Barb. Her daughter, Leslie, was in her early twenties when she died unexpectedly.

"Leslie was really sick," I described during the reading. "I'm experiencing sensations which indicate she was dizzy, nauseated, and very hot — feels like a high fever. There's a lot of pain just above my hips on both sides; this feels like a problem with her kidneys."

"That's spot-on, Mark. Please continue."

"Leslie wants you to know, *'He didn't kill me, but it was his fault.'* Does that make sense, Barb?"

"Yes, it does."

"Leslie's spirit is receding, but she has one final message. 'My life was not in vain. There will be a law to change this, but it will take time. It will not happen right away.'"

"I understand Leslie's message. The law does need to change. Since the reading is over, I'd like to explain why I came to you," Barb replied.

"Go ahead."

"I felt guided to contact you, Mark, because in your book *Never Letting Go*, I discovered you're an attorney as well as a medium. I had a feeling your legal expertise could help resolve some of the disturbing issues surrounding Leslie's death."

"Tell me about these issues."

"Leslie was dating a young man who lived an hour away, so occasionally she would stay at his place. His mother was the county coroner where he lived. While she was there, Leslie started running a really high fever — over 102 degrees. Instead of taking her to the emergency room, the boyfriend called his mother, the coroner. Technically, she's a doctor, and she gave Leslie some aspirin and said if her fever continued to climb, she should seek urgent care."

"Somehow it seems he never took her to urgent care."

"No, he didn't. Instead, he went to a party that night and left her alone. Leslie texted him three times begging him to check in on her, but he never responded."

"The next day was Sunday. Even though Leslie was getting worse, he left her alone again so he could go out with his friends. Leslie's condition worsened, and by Monday morning she had developed slurred speech and was so weak she could barely walk. The continuous fever, kidney pain, and slurred speech are all signs of sepsis."

"That validates the symptoms Leslie transmitted to me."

"Leslie's condition was critical, but he never took her to an emergency room. According to the police report on the following day, Tuesday, she was still alive when he left her alone at 1 p.m., but when he came home later at 6 p.m., he found Leslie dead."

"That's horrible!"

"The police report also said his first phone call was to his mother — the coroner! And get this — she conducted the inquest and medical examination of Leslie's cause of death!"

"What?"

"My husband is a dentist, and I'm a dental hygienist. We understand and abide by professional ethics. Because of the obvious conflict of interest, we insisted she recuse herself from the investigation of Leslie's death, but she refused."

"Barb, this goes way beyond unethical."

"Her report concluded that Leslie died of natural causes, thus exonerating her son of any neglect that may have led to Leslie's death."

"So that's what Leslie's spirit meant when she said, '*He didn't kill me, but it was his fault!*' He did not cause her death, but he didn't take her to the emergency room when he should have."

"That's true, Mark. I'm sure if he thought Leslie was as sick as she was, he would have brought her to the hospital. From the police reports, we noticed that this coroner didn't construct a twenty-four-hour timeline of the events leading up to Leslie's death. My understanding is that this is standard operating procedure where a healthy young person is found dead."

"Barb, I can't see how this can possibly be legal."

"The medical and legal professions are governed by a strict code of ethics. I've checked, and *not one* of the fifty states in this country has a law requiring a coroner to be recused in an investigation that involves a coroner's family member."

"There's got to be some recourse, Barb."

"You would think so, but there isn't. We presented our complaint before the county board, but since the coroner is appointed and not elected, they won't take action."

"Seriously?"

"We reported this to the state coroners and medical examiners society. We were told there's no law requiring recusal of a coroner, so we have to trust the *integrity* of the coroner.

"Our last resort was the attorney general, who told us they couldn't help because there would have to be a legislative change to the statute. Now we've been shuffled off to the legislature, and no one is returning our calls, emails, or letters. No one cares, and none of these people know how much it hurts to lose a child. So much for justice in the great state of Illinois!"

"Wait — did you say Illinois?"

"Yes, why?"

"I know an Illinois state senator who will listen."

"How can you be so sure?"

"He knows the pain of losing a child."

Two years later, after a long and grueling political battle, the pieces of this puzzle came together when Illinois compiled Statute 55 ILCS 5/3-3009, sponsored by Guillermo, became law.

This groundbreaking statute was the first of its kind in the United States. It requires that "a coroner [who] has an economic or personal interest that conflicts with his or her official duties as coroner ... *shall* disqualify himself or herself from acting at an investigation or inquest."

It is better known as "Leslie's Law."

WHILE SPIRIT INTERVENTION MAY BE SUBTLE and take years, in other instances it occurs at lightning speed. It may even involve manipulation of matter and energy.

Several spirits of family and close friends came forward for Alyssa during a session with me, but the final spirit to communicate was her brother.

"Interesting," I said. "Your brother is projecting an image of the archangel Gabriel."

"His name is Gabriel, but we called him Gabe. I was hoping to hear from him!"

"Gabe's spirit keeps mentioning Cameron."

"Cameron is my teenage son. But he's here in this world, Mark."

"I'm sensing Gabe and Cameron were very close."

"Cameron was only six years old when Gabe died, but yes, they were very close."

"Gabe's spirit has a message for Cameron: 'Look both ways when crossing the road.'"

The next day Alyssa called me.

"Mark, my son, Cameron, is on the line with me, and he wants to talk to you."

"Hi, Cameron. How can I help you?"

"Hey, Mr. Anthony. My mom told me about the reading you did for her and how my Uncle Gabe's spirit warned me to look both ways when crossing the street."

"That's right."

"After she told me that, I went to my girlfriend's house a block away."

"And?"

"I was listening to music through my earbuds. I was focused on that and not paying attention when I was crossing the street. All of a sudden I saw this car hauling butt right at me."

"What happened?"

"I froze! I thought I was going to die! And then something really intense shoved me so hard I flew backward, right off my feet. The car just barely missed me!

"I know it sounds crazy," Cameron choked up, "but I *knew* it was Uncle Gabe."

"Mark," Alyssa interjected, "Does this mean my brother Gabriel is like a guardian angel protecting my son?"

"In a sense, but please *DO NOT* test that theory. There may not be a next time when a spirit intervenes so directly. What did you learn from this, Cameron?"

"Definitely to look both ways — and to always be aware of what's happening around me."

AS PURE QUANTUM ELECTROMAGNETIC ENERGY, spirits transmit messages to us in many ways. RAFT (recognizing, accepting, feeling, and trusting) is the key to developing spiritual situational awareness. As Cameron learned, being aware of your surroundings is a personal decision. Spirit intervention isn't about spirits controlling us; rather, they're guiding us on the journey between the day we're born and the day we leave this material world. Ultimately, it's our individual free will that determines what we do with the time in between those days.

Chapter 10

THERE'S NO PLACE LIKE HELL

THE STATE DEPARTMENT OF CORRECTIONS announced that Franklin "Freaky Frankie" Kleftis had died from a rare neurological disorder while he was an inmate on death row. The coroner's report indicated it was a slow and painful death. Within minutes of this press release, Joy was swamped with calls from reporters who wanted her reaction to Frankie's death.

Even though it had been over twelve years since Freaky Frankie had murdered Rudy and critically wounded Joy, this was still a hot news story. Two criminal defense attorneys shot by a hardened criminal, leaving one dead and the other clinging to life, was big news.

Immediately after the shooting, Joy became a "famous victim." Since then, reporters continually sought her opinion whenever a story about a death row inmate hit the news.

On the plus side, this initially gave Joy a platform to advocate for the rights of victims in the criminal justice system. The flip side of the karmic coin was that Joy's high-profile status made her a media target. Reporters constantly probed for details about her personal life. They never stopped reiterating the irony that she and Rudy were public defenders whose job was to defend hardened criminals, not be brutalized by them.

Eventually Joy had enough of the unfettered access the media had to her as a government employee. Seeking a lower profile, she left the public defender's office and accepted a job in private practice with a prestigious civil law firm. While it didn't eliminate her exposure to the media, it provided some insulation. Unlike a public defender, who worked for the government, an attorney in private practice didn't have to talk to the press.

The civil firm where she now worked was housed in a stately, colonial-style red brick mansion. As soon as the news about Frankie's death broke, reporters laid siege to the front entrance of the building, demanding a press conference with Joy. Even behind the brick walls and imposing ten-foot-high wooden doors flanked by rows of white Greek-style marble columns, she felt vulnerable.

From her second-story office window, Joy watched with disdain as reporters from TV, radio, and print media swarmed at the foot of the granite steps that led up to the law firm's entrance. She was sick of their probing and tactless questions into every facet of her being. They wanted a show, so she was going to give them one today.

The reporters were taken off guard when the front doors of the law firm were flung open by two muscular, broad-shouldered men. While fresh out of law school, they were hardly boyish. Both were ex-military and looked it. They glared at the reporters, which gave Joy time to emerge through the doorway. Flanked by these two intimidating veterans in suits, she walked to the edge of the top step and faced the press.

"I HOPE HE BURNS IN HELL!"

The reporters gaped.

Joy paused for dramatic effect and then withdrew into the sanctity of the law firm. The two burly associates followed, locking the doors behind them. The press conference was over.

The reporters' shock morphed into delight. Her one-line zinger was powerful, to the point, and even better than what they'd hoped for.

"Thanks, guys." Joy smiled at the two brawny attorneys and then retreated to her second-floor office. Closing the door after her, she sank into the red leather chair behind her large oak desk.

Her brave face faded as her mind did what it always did — drag her back in time to the hell of that one dark night. Her mind's eye replayed Rudy shielding her with his body from the killer's bullets. Her mind's ear was flooded with gunshots as she felt Rudy's body convulsing above her.

The next wave of relentlessly hellish memories was shrouded in a nightmarish haze. She'd snapped awake in the intensive care unit, heavily sedated for the pain. Sketchy images of her parents by her bedside faded into those of police detectives questioning her, interspersed with the continual procession of nurses and doctors.

One memory burned a hole through her mental fog. Rudy's parents had come to her bedside. Joy's father attempted to console them with a Bible verse, John 15:13: "Greater love has no one than this: to lay down one's life for one's friends." Sadly, her dad's attempt to comfort only made Rudy's mother cry and made Joy feel guilty, wishing she were the one who died, not Rudy.

News reporters besieged the hospital, seeking every detail possible about the two public defenders gunned down by a hardened criminal. The bonus for the media came three days later, when the police found Freaky Frankie passed out drunk in

215

a public park, the murder weapon wrapped in a filthy shirt next to him on the ground.

The press labeled Rudy a hero, reporting how just as the gunman opened fire Rudy sacrificed his life by shielding Joy with his body. The media hailed Joy's survival as a miracle.

The press had no clue as to just how miraculous her survival was. Reporters knew that Joy had escaped the scene of the shooting to go for help but couldn't understand how she knew to avoid the nearby cabin, which was actually the killer's hideout. Joy told them that the cabin looked abandoned, so she headed for the motel instead. Despite being in shock and heavily sedated, she knew better than to say Rudy's spirit warned her about the cabin. This was her secret and hers alone.

For weeks Joy lingered in shock, feeling she was outside of her body, watching herself through a fog. Eventually the shock faded and the reality of what happened set in. After three surgeries and extensive physical therapy, Joy's gunshot wounds healed, leaving scars and some residual pain. But the scars of psychological trauma penetrated her more deeply and painfully than any bullet ever could.

The next round of hellish memories pulled her to the misery of being the prosecution's star witness in this highly publicized trial. She felt exposed and violated, being forced to relive that one dark night before a judge and jury in a courtroom packed with gawking onlookers and reporters.

The stakes couldn't have been higher for Frankie. Charged with kidnapping, carjacking, armed robbery, attempted premeditated first-degree murder, and premeditated first-degree murder, he faced the death penalty. Frankie's only hope was for the jury to find reasonable doubt.

Because the prosecution's victim and star witness was a public defender, it was clearly a conflict of interest for the public defender's office to defend Frankie. Therefore the court appointed a private criminal defense attorney to represent him. Joy's heart sank when she heard it was attorney Rikki Newoc.

Unlike Joy, Rikki caught the eye of many men. In her late forties, Rikki was a thin and athletic woman, who always dressed to the nines. She was a seasoned trial lawyer and an expert at creating reasonable doubt. Rikki was also the most obnoxious, arrogant, and aggressive attorney Joy knew and, after Frankie, one of her least favorite people on the planet.

During Frankie's trial, when Joy took the witness stand, she couldn't help feeling that there were two sociopaths seated at the defense counsel table. One a murderous thug and the other a vicious viper bent on destroying her on the witness stand. Frankie had been cleaned up for trial. Joy recognized his cheap suit as one the public defender's office kept on hand for their clients. His eyes twitched, and his hands shook. The rumors from the jailhouse were true — something was seriously wrong with him. Be that as it may, it certainly didn't stop him from glaring at Joy with seething hatred.

The prosecutor's direct examination of Joy concluded. Her gripping testimony brought tears to many eyes in the courtroom, but then it was Rikki Newoc's turn to question Joy. She stood, gave the jury a dose of her signature phony smile, took her time walking to the podium, cleared her throat, and zeroed in on Joy.

"You've never been married, have you?"

"Uh — no." Joy was taken off guard.

"In fact, you've never even had a long-term relationship, have you?"

"How is that relevant?"

"Forgive me, dear — and I certainly don't mean to be unkind — but your dance card hasn't exactly been full."

"What's that supposed to mean?"

"Rudy was a very handsome young man, wasn't he?"

"Y — yes — I suppose he was."

"Sexual relations with a coworker *is* a violation of the public defender's office policy, is it not?"

"That's my understanding," Joy replied.

"That means you could get fired for having sex with a co-worker — right?"

"I guess that was possible."

"So if two people at the public defender's office were intentionally violating office policy, it would be best if no one else knew about it — don't you agree?"

"I don't see —"

"My client surprised you and Rudy in this secluded area near the cabin where he sought shelter, didn't he?"

"That's not how it happened. He held us up at gunpoint in the parking lot of the Sand Trap Bar — then he forced Rudy to drive there."

"Yes, we've all heard your cover story, but it has been established by very credible police investigators who were called by the prosecution that Franklin Kleftis was homeless and had no means of transportation."

"He was at the Sand Trap!"

"It has also been established as a fact by these very same police detectives that Mr. Kleftis had been seeking shelter in an abandoned cabin near the scene of the incident."

"Incident? You mean where he murdered Rudy!"

"And it was near that cabin in the woods where he stumbled upon you and Rudy engaging in a sexual act in Rudy's car!"

"That's absurd!"

"Is it? When you recognized my client, Franklin, you threatened him, didn't you?"

"Threaten him? He had a gun!"

"You called my client 'Freaky Frankie' because you *knew* his street name!"

"EVERYONE KNEW HIS STREET NAME!"

"Not everyone, only people like you. People in the criminal justice system!"

"So what!"

"Let's face it — Rudy was a handsome man. Probably the only one in your life who ever paid any attention to a girl like you."

"HOW DARE YOU!"

"You were both powerful people. Not just regular people, but criminal defense attorneys. With one phone call, you could have him arrested! And you threatened to have *this* man arrested, to get him out of the way, didn't you!"

"YOU'RE OUT OF YOUR MIND!"

"You were afraid of losing your job, but Rudy was afraid people would find out he was having sex with *YOU!*"

"OBJECTION! ARGUMENTATIVE!" The prosecutor jumped to his feet.

The judge immediately sustained the prosecutor's objection and called for recess, ordering both attorneys to see him in his chambers. One bailiff escorted the jury out of the courtroom, while another took Frankie back to the holding cell.

Joy remained on the witness stand so she wouldn't have to answer questions from reporters. She was furious and disgusted with Rikki's underhanded tactics and even more so with the prosecutor for not objecting sooner. Her head was pounding. She wanted to scream. It was bad enough getting shot, but then to be subjected to this humiliation! Victim! She was always a victim! This was hell!

Pulling herself together, she took a deep breath. Her head cleared, and she began to think like a lawyer. The prosecutor was a good trial attorney. He must have been biding his time and waiting for the right time to object. He was running interference and kept her from coming totally unglued on the witness stand.

Okay, fine, but what was Rikki up to? Of course! There's an old adage in the legal profession: "When you don't have a case, go after the other side."

Rikki had a two-pronged attack. First, antagonize and embarrass Joy during cross-examination. Angry witnesses lose emotional control and are prone to making inconsistent statements about the crime. Then Rikki could argue that reasonable doubt existed based on conflicts in the state's evidence.

The second prong of the defense strategy was to turn the tables and put Joy on trial, portraying her not as a victim, but as a vindictive woman who would do anything to protect this alleged clandestine sexual relationship with Rudy. Calling Freaky Frankie by his street name showed that Joy knew he had a criminal history. Rikki could then contrive a story about how Joy threatened to have him arrested, which would violate his parole and send him back to prison.

It was a long shot, but if Rikki could raise at least a suspicion about any of this, then she might pull it off. She could then argue because of his neurological illness and mental instability, Joy's threat caused such fear within Frankie that he flew into a rage, which amounted to a form of temporary insanity. This would mean that Frankie lacked the requisite mental intent to commit premeditated first-degree murder. The best scenario would be acquittal, but the most likely outcome was he'd be found guilty of a lesser offense and thereby escape the death penalty.

When the recess was over, Rikki returned to resume her cross-examination of Joy. Except now the tables were turned on

Rikki. She no longer faced a frightened victim on the witness stand, but an attorney who was extremely intelligent, competent, and in control. Joy calmly responded to Rikki's belligerent questions and deflected the relentless waves of hatred vibrating from Frankie.

Rikki's strategy backfired, and Frankie was convicted on all counts. As guilty verdicts were announced to a standing-room-only courtroom, the look Frankie shot his attorney left little doubt that given the chance, Rikki would have been his next victim. The thrill of victory surged through Joy, but it immediately vanished when she saw the agony in the eyes of Rudy's parents, who were seated just behind the prosecution's counsel table.

A month later, during the penalty phase, which formally concluded the trial, Frankie was sentenced to die by lethal injection. Despite her loathing of Frankie, none of this brought Joy comfort. Being sentenced to death triggered an automatic right to appeal to the State Supreme Court. But if the prosecution won the appeal, it could even go to the United States Supreme Court, meaning it would be years, if ever, before Frankie was executed. In the meantime, he would sit in prison on death row.

These hellish memories replayed over and over in her mind like waves relentlessly pounding a rocky beach. Momentarily they subsided, as Joy stared down through her office window at the reporters scurrying away.

Frankie was dead. As far as she was concerned, he got what was coming to him. Joy was glad that he suffered a slow and agonizing death instead of escaping with a painless execution by lethal injection. If there really was a hell, she hoped he would burn in it forever.

Joy reflected on her life since the shooting. In public she did her best to exude the facade of the successful and dedicated attorney. Beyond the brave face, things were another matter entirely. She felt isolated and totally alone. No one, not even her family, could relate to or even begin to understand the hell she'd been through, the hell she was going through, and how every moment of her life was hell. Terrified something like this might happen again, she qualified for a weapons permit and always carried a Glock semiautomatic pistol with her.

Nighttime was the worst. Petrified of the dark, she slept with the door bolted, night-lights on everywhere, and the Glock beneath her pillow. When she did sleep, it was seldom restful. She was constantly plagued by a recurring nightmare in which Rudy lunged between her and Frankie's gun. Just as the killer fired, she'd lurch awake.

Joy returned to the present and looked at the resignation letter on her desk. She was leaving the law firm. The firm's senior partners would be relieved. Sure, she brought publicity to the law firm, but not the kind they really wanted. The town she'd lived in her entire life was no longer home. The memories of the past, of that one dark night, mercilessly haunted her. Maybe if she started over fresh in a new part of the country where no one knew her, things would be different.

Joy knew she'd escaped the scene of the murder thanks to the intervention of Rudy's spirit. Since then, the only time she perceived him was in her nightmares. Why weren't there other signs from him? What had happened to her keen intuitive sense, which she always trusted?

Joy was exhausted. She was tired of strangers probing into her life, tired of the nightmares, tired of being angry, tired of feeling guilty, tired of being afraid, and tired of feeling her life meant nothing. Most of all, Joy was tired of feeling she deserved to be sentenced to a lifetime in hell.

HELL IS SYNONYMOUS with unending suffering. But does it really exist? There's no place like hell, because it holds the unique position of being myth, metaphor, and painfully real.

All souls are judged after death, and those who were wicked will be condemned to a fiery pit ruled by an evil supernatural entity. Sound familiar? While many believe that this form of eternal punishment is a Christian and Muslim concept, it actually predates these religions by centuries.

Our quick tour of the mythical origins of eternal damnation takes us back to the Bronze Age 3,500 years ago in Persia (modern-day Iran), and the world's oldest monotheistic religion: Zoroastrianism. The founder of that religion, Zoroaster, taught people to honor the one God through good thoughts, good words, and good deeds. If you did not, Zoroaster warned that you would be condemned to eternal suffering.

The concept that evil people would be condemned to eternal suffering certainly had a big impact upon other religions throughout the Middle East. Like today, in ancient times, cultures influenced one another. By the sixth century BC, Zoroastrianism was the official religion of the mighty Persian Empire and influenced belief systems from the Himalayan Mountains to the Mediterranean Sea.

Unlike its Persian counterpart, Judaism embraces the afterlife, but not the concept of eternal damnation. Texts from all eras of Judaism recognize a realm where souls go after death. In the Hebrew Bible, it is called *Sheol*, but the rabbinical tradition refers to it as *yeshiva shel mallah* (the school on high) and *shamayim* (heaven). According to Jewish scholar Rabbi Evan Moffic, "Heaven is not a gated community. The righteous of any people and any faith have a place in it. Our actions, not our specific beliefs, determine our fate. No concept of Hell exists in Judaism. The closest we get is the fate of [the] apostate (a person who renounces God, faith and morality in this world), who is said to be 'cut off from his kin.'"

In ancient Judea, not far from Jerusalem, lay the Hinnom Valley. At a place there, called Gehenna, the bodies of criminals, the dishonored, and those who could not afford a proper burial where burned in sulfur pits. Sulfur is also known as brimstone — hence "fire and brimstone." While it was not part of religious doctrine, over the centuries the fear factor of ending up in Gehenna became entrenched in the culture. By the first century BC, it was used to scare people into avoiding sinful behavior lest they be "cut off from their kin," and their final resting place would be a dishonorable one of fire and brimstone.

The ancient Greco-Roman religions contained a version of the dreaded realm ruled over by Hades, god of the underworld. These cultures even believed that a portal to it existed in what is now Turkey. It was described by the Greek geographer Strabo: "This space is full of a vapor so misty and dense that one can scarcely see the ground. Any animal that passes inside meets instant death. I threw in sparrows and they immediately breathed their last and fell." Recent archaeological discoveries in Turkey have not only discovered the feared "Mouth of Hades" but found that it emits lethal concentrations of carbon dioxide gas from deep within the earth.

The Roman Empire not only conquered other cultures, it also assimilated them. In 37 BC, the Romans appointed Herod the king of Judea, which included Israel. As a "client king" of the Roman Empire, his position was tenuous, but the wily Herod knew how to appease Rome in order to keep both his head and the crown he wore on it. Unfortunately, his successors were not as politically savvy, and a few years after Herod's death, the empire annexed Judea/Israel. Although the Jewish people tended to resist Roman culture, they did influence each other, and tales of Gehenna spread throughout the empire.

The teachings of Jesus, which began in Israel, expanded throughout the Roman Empire. Christians were initially persecuted by the Roman government. However, three centuries later, in AD 313, Emperor Constantine the Great issued the Edict of Milan, which ended the persecution of Christians. Then in AD 325, the Council of Nicaea issued the doctrine of the Trinity, which led to Christianity becoming the de facto religion of the empire. Constantine and his successors were hailed as the "Equal of the Apostles and God's Vicegerent on Earth."

When Emperor Theodosius declared Christianity the official religion of the Roman Empire in AD 390, this cemented the status of the emperors as God's representatives on earth. Demigod status for Roman emperors was nothing new, but this added a whole new dimension to that exalted status. This didn't exactly motivate emperors to start behaving like Jesus or his apostles and transform the Roman Empire into a peaceful, non-oppressive, love-your-neighbor-as-yourself utopia. Instead the new religion was twisted into an extension of imperial authority. Disloyalty to the emperor and disobeying the laws of the empire now meant disobeying God's earthly representative. The ultimate punishment, after torture and/or execution, now included condemnation to eternal suffering in fire and brimstone.

In the fifth century AD, the Western Roman Empire was conquered by invading tribes from Germany and Scandinavia. The surviving Eastern Roman Empire, better known as the Byzantine Empire, continued on until 1453. To the very last day of its existence, as Turkish troops breached the walls of its capital city, Constantinople, the last Byzantine emperor, Constantine XI, was still hailed as "Equal of the Apostles and God's Vicegerent on Earth."

This divine authority to rule, with its threat of eternal damnation, continued long after the Roman and Byzantine empires collapsed. Christian rulers throughout Europe and Russia, as well as their Muslim counterparts in the Middle East, routinely claimed their rule was ordained by God.

The final touches for eternal damnation were incorporated from northern Europe. The Nordic people, who included the Vikings, came from what is now Germany and Scandinavia. These warrior cultures, who invaded and conquered the Western Roman Empire, were among the last Europeans to convert to Christianity. However, their ancient beliefs retained their influence.

According to the ancient Nordic religion, to die with honor in battle was a soul's one-way ticket to Valhalla, the halls of the gods. People who killed for dishonorable reasons, meaning not in battle, were deemed murderers. Along with adulterers and perjurers, these souls went to the world of the dead, presided over by the goddess of death, whose name was Hel.

Hel was the daughter of Loki, the god of fire and magic. Loki was the malevolent trickster of the gods, who was able to assume different shapes and forms. Over the centuries the characteristics of Loki merged with those of Lucifer, which is one of the names for the Devil in Judaism and Christianity. Eventually, Hel vanished as an entity, although her name became synonymous with this realm of eternal suffering, with Loki/Lucifer as its ruler.

It is part of human nature to want justice. Let's face it, we all want the bad guys to get what's coming to them, don't we? The souls of wicked people condemned to an eternity of suffering as punishment for their evil deeds is the ultimate form of justice.

NDE research has discovered a small percentage of people, like Thor in chapter 6, who had a distressing near-death experience (DNDE). This phenomenon is better known as a hellish NDE because it is negative, unpleasant, and even horrifying. Those who have had a hellish NDE have described it as a life-changing experience, which alters their subsequent behavior for the better. This has triggered discussion and debate in NDE and afterlife research circles about whether a hellish NDE is a glimpse of eternal damnation or part of the electromagnetic soul's life review, which concludes that person needed a wake-up call. In either event, fear of eternal damnation is certainly a great motivator for rethinking one's behavior in life.

After years of studying belief systems around the globe and contact with thousands of spirits, my observation is that the infinite love of the Divine Energy we call God does not condemn souls to eternal suffering. That is why hell, as a form of eternal damnation in the archetypal sense, is a myth. Hell is a metaphor in that it has been used to deter people from committing negative acts. In other words, watch out for your bad behavior, or you will go to hell.

That being said, hell is real. It is not eternal; it is temporary, because it exists in the material world. Many people in the material world are immersed in a painful reality, and they simply cannot break free of the cycle of mental and emotional pain, believing there is no escape from it. That *is* hell.

What about people who are predators and inflict harm upon others? Does this mean there is no justice? The ultimate form of justice does exist. It is achieved through the operation of karma — and metaphorically speaking, karma can be hell.

Most of us have heard of karma, the proverbial "what goes around comes around." Yet it is more complex than that. *Karma* is an ancient Sanskrit word, which means "action" and "intent." Positive actions, in concert with positive intentions, generate good karma, while negative actions coupled with negative intentions create bad karma.

Notwithstanding its Hindu origin, the concept of karma exists in one form or another in the world's major belief systems.

Judaism, Buddhism, Jainism, Christianity, Islam, Sikhism, Taoism, African traditional religions, Zoroastrianism, and Mormonism all teach that a person is responsible for and unable to escape the consequences of his or her negative actions.

Although the laws of physics provide the scientific basis for the existence of the afterlife and spirit communication, many people confuse karma with Newton's third law of motion: "For every action, there is an equal and opposite reaction."

Wait a nanosecond! Doesn't karma mean that whatever you do comes back on you? Isn't that the same as "for every action, there is an equal and opposite reaction?"

Actually, that isn't what karma means. Be thankful it doesn't. If karma were the same as Newton's third law of motion, we'd be constantly bombarded by instant karma. As soon as you did something positive, immediately something negative would happen to you and vice versa. This would certainly give credence to Oscar Wilde's sarcastic remark, "No good deed goes unpunished."

Why then isn't karma the same as Newton's third law? The distinction is the word *action*. Newton developed his laws of motion in the seventeenth century using the vernacular of his time. His meaning of *action* wasn't "a thing that is done," but what is more accurately described in twenty-first-century terms as "force."

When force is applied to one object, the immediate reaction is an opposite force of the same magnitude applied to the second object. The direction of the force applied to the first object is in the opposite direction of the force applied to the second object.

To simplify, think of paddling a canoe. To make the canoe move forward, you use the paddle to push the water backward. The equal and opposite reaction is that the canoe is propelled forward in the water.

In the twenty-first century, understanding Newton's third law of motion is essential for aerospace technology. During a rocket launch, when the fuel in the rocket's engines is ignited, it exerts a force that pushes the exhaust from the engine downward. The equal and opposite reaction is that the rocket is immediately propelled upward with the same amount of force.

Unlike Newton's third law, karma isn't about an instant change in the force that an object exerts on another object; it is about the repercussions of one's behavior and intentions. Think of the ripple effect, illustrated by dropping a pebble into water. The concentric circles caused by the pebble's impact on the water's surface expand and touch plants, animals, and other substances in the water.

The ripple effect of karma may sound like a purely philosophical construct, except we now know that the Earth itself is touched and influenced by the ripple effect. In 1916 Einstein theorized gravitational waves existed. A century later, in 2015, scientists from California Institute of Technology and Massachusetts Institute of Technology reported that LIGO (the Laser Interferometer Gravitational-Wave Observatory) detected gravitational waves. Overnight, Einstein's theory became scientific fact.

According to NASA's Jet Propulsion Laboratory, "Gravitational waves are invisible. However, they are incredibly fast. They travel at the speed of light [186,282 miles or 299,792 kilometers per second]. Gravitational waves squeeze and stretch anything in their path as they pass by." Einstein predicted that something special happens when two bodies — such as planets or stars — orbit each other. He believed that this kind of movement could cause ripples in space. These ripples would spread out like the ripples in a pond when a stone is tossed in. The gravitational waves detected by LIGO were created when two black holes crashed into one another. The collision happened 1.3 billion years ago. But the ripples didn't make it to Earth until 2015!

If Earth is touched and influenced by the ripple effect of gravitational waves that took over a billion years to get here, then by analogy the ripple effect of our actions influences karma, but not always immediately. This is why Hinduism and Buddhism, which embrace the doctrine of reincarnation, believe that the ripple effect of karma can span lifetimes.

There are three basic levels of karma. The first level is *individual karma*, which is incurred by a single person's actions. The second level is *collective karma*, which people incur as members of a group. The third is the *karma experience*, which includes the repercussions of being interconnected to everyone and everything living on this particular planet in this particular dimension.

Karma can be either positive or negative. Obviously we all want to accumulate positive karma. That's why our focus will be upon individual karma, the level we have the ability to influence. I avoid using the word *control*, because, as much as we like to think we're totally in control of our own destiny, we must also acknowledge that our lives are influenced by the lives and actions of those around us — and that includes spirits. There are a lot of pebbles being thrown into the pond of our lives, and all their concentric circles are overlapping and influencing each other — once again, an indication that everyone and everything is energetically interconnected.

Despite the visceral desire for instant karma upon those who harm others, karma can take years, even lifetimes, to resolve. Often it appears that people who commit negative acts and aren't held accountable for them are somehow getting away with them. This isn't true: we're just not immediately aware of when their negative karma will come due.

Creating negative karma perpetuates an ongoing cycle of negativity, which can land you right back into the reality of suffering here in the material world. Make no mistake — that can be hell. The way to escape the hell of negative karma is by not creating it in the first place. This is achieved by manifesting positive intentions, which lead to positive actions.

Essentially, the ethical teachings of all the world's great spiritual teachers can be summed up in two words: "Be nice." This is easy to say but difficult to do, because no one is perfect. Humans are prone to actions that can lead to anger, bigotry, judgment, hatred, and violence. That is why the spiritual teachers have set the bar as high as they have, because these negative impulses are what we must strive to avoid.

Why, then, do bad things happen to good people? Why are so many victimized by predators? Why must someone who was always kind and good have to endure a long and painful terminal illness? How do we even begin to make sense of the hell parents endure for the rest of their lives after the death of a child?

Hell does exist, but it is here in the material world. At some point in everyone's life, mine included, we are cast into hell. Yet hell, like the material world where it exists, is not a permanent state, although it may sure feel like it.

Is the temporary state of hell a punishment or part of the ripple effect of karma? Both Hinduism and Buddhism agree that you should never assume that when something bad happens to someone, it's because of the law of karma, and that person had it coming.

Nancy Evans Bush, the world's foremost authority on the distressing (hellish) NDE, has observed, "Hell lives inside us, burning as the fires and torments of our shadow. That is what we meet in a distressing NDE. We have to be brave enough to confront our shadow, our demons, our darkness, and move through it. It is not punishment; it is an invitation to growth, to wholeness."

Perhaps hell is a lesson as opposed to a punishment. This is certainly not meant to marginalize or minimize the pain anyone endures. Yet bad things happen to good people, and the lesson may be learning to accept there is nothing you can do about the negative things that have happened to you. You cannot change the fact someone you love has died. But what you can do is change how you react to that pain. Some people turn to drugs, alcohol, and impulsive and even violent behaviors in response. Others embrace their faith and spirituality and strive to become more compassionate and understanding of others. The choice is up to the individual.

Musician Steve Miller had a point when he wrote, "You know you got to go through hell before you get to heaven." We grow and evolve spiritually and personally in response to adversity. If everything were easy and positive all the time, there would be no incentive to improve and excel. Understanding this doesn't make devastating events in our lives easier, but it may help to give a different perspective when one is coping with the pain of loss.

How you respond to life events and how others treat you influences karma. When someone has wronged you, it is important not to take justice into your own hands. Society has laws and a system of justice, albeit imperfect, for a reason. A system of justice based upon the due process of law attacks the problem, not the person, whereas taking it upon yourself to judge and exact revenge entangles you into that person's karma. In Matthew 7:1–2, Jesus is quoted as saying, "Do not judge, or you too will be judged. For in the same way you judge others, you will be judged, and with the measure you use, it will be measured to you."

Because collective consciousness communication demonstrates we are all energetically interconnected, the operation of karma is integral to spirit intervention. Karma is not immediate, has no expiration date, and never loses an address, and so one never knows when or where karma will surface.

~

WHILE ON A SPIRIT COMMUNICATION TOUR of New England, I was invited to appear as a guest on a national radio show. The host was a hard-core skeptic about mediums; nevertheless, he asked me to be on his show. The show airs at midnight and is broadcast in forty states simultaneously. I entered the studio and took my seat.

As I was putting on my headphones and adjusting my microphone, the host said, "You'll take calls from listeners and do readings on the air, right?"

"I look forward to that."

He hit the switch unmuting our microphones. We went live on air. "Tonight we have a special guest, Mark Anthony, the *so-called* Psychic Lawyer."

"That's what I've been labeled by the media."

"You say you talk to dead people?"

"I communicate with spirits, that is correct."

"I don't believe that's possible."

"I'm happy to provide proof by taking calls from listeners."

"Not so fast. Do a reading for me first."

"A female energy is coming through. She's on your generational level, meaning a sister, cousin, wife, or friend."

"Well, Mark, that's pretty general. That could be anybody."

"This woman looks like she was in her late thirties, possibly early forties when she died — very suddenly, abruptly — hit her like a ton of bricks — meaning she didn't have any warning.

From the pain in my chest and the numbness running down the left side of my body, it feels like she died from a sudden heart attack."

"Uh — okay," the host stiffened.

"Elaine — could be Eileen — is the name she's projecting to me."

Color drained from his face.

"The two of you were very close emotionally — you were more than friends — she loved you very —"

"We have to take a commercial break!" he interjected and immediately muted our microphones. A prerecorded commercial filled the airwaves.

"What the hell are you trying to do to me, Mark?"

"You asked for a reading."

"I had an affair with Eileen. She died suddenly of a heart attack!"

"I'm sorry for your loss."

"You don't understand. My wife believes in all this stuff, and she's listening tonight! She didn't know I cheated on her with Eileen! No one knows that!"

The commercial ended, and the host unmuted our microphones. "We're back on the air with Mark Anthony, the Psychic Lawyer. We're going to the phone lines now, and he'll be taking calls from listeners."

The last day of the New England tour, I was the guest on a TV morning talk show. It was announced I'd be conducting an evening of spirit communication that night at a popular bookstore just north of Salem, Massachusetts.

The venue seated a hundred people and was sold out. After two hours of interdimensional communication, I felt the evening was winding down. Apparently the collective consciousness had other ideas.

"I'm picking up on the spirit of a little dog — looks like a Yorkshire terrier. Does that resonate with anyone?"

About half a dozen people raised their hands.

"There's something about pepper — does pepper make sense?"

A woman seated at the back of the room stood.

"My mother gave me a Yorkie. Her name was Pepper, and she died about a month ago. I miss her so much." Her accent was out of character for Massachusetts.

"I'm sorry for your loss. Hold on — there's another spirit with Pepper. Human spirit — male — looks like he was in his twenties."

She stared at me.

"I'm feeling an impact sensation, indicating his passing was quick and unexpected — does that make sense?"

"It does."

"His death happened at night — seems like it was really dark that night."

She nodded.

"I taste blood — and I smell gunpowder."

"Yes — go on."

"My mind's ear is flooded with BANG — BANG — BANG — like gunshots."

She began to tremble.

"This wasn't self-inflicted — someone did this to him. I believe this was a murder."

She closed her eyes and nodded.

"He's showing me a red gemstone. Ruby is the birthstone for the month of July — but it can reference a name, like —"

"Rudy!" she gasped.

"'Don't do it — put it down — don't do it!'"

"What did you say?"

"Rudy keeps repeating, 'Don't do it — put it down — don't do it!' But there's another message — your TV remote needs new batteries. Does that make sense?"

"This morning" — Joy was fighting tears — "I was sitting on the sofa in my living room. The remote control for the TV was on the coffee table in front of me ..."

"Go ahead."

"This sounds insane, Mark."

"It's all right."

"The TV was on — I wasn't listening — it was just background noise — it was irritating me — I — I needed some peace and quiet — I picked up the remote to turn the TV off." She was trembling. "It wouldn't turn off — the batteries in the remote were dead. I just dropped it on the coffee table, and then there you were, on that show this morning, talking about how spirits communicate."

Tears welled up in Joy's eyes.

"And then — I heard his voice — for the first time since that horrible night. I clearly heard Rudy's voice, and he said, 'Don't do it — put it down — don't let him win.'"

Every ear in the room was focused on Joy.

"I had a gun in my hand!"

Gasps flew through the crowd.

"Rudy wants you to know it's about time he got through to you."

She looked at me through her tears. "My dreams! It feels like somehow he always brings me back to that — that night — to that horrible night!"

"Rudy says he doesn't bring you there. You live there."

Joy shook as tears streamed from her eyes. "That's what it feels like — like I live there. He's the one who died, but I'm the one who lives in hell!"

"Rudy has a parting message." I gave Joy a moment, then continued, "'Until you accept that you're powerless to change what happened, you will always live there.'"

With that, Rudy's spirit let me go.

After the event, Joy asked to speak with me. She told me in detail what happened the night she and Rudy were shot and what her life had been like since then.

Joy was one of the most courageous and heroic people I've ever been privileged to meet. She related how she had always felt receptive to the presence of spirits, but since Rudy's death, for her that sensitivity had been blocked. The negative emotions that had overwhelmed her since the shooting were a form of the No, No, No syndrome, which unintentionally created a block to the afterlife frequency and thwarted her natural sense of spiritual situational awareness. The block lifted the morning she contemplated taking her own life.

In the blink of an eye, Joy's intuitive sense opened up, and she instinctively employed RAFT. She recognized the contact from Rudy's spirit. Immediately she accepted the signs as real: first the TV remote, then Rudy's voice, and then the TV morning show about spirit communication. She instinctively trusted she was being guided to be at the spirit communication event.

"Mark, you said that it takes hours, days, weeks, and even longer for the full impact of a message to unfold."

"That's correct."

"I wanted to talk to you about Rudy's message that until I accept I'm powerless to change what happened, I will always live there."

"What is your interpretation of that message, Joy?"

"I've been in counseling for years, and I know I suffer from PTSD and survivor's guilt — and I've been through more sessions with shrinks than I care to think about, and their mantra is that I'm powerless over the actions of that psycho creep — yes, psycho creep!"

"Joy, I can totally understand why you're angry."

"Damn right I'm angry — but hey — think of me as a work

in progress, and I'm dealing with anger issues. I have to admit, I'm not exactly upset he died a horribly painful death in prison. Maybe that was his karma."

"That's entirely possible."

"In counseling, the focus has always been on how I'm powerless over Freaky Frankie's actions — I get that — but Rudy's message meant more than that."

"This sounds like a multiple meaning message."

"Exactly, Mark! It dawned on me that there is more than one way to interpret what Rudy was conveying. Mentally I keep returning to that night. I get it that no one brings me there. I create my own hell by psychologically returning there over and over to punish myself — but it's deeper than just feeling guilty that I survived."

"How so?"

"Rudy and I loved each other — maybe not in the romantic sense — but it was more than just being friends. We were totally in tune with each other and were connected in a way I never have been with anyone else. Rudy came through when for a few seconds I was thinking about ending it all, but it was also about not letting that thug win. His message also meant that it was now my decision to not just survive but to move forward in my life."

"Love is energy, Joy, and the two of you are definitely linked energetically."

"I always felt guilty when I thought about hearing my dad quote John 15:13 to Rudy's parents: 'Greater love has no one than this: to lay down one's life for one's friends.' But my dad was right — Rudy gave his life to save mine because he *loved* me. He's intervened spiritually to save my life since then because even as a spirit, he *loves* me."

"It is my belief, Joy, that love transcends physical death."

"Rudy was unique, and it was horrible how cops and guys at the office nicknamed him Fruity Rudy. Sometimes they even said it to his face. I saw how it hurt his feelings, but he never let it get him down. In the end he proved he was braver and tougher than all of those guys put together. Not one of them would've taken a bullet for me — let alone three bullets — but Rudy sure did."

"Sounds like he was a real hero, Joy."

"He was my knight in shining armor." A tear rolled down her face. "He still is, and it took time, but I now understand his message. Rudy didn't throw away his life that night. He made a choice to save mine. In a split second, he made that decision, and no matter what I did that night, what I do now, or how many times I play this over in my head, I have no power to change the outcome. And I've been punishing myself for his choice. Rudy wants me to know that I'll always be stuck in that hellhole of a night until I accept that I'm totally powerless over his choice."

"How does that make you feel?"

"Empowered! To finally get the hell out of hell!"

SPIRIT INTERVENTION is part of the ripple effect of karma. Sometimes it is subtle — other times it is more direct. Spirits can influence the chain of events we call synchronicity to intervene in our lives to guide and help us. Spirits are persistent and will get their message through one way or another.

Karma is not an instant process, it doesn't have an expiration date, and it never loses an address. It is a complex intertwining of energy that touches all of us. Karma can be inflicted by others or self-inflicted, and releasing oneself from its grasp can take lifetimes.

Bad things happen to good people. This is a sad and unfortunate fact of living in the material world. These negative events can be emotionally devastating, as it is for parents who have lost a child, families of murder victims, and people who live through military combat. Many who suffer from PTSD cannot mentally escape the emotional anguish caused by the pain, loss, and horror inflicted upon them. They feel as if they've been sentenced to a lifetime in hell.

Hell is a myth, a metaphor, and unfortunately very real, but it isn't a stagnant or permanent state, and sometimes it takes the power of love, through spirit intervention, to light the way to an early release from the prison of hell.

Chapter 11

ETERNAL LIGHT, ETERNAL LIFE

WHAT AT FIRST MAY SEEM to be a simple moment may actually be the most profound. Such an event occurred when I was four years old. It was an October evening a few months after my near-death experience. The heat and humidity of the Florida summer had given way to the milder and drier air of autumn in Orlando.

My brother, sister, and I were excited because it was Saturday, and that meant pizza night. This wasn't a delivery or store-bought pizza, but one our mother, Jeannie, made from scratch. Even though every window in our house was open, the aroma of freshly baked pizza wafted through our home.

After dinner, my mother, father, brother, sister, and I stood in the driveway out front of our house to watch the full moon rise. The sky was cloudless. The waning rays of sunlight receded into the western sky as the bright-pink full moon rose in the east. On its sojourn across the sky, the moon's color faded from pink to orange, then yellow, and finally white. As day became night, stars emerged in the deepening hues of the evening sky.

Dad went to his car, returned with a bag of flashlights, and gave one to each of us. We all switched on the flashlights and pointed them in all directions. I was spotlighting an ant crawling across the driveway when suddenly I heard an eerie sound directly behind me.

"Woo-ooo-ooo!"

I turned and faced a grotesque and horrifying apparition.

"Earl, knock it off!" Dad interjected. "You're scaring your little brother."

It was my big brother, Earl Joseph. He'd snuck up behind me, making spooky sounds while he held his flashlight at the bottom of his chin, shining the light upward, giving his face a contorted and monstrous appearance.

It appears to be standard operating procedure among children worldwide for big brothers to enjoy scaring the daylights out of their younger siblings. On the other hand, it was hilarious, and the entire family, including me, burst into laughter.

Redirecting our attention, Dad said, "Point your flashlights at the sky."

I marveled at how the beam of light from my flashlight shot through the night sky.

"Point your flashlight at the moon. It takes less than two seconds for the light from your flashlight to get there."

"Whoa!" my brother, sister, and I exclaimed.

"Now point them at the stars."

My mother, father, brother, sister, and I simultaneously targeted the same bright star. The rays from our five flashlights converged into one great tower of light.

In that moment, everything in my world was perfect. My family loved each other. We may have just been playing with flashlights in our front yard, but we were all together. Everyone was happy, healthy, and having fun. For my four-year-old self, nothing could have been better.

Then Dad said, "The light from our flashlights can go on forever."

I looked up at him.

"Mark, when you were in the hospital, you wanted to know what 'eternal' meant."

I nodded.

"Look at the stars. They're very far away, and many of them burned out a long time ago."

I must have looked concerned, because my father knelt down on one knee next to me to explain.

"It's okay, Mark," he said gently, "the stars may have burned out, but their light didn't. The stars are so far away it takes a very long time for their light to reach us, and their light travels on into eternity. It's the same with your flashlight. The light from that can go on forever."

This was a lot for my four-year-old self to digest, but I ate it up and kept pointing my light at the stars, wondering where it would go, and if it really would go on forever.

THE MYSTERY OF SPACE constantly reminds us that there will always be things currently beyond human understanding, because the human brain is only capable of finite perception. From our finite perspective, everything we know and can comprehend has a beginning, a middle, and an end. We are born, we live for various lengths of what we perceive as time, and ultimately we die. That is part of our finite existence of living in the material world.

This does not mean we should underestimate the amazing capabilities of the human brain. The brain acquires, then processes and synthesizes, vast amounts of information, which can result in incredible discoveries and creations. Just because we may not be able to perceive or comprehend something doesn't mean we aren't aware of its existence. The human brain may not be able to perceive or comprehend "eternity" or "always was, always will be," but the brain is capable of accepting its inability to comprehend these concepts while acknowledging they exist.

One of the most intriguing talents of the human brain is the ability to question the unknown. A mystery can be something we fear, or a challenge for us to explore the unknown.

My dad didn't fear the unknown, because he didn't believe in mysteries. He was a NASA engineer who considered a mystery just a question that we haven't answered yet, or one we can answer once we develop the science and technology to enable us to arrive at the solution. He believed that with enough money, talent, and research applied to a mystery, it was possible to find an explanation for everything. If the answer isn't readily available, it is still important to pose the question, for that will lead you on the quest to discover the answer.

Think about how people viewed the stars before the invention of the telescope. There were all sorts of theories: that they were spirits or gods or that the light of heaven was shining through holes in the fabric of the sky. Those ideas vanished after the arrival of the telescope. The science of astronomy flourished, as humans were now able to observe these mysterious points of light in the sky. This led to the discovery that they were an infinite variety of things. Some were planets and asteroids, which orbit our sun like Earth. As telescopes became more sophisticated, humans observed nebulae, other galaxies, and beyond our solar system, other suns, which have planets orbiting them.

Diseases have also been a source of fear, and for good reason. Plagues kill millions of people. What did people think caused disease before the invention of the microscope? Pretechnological explanations said that disease was caused by witchcraft, demonic possession, or noxious vapors which seeped up from the ground at night. These superstitious beliefs were dispelled when the microscope brought a whole new dimension to the study of biology. It was discovered that many diseases are caused by cellular mutation, viruses, bacteria, and other microscopic organisms. This eventually led to the development of the electron microscope, and humans were able to view DNA and other protein molecules within cells. This in turn led to the study of genetics. In short, science and technology provide the answers to many mysteries, but in so doing, they also open the door to more questions about the unknown.

Death is the great unknown. Since the dawn of recorded history, humans have always wondered if who and what we are continues on beyond the material world. In approaching this mystery, it is essential to avoid confusing the limited capacity of the finite human brain with the infinite electromagnetic soul. The brain doesn't create the electromagnetic soul. The brain houses the electromagnetic soul the way a computer hard drive houses information. When the body, which includes the brain, physically ceases to function, the information contained on that hard drive — the electromagnetic soul — is uploaded to a different dimension.

Faith embraces mysteries, whereas science explains them. But faith and science may converge when it comes to survival of the soul and the afterlife. People of faith accept the existence of the soul and eternal life as true, while simultaneously accepting it as a mystery. People of science accept the existence of the brain's electrical field and that energy is neither created nor destroyed, only transferred from one form to another. The existence of the soul and the afterlife is a mystery, challenging scientists to develop the technology to solve this mystery.

Do you ever have days when you just don't feel like you're

"all here"? The truth is, you're never "all here," because the electromagnetic soul is constantly touching the higher frequency of another dimension.

This idea is not as far-fetched as it may seem. Everything is composed of molecules, which are made of atoms, which in turn are made of subatomic particles known as electrons, protons, and neutrons. Electrons disappear and reappear constantly without passing through the matter in between. U. Satya Sainadh, PhD, of the Indian Institute of Science and the Israel Institute of Technology, has explained, "For quantum particles, such as electrons, when you say they can tunnel through barriers, we don't refer to physical obstacles, but barriers of energy." This process is known as *quantum tunneling* and has been re-created in clinical conditions at the Max Planck Institute for Nuclear Physics in Heidelberg, Germany.

So where do these particles go? The Schwarzschild quantum lattice theory may provide the answer. In the early twentieth century, German physicist Karl Schwarzschild theorized that subatomic particles travel constantly between our dimension and another dimension through tiny "black holes" which puncture space. This is known as the *quantum lattice theory*, because the crisscrossing of subatomic particles has been likened to a lattice pattern created by the stitching of a sewing machine.

In the early twenty-first century, physicist and parapsychologist Evan Harris Walker applied the Schwarzschild quantum lattice theory to his explanation that consciousness was not created by the brain. Walker's theory proposes that consciousness (aka the electromagnetic soul) is not physical, because these subatomic particles slip back and forth between our material world dimension and another dimension.

The brain doesn't create the electromagnetic soul: it merely hosts it while we are living in the material world. By analogy, when a computer hard drive linked to the "cloud" crashes and ceases to function, the data on the computer is transferred to the cloud. It isn't lost; it's just uploaded to a vast database. Similarly, when a person's body dies, the energy of the electromagnetic soul is no longer tethered to the organ of the brain. This energy cannot be destroyed, only transferred to the dimension we refer to as the Other Side, where it becomes interconnected with the collective consciousness.

Until one's electromagnetic soul transitions to the Other Side, everyone living in the material world will experience days and times when one just doesn't feel "all here." This sensation is never more apparent than after the death of a loved one. Is this just a symptom of grief, or is it something more?

Grief is devastating emotionally, physically, mentally, and spiritually. Losing a loved one pulls the rug of stability right out from under your feet. The journey through grief is a path no one wants to take, but it is one that we're all forced down at some point in our lives. It must be treated; it cannot be avoided or self-medicated away. Grief enhances feelings of isolation and loneliness, and no one should go through this alone. This is the time to reach out for support from family and friends, your faith community, grief share groups, and counseling.

While there are several stages of grief, my observations indicate that there are two phases of grief: shock and trauma. Shock occurs immediately after the death and may last a few weeks and sometimes longer. This is the nightmarish haze of being unable to accept what happened and feeling you are outside of your body as you watch events drift by. Eventually shock fades into the trauma phase. Trauma is the excruciating pain of the loss, which we must learn to live with. This isn't easy and can take a lifetime to achieve.

It is during the initial shock phase that people are the most prone to feeling not "all here." Shock may be a symptom of grief, but it can also remove the No, No, No syndrome blocking interdimensional communication. This may explain that while not everyone is a medium, everyone is capable of having an interdimensional communication experience.

People worldwide report how in the initial aftermath of the death of a loved one, they sense that person's spirit. In many instances, they see and hear messages from the spirit, often including intricate details and verifiable information. This phenomenon may occur for a few weeks and sometimes longer. People are usually not aware that the subatomic particles of their electromagnetic souls constantly quantum-tunnel between the material world and the Other Side. However, the hypersensitive emotional state triggered by grief enhances spiritual situational awareness. In other words, you lower the deflector shields. Spirits, recognizing that your shields are down, reach out to you by aligning their frequency with your brainwave frequency. The result is interdimensional communication.

~

MY LIFE HAS BEEN DEDICATED TO using my abilities as an evidential medium to help those suffering with the pain of loss understand that who and what we are survives physical death. Yet this doesn't mean that those of us who can communicate with spirits are immune from the pain of loss.

In my capacity as an attorney and also as a psychic medium, I've been at the bedside of many terminally ill people whose transition to the Other Side was imminent. This is never easy, but it was never more difficult for me than when that bedside was my father's.

Ten years after my mother had passed suddenly from a heart attack, my father was diagnosed with an aggressive cancer. He received the news stoically, and although he knew the outcome was inevitable, he wasn't going down without a fight. Navy SEALS are tough guys, and Dad was no exception.

There was never any question that my family would pull together to care for him. Serving as the caretakers for our terminally ill father was the most exhausting, difficult, and emotionally painful experience of our lives. It was also the greatest honor we as a family have ever been called upon to fulfill.

Cancer is an insidious disease. Some of its victims are taken quickly; others are consumed a piece at a time. For several months, his condition stabilized but then took a turn for the worse.

Everyone pitched in, and we took turns being with Dad round the clock. My niece and nephew had a great relationship with their grandfather, "Pop Pop." My niece spent time with him constantly, and my nephew who was living overseas flew in for a week to help out. My nephew set up the bed provided by hospice in the living room of Dad's house. He wanted to make sure his Pop Pop would always be surrounded by loved ones during his final days.

As the cancer invaded his brain, my father struggled to maintain his mental clarity. To see this happen to such a brilliant man was crushing. Although the cancer was overwhelming him, the Wednesday before he passed, the Dad we knew emerged. He told my brother, sister, and me how he appreciated our taking care of him, how proud he was of us, and how much he loved us. After that, he drifted into an unconscious state.

Dad's house was a few hundred feet from the ocean. It was early November, and the autumn weather along Florida's east coast was mild and breezy. Dad always enjoyed hearing the ocean waves crashing on the beach. We kept all the windows of his house open so he could hear them.

By Friday night, his breathing became erratic. That night was a long one as we stood vigil by his side. I felt the presence of several spirits converging around my father. The intense energy of this collective consciousness was like a vast electrical arc spanning the room from his bed to the redwood beams of the cathedral ceiling.

The night faded into a sunny Saturday morning. The scent of the salty sea air wafted through the house as the melody of the surf crashed in the background. It was a beautiful day. Somehow it would have felt more appropriate for there to have been torrential rain, thunder, and lightning. Maybe that expectation mirrored the storm of the emotional pain all of us were feeling.

My siblings, Earl Joseph and Roxanne, had been joined by three close family friends: Tevan, Joe, and Nancy. Tevan's little dog, Charlie, loved my dad and stood sentinel by his bedside.

Waiting for the inevitable can feel like an eternity, and we were enduring the situation as best we could. The kitchen is adjacent to the living room, so we were drinking coffee and making small talk. My sister held my father's hand and gently massaged his arm, telling him, "I love you, Daddy."

Suddenly everyone stopped. For an instant the room got brighter.

I was taken off guard when I saw a burst of light surge out of my father's body and beam right up through the cathedral ceiling.

"Did you see that light?" Joe exclaimed.

"I saw it too!" Nancy added. Everyone saw it.

For a second, our attention was drawn to Charlie, who cowered in a corner, howling.

Then we realized Dad wasn't breathing.

My father was the bravest man I've ever known. He'd fought many battles in the material world — not just in war, but in corporate boardrooms and against the obstacles and challenges life threw at him. His last battle was against cancer, and even though all battles must come to an end, he went down fighting. I couldn't be more proud of him.

When the funeral home workers arrived, they draped his body bag in an American flag to honor him as a Navy veteran. Neighbors and people we didn't even know stopped and saluted as the hearse carrying his body departed slowly down the length of the street.

One of the most important lessons my father taught me was that men have hearts and tear ducts for a reason. "Mark, a real man," he once told me, "is never afraid to say, 'I love you,' or to cry for those he loves when they die."

Apparently I got that memo. Like everyone else, I was crying. Being a medium comes with being hypersensitive, not just to frequency, but also emotionally.

The shock of watching my father die and then seeing his energy shoot out of his body was overwhelming. This was beyond being sensitive — I felt like an exposed nerve ending. My head was pounding and I definitely wasn't feeling "all here."

I felt guided to get away and be alone. I retreated to a bedroom, closed the door, and sat down. Tears streamed from my eyes. Then I felt cold chills and tingles resonate through my body. I knew this sensation well — it was the presence of spirits, and it was coming through really strong.

I looked up and gasped.

There before me stood my mother and father. Dad looked about twenty years old. He was wearing his Navy uniform, his body tight and muscular, and his torso reflecting a perfect V shape under his uniform. Next to him stood Mom, and she too looked maybe twenty years old. She was wearing a silky, flowing light-beige gown, which appeared to sparkle. My mother was shapely and beautiful. I always thought of Mom as, well, Mom, but she was a total knockout!

I was stunned because I never saw my parents look that age. They had me when they were in their late thirties. I never knew them when they were that young.

Although I was awestruck, this was no time for me to fall apart. I'm used to being objective while facilitating interdimensional communication for other people, but this was happening to me!

I took a deep breath, centered, and focused myself.

Okay, thank you for reaching out. What are you trying to tell me?

The spirits of my parents knew they had my attention. They looked me in the eye and smiled, then they turned to each other and joined hands. They'd been ballroom dancers, so were they going to do a waltz?

It certainly wasn't like any waltz I'd ever seen. In a flash the energy in the room intensified as they began to revolve around each other in a spinning motion. They spun so fast that I couldn't distinguish them as bodies. Instead their energy transformed into a vortex of a glowing copper color, which immediately shifted to gold, then silver, culminating in an explosion of intense white light.

They vanished.

All of this occurred within seconds. Trying to process this powerful contact experience was overwhelming. Excited, I leaped up and ran to the living room.

"I just saw Mom and Dad!"

"WOULD YOU SHUT THE HELL UP!" my brother roared.

Abruptly I halted. It felt like I'd been smacked in the face. Everyone else was stunned by my brother's reaction.

Then I saw why. Tears welled up in my brother's eyes. Earl Joseph was emotionally devastated and physically exhausted.

"I'm sorry, Mark." He approached me, put his hands on my shoulders, and whispered, "What did you see?"

Hours later, as day drifted into night, it occurred to my brother, sister, and me that the last eighteen months of constant, round-the-clock care for our father had been immediately replaced by an empty void. We had to get out of the house and be near the ocean, so we went for a walk on the beach.

The full moon had just risen over the ocean, its reflection shimmering in the waves. Shining stars blazed brightly in the cloudless sky.

As we walked along the water's edge, Roxanne said, "It's a full moon. Just like when Mom died."

I remembered that day all too well.

"Do you guys remember that time in Orlando when we were kids and we pointed flashlights at the stars?" Roxanne asked. "It was a full moon that night too."

A tingling sensation ran up and down my spine.

"Yes," I replied. "All five of us put our beams together to make one big spotlight pointing into space."

"Wow — you remember that, Mark? You were like, what? Four?"

Earl Joseph added, "Ya know, it sounds corny, but that night was one of the happiest memories of my life. All five of us were together. Now there's just the three of us — well, here, anyway."

As soon as my brother said that, a tidal wave of understanding hit me. None of what had happened to us or was happening right now was coincidental. This was spiritual synchronicity.

My parents were both mediums. Dad was a science guy, and as he and I discussed so many times, the laws of physics teach us energy is neither created nor destroyed, only transferred from one form to another.

Mom was a woman of faith, who taught me that we are not these bodies. Our soul preexists the body, comes into the body, and lives on after the body dies.

Dad physically died today, and his energy had transferred to another dimension, but then he made a quantum leap from that dimension back to the material world, and he brought Mom with him.

Like my parents, I'm a medium, but I'm not immune from grief. Their children were grieving, and they responded to our frequency beacon. My parents appeared to me as young and beautiful because they are pure energy! Energy doesn't get old, it doesn't get sick, and it cannot die.

Eternal Light, Eternal Life.

The voice I heard during my near-death experience resonated through me and its meaning unfolded. As I gazed at the stars and recalled those flashlights from so long ago, it all made sense. After we leave this dimension, the light of our electromagnetic soul, like the light of stars that burned out long ago, doesn't cease to exist — it shines on forever, into eternity.

This isn't philosophy — this is physics.

ACKNOWLEDGMENTS

AN ATTORNEY I WORKED WITH had a sign in his office: "Everyone brings joy into my life, some when they enter, and others when they leave." Cynicism aside, he had a point, because everyone in our lives is there for a reason. That is why I want to honor those who have brought joy into my life and who have been part of my journey while creating this book.

Thank you to my amazing literary agent, Wendy Keller of Keller Media — you're the best! Special thanks to Karen Wolny for your insights and guidance.

Georgia Hughes and the entire team at New World Library are second to none. Thank you to Marc Allen, Tracy Cunningham, Kristen Cashman, Kim Corbin, Munro Magruder, Tona Pearce Myers, and Richard Smoley.

My business and tour manager Rocky Trainer, thanks for always being by my side and constantly finding a way to transform lemons into Italian lemon ice.

Thank you to my friend Deborah Duncan, the coolest host of Houston's hottest TV Show, *Great Day Houston*. Kudos to

Ralph Garcia, Cristina Kooker, Kathy Richey, Jennifer Altheide, and the entire KHOU team.

My Los Angeles team is my extended family. Love and thanks to McKenzie Van-Dorne Rice of Liquid Studios Entertainment, Steve Rice, and rising star Zach Rice. Special thanks to Nancy Gershwin, Judy Shields, Corey Allen Kotler, and Thomas Uncles. Thank you, Jana Short, editor of *Best Holistic Life* magazine, who teaches all of us we can make the world a better place if we first start by improving ourselves.

On the East Coast, special thanks to Mark Lewis and the Tightline Productions team: James Angy, Dmitriy Pi, Damien Milner, and Stephanie Gabel. Thank you, Mike Misconi of Digital Zoetrope Productions.

Mahalo to my Hawaiian film family: Angie Loprete, Vince Lucero, Mike Prickett, Glen Kila, Christopher Olivera, and Hawaiian slack key guitarist and Grammy winner Jim Kimo West.

Radio has been a great medium for this medium. Very special thanks to Dr. Pat Baccili, my friend and cohost on *The Psychic & The Doc*. Thank you, Linda Firing, Jessica Henderson, Jacob Kappes, David Tortosa, and the Transformation Network team.

Special thanks to George Noory, Tommy Danheiser, Lisa Lyons, and the entire production teams of *Coast to Coast AM* and Gaia TV's *Beyond Belief*.

I'm honored to thank some very special friends in radio: the generals of the "Army of Darkness," Dave Schrader and Tim Dennis of *Darkness Radio*, Gary Mantz and Suzanne Mitchell, Brenda Michaels and Rob Spears, Christine Upchurch, Rob McConnell, Sunny McMillan, Jim Malliard, Tony Sweet and Captain Ron, John Pizzi and Mikey Sausage, Inez Bracy, Nancy Yearout, Tim Ray and Shannon McVey, Lisa Garr, Tom

Barnard and Winifred Schrader, Wendi Cooper, Scotty Rorek, Carol Adams, Carolan Carey, Dave Barnett, Brian Sullivan, Winifred Adams, Ericka Broussarhane, Emily Menshouse, Stephanie Barnhart, Gwilda Wiyaka, Hollis Chapman, Jeremy Scott, Jason Rigden, Jim Harold, Kat Hobson, Marlene Pardo, Mike Cavalli, James Creachbaum, Heather Horsley, Ted VanSon Jr., Andrea Peet, Roberta Grimes, Stan Long, Patricia Kirkman, Todd Wilcox, Chip Reichenthal, Auriel Grace, Robert Kalil, Mimi Pettibone, Barb Crowley, Patricia Baker, and Adrien Blackwell.

Kudos to my paranormally normal friends Shirley Bolstok, Mike Ricksecker, Nicole Antoinette, Jim Bruton, Joshua Chaires, Chuck Bergman, Patricia Kirkman, Beverly Lavender, and April Rane.

Thank you to my colleagues Dr. Gary Schwartz, Rhonda Schwartz, Dr. Bruce Greyson, Dr. Jeffrey Long, Jody Long, Kevin Todeschi, Nancy Evans Bush, P.M.H. Atwater, Col. Dr. John Alexander, Dr. Dean Radin, Dr. Pim van Lommel, William Buhlman, Dr. Raymond Moody, Dr. Kenneth Ring, Marcy Neumann, Dr. Eben Alexander, and Karen Newell.

IANDS has brought the light of understanding to the realm of near-death experiences. Thank you, Susan Amsden, Chuck Swedrock, Jeff Applewhite, Barbara and Victor Bartolome, Jacqueline Arnold, Gary Gilman, Beverly Brodsky, Debbie James, Angie Willson-Quayle, PhD, Daniel Endy, and everyone associated with IANDS and IANDS sharing groups worldwide.

It is an honor to work with Elizabeth Boisson, Irene Vouvalides, Mark Ireland, and Irene Weinberg of Helping Parents Heal, a refuge for "Shining Light Parents."

Thank you, Lisa Bonnice, Elana Maggal, Kaeza Fearn, Amanda Sutton, Vanessa Toro, and the entire Shift Network team.

I would also like to thank Linda Truax, Dr. Yvonne Kason, and Robert Bare of Spiritual Awakenings International.

It would take a book in itself to thank everyone who has been part of my public events, but I would like to spotlight some of them: Cheri Hart of Aquarian Dreams; Denise Welling, Susan Certain, Clyde Certain, Brad Certain, and Kevin Casey of Body, Mind & Soul Houston; Bhima Breckenridge and the team at East West Bookshop in Seattle; Diane Fresquez of For Heaven's Sake in Denver; Rev. Larry Swartz and Rev. Mary-Ellen Swartz of Unity Church of Tucson; Biba and Robert St. Croix of Gallery Biba; and Pat Krause of Universal Energy Holistic Services.

I've been blessed with many special friends in this life: Andrea Beckel (you'll always be Ginger to my Professor), Mary and Mike Goodwin, Carole Rooksberry, Marla Grabill, Sue Rice, Stephanie Rolls, Eve Dolan, Peter Nason, James Roland, Nancy Rowe, Louise Kleba, Kelly Dunn, Juen Joyce, William and Iris Delgado, Louis "Chip" Bock, and Nancy Bock.

Roxanne, Earl III, Joe, Laura and Earl IV, I love you beyond measure. Special thanks to the cousins in my corner: Denise, Diane, Barbara, Joanie, Anthony, Laurie, and Ana.

Love and eternal gratitude to my parents, Jeannie and Earl — thank you for being my guiding lights from the Afterlife Frequency.

ENDNOTES

Introduction

p. 3   *"The public has a distorted view of science"*: Freeman Dyson, "How We Know," review of James Gleick, *The Information: A History, a Theory, a Flood*, in *The New York Review of Books*, March 10, 2011, https://mast.queensu.ca/~math474/How-We-Know-Freeman -Dyson-NYREV-march11.pdf.

Chapter 1: Spiritual Synchronicity

p. 8   *"Once you eliminate"*: Arthur Conan Doyle, *The Sign of the Four* (1890; repr., Beeching Park, UK: House of Stratus Books, 2008), 2.

p. 8   *"The idea of the universe"*: Dean Radin, *Entangled Minds: Extrasensory Experiences in a Quantum Reality* (New York: Paraview, 2006), 3.

p. 9   *"All of our observations"*: Cathal O'Connell, "Universe Shouldn't Exist, Say CERN Physicists," *Cosmos*, October 22, 2017, https://cosmos magazine.com/physics/universe-shouldn-t-exist-cern-physicists -conclude.

Chapter 2: The Light of the Electromagnetic Soul

p. 23   *"What came first"*: D. Wootton, "History: Science and the Reformation," *Nature* 550 (2017): 454–55, https://doi.org/10.1038/550454a.

p. 29　*"I think, therefore I am"*: René Descartes, *Discourse on the Method for Conducting One's Reason Well and for Seeking Truth in the Sciences*, trans. Donald A. Cress (1637; repr., Indianapolis: Hackett Publishing, 1998), 18.

p. 33　*"It is entirely feasible"*: Shelli Joye, *The Electromagnetic Brain: EM Field Theories on the Nature of Consciousness* (Rochester, VT: Inner Traditions, 2018), 236.

p. 33　*"Eternal life does not violate"*: In Philip Bethge and Rafaila von Bredow, "Eternal Life Does Not Violate the Laws of Physics," *Spiegel International*, September 28, 2012, https://www.spiegel.de /international/world/interview-with-the-american-futurologist -michio-kaku-a-857860.html.

p. 34　*"The beauty of science"*: In Jessica Orwig, "Neil deGrasse Tyson's Best Quotes May Make You Fall in Love with Science All Over Again," *Business Insider*, November 22, 2015, https://www.businessinsider .com/15-inspirational-quotes-from-neil-degrasse-tyson-2015-11.

p. 38　*This phenomenon has been labeled* terminal lucidity: Michael Nahm, "Terminal Lucidity in People with Mental Illness and Other Mental Disability: An Overview and Implications for Possible Explanatory Models," *Journal of Near-Death Studies* 28, no. 2 (Winter 2009): 87–106. See also Michael Nahm, Bruce Greyson, Emily Kelly, and Erlendur Haraldsson, "Terminal Lucidity: A Review and a Case Collection," *Archives of Gerontology and Geriatrics* 55, no. 1 (July 2011): 138–42, https://doi.org/10.1016/j.archger.2011.06.031.

p. 39　*As observed by Professor Alexander Batthyány*: See Marilyn Mendoza, "Terminal Lucidity Revisited: The Mystery Continued," *Psychology Today*, September 30, 2019, www.psychologytoday.com/us/blog /understanding-grief/201909/terminal-lucidity-revisited.

p. 39　*"I do have my doubts"*: In Zaron Burnett III, "Terminal Lucidity: The Researchers Attempting to Prove Your Mind Lives On Even after You Die," *MEL Magazine*, September 26, 2018, https://medium.com /mel-magazine/terminal-lucidity-the-researchers-attempting-to -prove-that-your-mind-lives-on-even-after-you-die-385ac1f93dca.

p. 40　*"the electromagnetic spectrum is the range"*: NASA, Goddard Space Flight Center, "The Electromagnetic Spectrum," Imagine the Universe, March 2013, https://imagine.gsfc.nasa.gov/science/toolbox /emspectrum1.html.

p. 40　*"Matter is energy"*: In S. Vashisth, "A Beautifully Refreshing Perspective of Quantum Consciousness," *International Journal of Science and Consciousness* 3, no. 4 (October 2017): 93–100, http://ijsc.net/docs/issue10 /beautifully-refreshing-perspective-quantum-consciousness.pdf.

p. 41   *"though the bush was on fire it did not burn up"*: Exodus 3:2, New International Version.

p. 42   *"The lamps are different"*: Mevlana Jalaluddin Rumi, *The Rumi Collection*, ed. Kabir Helminski, trans. Andrew Harvey (Boston: Shambhala, 1998), 112.

p. 43   *"Biophoton streams consist of"*: MIT Technology Review, "Biophoton Communication: Can Cells Talk Using Light?," May 22, 2012, https://www.technologyreview.com/2012/05/22/185994/biophoton-communication-can-cells-talk-using-light.

p. 43   *"Biophoton emission is a general phenomenon"*: Fritz-Albert Popp, "About the Coherence of Biophotons," abstract, *Macroscopic Quantum Coherence: Proceedings of the International Conference* (Singapore: World Scientific, 1998), 130–50, https://inis.iaea.org/search/search.aspx?orig_q=RN:31042082.

p. 44   *"Practically every neurology textbook"*: Eben Alexander, "Near-Death Experiences," lecture, International Association of Near-Death Experiences annual conference, September 2017.

p. 44   *"the 'hosting hardware' of our consciousness"*: Evan Harris Walker, *The Physics of Consciousness: The Quantum Mind and the Meaning of Life* (New York: Basic Books, 2000).

p. 45   *"Death of consciousness"*: Robert Lanza with Bob Berman, *Biocentrism: How Life and Consciousness Are the Keys to Understanding the True Nature of the Universe* (Dallas: BenBella Books, 2009).

p. 45   *"The origin of consciousness reflects our place"*: "Discovery of Quantum Vibrations in 'Microtubules' inside Brain Neurons Supports Controversial Theory of Consciousness," ScienceDaily, January 16, 2014. https://www.sciencedaily.com/releases/2014/01/140116085105.htm.

p. 45   *the human brain may account for only 2 percent of the weight*: Marcus E. Raichle and Debra A. Gusnard, "Appraising the Brain's Energy Budget," *Proceedings of the National Academy of Sciences of the United States of America* 99, no. 16 (2002): 10, 237–39, https://doi.org/10.1073/pnas.172399499.

p. 45   *"When I die"*: In Rolf Fröböse, "Scientists Find Hints for the Immortality of the Soul," *HuffPost UK*, August 16, 2014, https://www.huffingtonpost.co.uk/rolf-froboese/scientists-find-hints-for-the-immortality-of-the-soul_b_5499969.html.

Chapter 3: Collective Consciousness Communication

p. 47   *"If I'd lived in Roman times"*: In Jonathan Cott, *Days That I'll Remember: Spending Time with John Lennon and Yoko Ono* (New York: Anchor, 2013), 154.

p. 54 *"Energy is directly proportional to frequency"*: In James Stein, "Planck's Constant: The Number That Rules Technology, Reality, and Life," *Nova*, October 24, 2011, https://www.pbs.org/wgbh/nova/article /plancks-constant.

p. 55 *Stephen Hawking coauthored a paper*: S.W. Hawking and Thomas Hertog, "A Smooth Exit from Eternal Inflation?," *Journal of High Energy Physics* 27 (2018), https://doi.org/10.1007 /JHEP04(2018)147; https://arxiv.org/pdf/1707.07702.

p. 56 *Theoretical physicist Laura Mersini-Houghton*: Laura Mersini-Houghton and Rudy Vaas, eds., *The Arrows of Time: A Debate in Cosmology* (New York: Springer Heidelberg Dordrecht, 2012).

p. 57 *"As we watch"*: Thomas Banchoff, *Beyond the Third Dimension* (New York: Scientific American Library, 1990), 1.

p. 57 *astrophysicist Neil deGrasse Tyson has suggested*: Neil deGrasse Tyson, in Cecille de Jesus, "Physicists Weigh In: Could We Ever Travel to a Parallel Universe?," Futurism.com, December 31, 2016, https://futurism.com/physicists-weigh-in-could-we-ever-travel-to -a-parallel-universe.

p. 60 *a change in one particle instantly creates a change*: Chelsea Gohd, "Ancient Quasars Provide Incredible Evidence for Quantum Entanglement," Space.com, August 21, 2018, https://www.space .com/41569-ancient-quasars-evidence-quantum-entanglement.html.

p. 67 *"we have feelings and tear ducts for a reason"*: Mandy Oaklander, "The Science of Crying," Time.com, March 16, 2016, https://time .com/4254089/science-crying.

Chapter 4: RAFT

p. 70 *"This could well be related"*: S.M. Roney-Dougal and G. Vogl, "Some Speculations on the Effect of Geomagnetism on the Pineal Gland," *Journal of the Society for Psychical Research* 59, no. 830 (1993): 1–15.

p. 70 *A French-Israeli study*: Simon Baconnier, Sidney B. Lang, and René de Seze, "New Crystal in the Pineal Gland: Characterization and Potential Role in Electromechano-Transduction," August 2002: https://www.researchgate.net/publication/278736874_New_crystal _in_the_pineal_gland_characterization_and_potential_role_in _electromechano-transduction.

p. 71 *McFadden proposes that neurons engage in a feedback loop*: Johnjoe McFadden, "The CEMI Field Theory: Seven Clues to the Nature of Consciousness," in Jack A. Tuszynski, ed., *The Emerging Physics of Consciousness* (Berlin: Springer, 2006), 387–406: https://www .researchgate.net/publication/226078423_The_CEMI_Field_ Theory_Seven_Clues_to_the_Nature_of_Consciousness.

p. 71   *According to McFadden, this indicates*: Joye, *The Electromagnetic Brain*, 20–24.

p. 72   *the human body's "second brain"*: Michael Gershon, *The Second Brain: The Scientific Basis of Gut Instinct and a Groundbreaking New Understanding of Nervous Disorders of the Stomach and Intestines* (New York: HarperCollins, 1998).

p. 72   *"In evolutionary terms, it makes sense"*: In "The Enteric Nervous System: The Brain in the Gut," King's Psychology Network, 1996, https://webprojects.oit.ncsu.edu/project/bio181de/Black/endocrine2 /endocrine2_news/id36.htm.

p. 73   *"The gut converses with the brain"*: In Dan Gordon, "Understanding the Constant Dialogue That Goes On between Our Gut and Our Brain," UCLA Newsroom, July 25, 2017, https://newsroom.ucla.edu /stories/understanding-the-constant-dialogue-that-goes-on-between -our-gut-and-our-brain.

p. 82   *Molnar confirmed that this particular alignment*: Michael Molnar, *The Star of Bethlehem: The Legacy of the Magi* (New Brunswick, NJ: Rutgers University Press, 2013), 89.

p. 82   *These findings were confirmed*: In Brendan O'Shaughnessy, "Royal Beauty Bright: Notre Dame Astrophysicist Researches the Christmas Star," University of Notre Dame Stories, Office of Public Affairs and Communications, November 30, 2018, https://www.nd.edu /stories/royal-beauty-bright.

Chapter 6: Near-Death and Shared Death Experiences

p. 118   *"Most near-death survivors"*: In Mark R. Pitstick, *Toward Heaven on Earth: Remembering Your Soul* (self-published, 1997), 51.

p. 118   *"even the word 'God'"*: Alexander, "Near-Death Experiences."

p. 118   *Yet NDE researcher Dr. Kenneth Ring*: Kenneth Ring and Sharon Cooper, *Mindsight: Near-Death and Out-of-Body Experiences in the Blind* (Palo Alto, CA: William James Center for Consciousness Studies Institute of Transpersonal Psychology, 1999).

p. 118   *"As our medical and surgical skills"*: John C. Hagan III, ed., *The Science of Near-Death Experiences* (Columbia, MO: University of Missouri Press, 2017), 3.

p. 119   *it is estimated that 774 NDEs occur daily*: Jeffrey Long, "How Many NDEs Occur in the United States Every Day?," accessed June 21, 2021, https://www.nderf.org/NDERF/Research/number_nde_usa.htm.

p. 119   *One of the most intriguing ancient accounts of an NDE*: Plato, *Republic*, 614b–621d.

p. 119   *Er left this world and went into a transcendent reality*: In N. S. Gill,

"The Myth of Er from the *Republic* of Plato: English Translation by Jowett of Plato's Myth of Er," ThoughtCo.com, April 3, 2019, https://www.thoughtco.com/the-myth-of-er-120332.

p. 120 *"I know a man in Christ"*: 2 Corinthians 12:2–3, New International Version.

p. 120 *In his book* Anecdotes de médecine: Pierre-Jean du Monchaux and Jacques Barbeu du Bourg, *Anecdotes de médecine* (1762; repr., Charleston, SC: Biblio Bazaar, 2011).

p. 126 *"When I was eighteen"*: Maria Popova, "George Lucas on the Meaning of Life," BrainPickings, March 17, 2014, https://www.brainpickings.org/2014/03/17/george-lucas-meaning-of-life.

p. 127 *"The Force is an energy"*: George Lucas, *Star Wars Episode IV: A New Hope*, Twentieth Century Fox, 1977, film.

p. 128 *Lucas sold* Star Wars: Brian Solomon, "Donating Star Wars Billions Will Make George Lucas One of the Biggest Givers Ever," *Forbes*, November 4, 2012, https://www.forbes.com/sites/briansolomon/2012/11/04/donating-star-wars-billions-will-make-george-lucas-one-of-the-biggest-givers-ever/?sh=2078c0822adb.

p. 134 *Researchers Dr. Bruce Greyson and Nancy Evans Bush*: In Hagan, *The Science of Near-Death Experiences*, 95–96.

p. 134 *"In the DNDE"*: Hagan, *The Science of Near-Death Experiences*, 7, 93–101.

p. 135 *"The kind of NDE"*: Nancy Evans Bush, *Reckoning: Discoveries after a Traumatic Near-Death Experience* (self-published, 2021), 170.

p. 135 *"frequent or key NDE phenomena"*: Michael Potts, "Does N,N-Dimethyltryptamine (DMT) Adequately Explain Near-Death Experiences?," *Journal of Near-Death Studies* 31, no. 1 (2012): 3–23, https://digital.library.unt.edu/ark:/67531/metadc937961.

p. 136 *"Bystanders or onlookers"*: Raymond A. Moody, "Getting Comfortable with Death and Near-Death Experiences: An Essay in Medicine and Philosophy," *Missouri Medicine* 110, no. 5 (2013): 368–71, https://www.ncbi.nlm.nih.gov/pmc/articles/PMC6179873.

p. 137 *One of the most compelling examples*: Kevin Williams, "A Group of Firefighters Near-Death Experience," Near-Death.com, September 20, 2019, http://near-death.com/firefighters-nde.

Chapter 7: After-Death Communication

p. 144 *"I have been at work for some time"*: In Kristin Tablang, "Thomas Edison, B.C. Forbes and the Mystery of the Spirit Phone," *Forbes*,

October 25, 2019, https://www.forbes.com/sites/kristintablang/2019/10/25/thomas-edison-bc-forbes-mystery-spirit-phone/?sh=7560bd8f29ad.

p. 144 *Other interviews, particularly in* Scientific American: Natalie Zarrelli, "Dial-a-Ghost on Thomas Edison's Least Successful Invention: The Spirit Phone," Atlas Obscura website, October 18, 2016, https://www.atlasobscura.com/articles/dial-a-ghost-on-thomas-edisons-least-successful-invention-the-spirit-phone.

p. 144 *"I do hope myself"*: In Shaw Desmond, "Edison's Views upon Vital Human Problems," *The Strand Magazine*, vol. 64, July–December 1922, 162.

p. 144 *Dr. Gary Schwartz and his team*: Mark Pitstick and Gary Schwartz, *Greater Reality Living: Integrating the Evidence for Eternal Consciousness into Your Daily Life* (N.p.: CreateSpace, 2018), 169–73.

p. 145 *"Dr. Schwartz's scientific research has definitely demonstrated"*: Mark Pitstick, email correspondence, June 2019.

p. 145 *"The next anticipated device is the* SoulKeyboard*"*: Pitstick, email correspondence, June 2019.

p. 145 *"When wireless is perfectly applied"*: In Damon Beres, "Nikola Tesla Predicted Smartphones in 1926," *HuffPost*, July 10, 2015, https://www.huffpost.com/entry/tesla-quotes_n_7771358.

p. 146 *"Those dying may report seeing or hearing dead family members"*: Jeffrey Long, phone conversation with author, 2020.

p. 152 *"If no one asks me"*: St. Augustine, *Confessions*, trans. J.G. Pilkington, 11.14.17, http://web.mnstate.edu/gracyk/courses/web%20publishing/AugustineBookXI.htm.

p. 152 *time remains one of the least understood*: See Paul Erker, Mark T. Mitchison, Ralph Silva, Mischa P. Woods, Nicolas Brunner, and Marcus Huber, "Autonomous Quantum Clocks: Does Thermodynamics Limit Our Ability to Measure Time?," *Physics Review* 10, no. 7 (July–September 2017), https://arxiv.org/abs/1609.06704.

p. 152 *"a mental construct or other illusion"*: In Dan Falk, "A Debate Over the Physics of Time," *Quanta Magazine*, July 19, 2019, https://www.quantamagazine.org/a-debate-over-the-physics-of-time-20160719.

p. 153 *"We can portray our reality"*: In Robert Lawrence Kuhn, "The Illusion of Time: What's Real?," Space.com, July 6, 2015, https://www.space.com/29859-the-illusion-of-time.html.

Chapter 8: The Unfolding and Avoiding the No, No, No Syndrome

p. 177 *One of the audience members, Paula, recognized*: KHOU Great Day Houston Psychic Readings, "Chesterfields," YouTube, May 4, 2016, https://www.youtube.com/watch?v=n4FEd-rxp9M&t=7s.

p. 185 *NASA and other space agencies*: Clara Moskowitz, "Star Trek's Deflector Shield Envisioned for Mars Mission," Space.com, November 19, 2008, https://www.space.com/6128-star-trek-deflector-shield-envisioned-mars-mission.html.

p. 185 *According to the European Space Agency*: R. Aceti, G. Drolshagen, J.A.M. McDonnell, T. Stevenson, and Mare Crisium, "Micrometeoroids and Space Debris: The Eureca Post-Flight Analysis," *ESA Bulletin*, no. 80, November 1994, http://www.esa.int/esapub/bulletin/bullet80/ace80.htm.

p. 186 *Professor Bryn James*: Staff writers of Space Daily, "Armor Could Form 'Force Field,'" Space Daily website, March 20, 2009, https://www.spacedaily.com/reports/Armor_could_form_force_field_999.html.

p. 186 *"method and system for shockwave attenuation"*: Brian J. Tillotson, Method and system for shockwave attenuation via electromagnetic arc, US Patent 8,981,261 B1, filed May 30, 2012, and issued March 17, 2015, https://pdfpiw.uspto.gov/.piw?docid=08981261.

Chapter 9: Spirit Intervention

p. 193 *"What one man calls God"*: Dobrica Savić, ed., *Tesla in His Own Words: Wisdom from One of the World's Greatest Inventors* (Vienna: self-published, 2019), 16.

p. 210 *"a coroner [who] has"*: Illinois General Assembly, Illinois statute 55 ILCS 5/3-3009 (from ch. 34, par. 3-3009; 2014 State Bar Edition), https://www.ilga.gov/legislation/ilcs/fulltext.asp?DocName=005500050K3-3009; italics mine.

Chapter 10: There's No Place Like Hell

p. 215 *"Greater love has no one than this"*: John 15:13, New International Version.

p. 223 *"Heaven is not a gated community"*: Evan Moffic, "Do Jews Believe in an Afterlife?," ReformJudaism.org, accessed June 23, 2021, https://reformjudaism.org/beliefs-practices/lifecycle-rituals/death-mourning/do-jews-believe-afterlife.

p. 224   *"This space is full of a vapor"*: Strabo, *Geography* 13.4, trans. H.C. Hamilton and W. Falconer, accessed May 14, 2021, http://www .perseus.tufts.edu/hopper/text?doc=Perseus:text:1999.01.0198 :book=13:chapter=4.

p. 224   *Recent archaeological discoveries in Turkey*: Rachel Tepper Paley, "Animals Dropped Dead Inside Roman 'Gate to Hell.' Scientists Just Figured Out Why," Time.com, February 22, 2018, https://time .com/5171047/turkey-gate-to-hell-pamukkale-hierapolis.

p. 225   *Constantine and his successors were hailed as*: John Julius Norwich, *Byzantium: The Early Centuries* (New York: Knopf, 1988), 337.

p. 225   *Byzantine emperor, Constantine XI, was still hailed*: John Julius Norwich, *Byzantium: Decline and Fall* (New York: Knopf, 1995), xxxv, 439.

p. 229   *In 1916 Einstein theorized*: NASA Science, "What Is a Gravitational Wave?," NASA Science Space Place, updated June 4, 2020, https:// spaceplace.nasa.gov/gravitational-waves/en.

p. 231   *"Hell lives inside us"*: Bush, *Reckoning*, 171.

p. 232   *"You know you got to go through hell"*: Steve Miller, "Jet Airliner," Capitol Records, 1977, https://www.discogs.com/The-Steve -Miller-Band-Book-Of-Dreams/release/774273.

p. 232   *"Do not judge, or you too will be judged"*: Matthew 7:1–2, New International Version.

Chapter 11: Eternal Light, Eternal Life

p. 246   *"For quantum particles, such as electrons"*: U. Satya Sainadh, "We Did a Breakthrough 'Speed Test' in Quantum Tunneling, and Here's Why That's Exciting," The Conversation, March 19, 2019, https://the conversation.com/we-did-a-breakthrough-speed-test-in-quantum -tunnelling-and-heres-why-thats-exciting-113761.

p. 246   *This process is known as* quantum tunneling: Nicolas Camus, Enderalp Yakaboylu, Lutz Fechner, Michael Klaiber, Martin Laux, Yonghao Mi, Karen Z. Hatsagortsyan, Thomas Pfeifer, Christoph H. Keitel, and Robert Moshammer, "Experimental Evidence for Quantum Tunneling Time," *Physical Review Letters* 119, no. 2 (July 14, 2017), https://doi.org/10.1103/PhysRevLett.119.023201.

p. 246   *This is known as the* quantum lattice theory: Richard Merrick, "The Physics of Consciousness," Token Rock, August 22, 2009, https:// www.tokenrock.com/blogs/the-physics-of-consciousness-378.

p. 246   *Walker's theory proposes*: Walker, *The Physics of Consciousness*, 29–40.

BIBLIOGRAPHY

Aceti, R., G. Drolshagen, J. A. M. McDonnell, T. Stevenson, and Mare Crisium. "Micrometeoroids and Space Debris: The Eureca Post-flight Analysis." European Space Research and Technology Center website, 1993. http://www.esa.int/esapub/bulletin/bullet80/ace80.htm.

Alexander, Eben. "Near-Death Experiences." Lecture. International Association of Near-Death Experiences annual conference, September 2017.

Anderson, John. *Life, Death, and Beyond.* Grand Rapids, MI: Zondervan, 1980.

St. Augustine. *Confessions.* Translated by J. G. Pilkington. *The Early Church Fathers and Other Works.* Grand Rapids, MI: Eerdmans, n.d. [1867]. http://web.mnstate.edu/gracyk/courses/web.percent20publishing /AugustineBookXI.htm.

Baconnier, Simon, Sidney B. Lang, and René de Seze. "New Crystal in the Pineal Gland: Characterization and Potential Role in Electromechano-Transduction." August 2002. https://www.researchgate.net/publication /278736874_New_crystal_in_the_pineal_gland_characterization_and _potential_role_in_electromechano-transduction.

Banchoff, Thomas. *Beyond the Third Dimension.* New York: Scientific American Library, 1990.

Becker, Carl. "The Centrality of Near-Death Experiences in Chinese Pure Land Buddhism." *Anabiosis* 1 (December 1981): 154–71.

Beres, Damon. "Nikola Tesla Predicted Smartphones in 1926." *HuffPost*, July 10, 2015. https://www.huffpost.com/entry/tesla-quotes_n_7771358.

Blackmore, Susan. *Dying to Live: Science and the Near-Death Experience.* London: Grafton, 1993.

Botkin, Allan. "The Induction of After-Death Communications Utilizing Eye-Movement Desensitization and Reprocessing: A New Discovery." *Journal of Near-Death Studies* 18, no. 3 (2000): 181–209.

Burnett, Zaron. "Terminal Lucidity: The Researchers Attempting to Prove Your Mind Lives On Even After You Die." *MEL Magazine*, September 26, 2018. https://medium.com/mel-magazine/terminal-lucidity-the -researchers-attempting-to-prove-that-your-mind-lives-on-even-after -you-die-385ac1f93dca.

Bush, Nancy Evans. *Reckoning: Discoveries after a Traumatic Near-Death Experience.* Self-published, 2021.

Camus, Nicolas, Enderalp Yakaboylu, Lutz Fechner, Michael Klaiber, Martin Laux, Yonghao Mi, Karen Z. Hatsagortsyan, Thomas Pfeifer, Christoph H. Keitel, and Robert Moshammer. "Measuring Time in a Quantum Tunnel." Max-Planck-Gesellschaft website, July 26, 2017. www.mpg.de/11419700/time-measurement-quantum-tunnel.

Cheung, Philip. "A Debate over the Physics of Time." *Quanta Magazine*, July 19, 2019. www.quantamagazine.org/a-debate-over-the-physics-of -time-20160719.

Cooper, Paul. "Animals Entering Ancient Rome's 'Gate to Hell' Killed by Gas, Not Gods." History.com, August 30, 2018. https://www .history.com/news/ancient-romans-gate-hell-mystery.

Cott, Jonathan. *Days That I'll Remember: Spending Time with John Lennon and Yoko Ono.* New York: Anchor, 2013.

de Jesus, Cecille. "Physicists Weigh In: Could We Ever Travel to a Parallel Universe?" Futurism.com, December 31, 2016. https://futurism.com /physicists-weigh-in-could-we-ever-travel-to-a-parallel-universe.

Del Maestro, Rolando. "Leonardo da Vinci: The Search for the Soul." *Journal of Neurosurgery* 89 (1998). 10.3171/jns.1998.89.5.0874.

Descartes, René. *Discourse on the Method for Conducting One's Reason Well and for Seeking Truth in the Sciences.* Translated by Donald A. Cress. 1637. Reprint, Indianapolis: Hackett Publishing, 1998.

Desmond, Shaw. "Edison's Views upon Vital Human Problems." *The Strand Magazine* 64 (July–December 1922): 155–62.

"Discovery of Quantum Vibrations in 'Microtubules' inside Brain Neurons Supports Controversial Theory of Consciousness." ScienceDaily, January 16, 2014. https://www.sciencedaily.com/releases/2014/01 /140116085105.htm.

Doyle, Arthur Conan. *The Sign of the Four*. Beeching Park, UK: House of Stratus Books, 2008 [1890].

Druback, Daniel, MD. *The Brain Explained*. Upper Saddle River, NJ: Prentice-Hall, 1999.

du Monchaux, Pierre-Jean, and Jacques Barbeu du Bourg. *Anecdotes de médecine*. 1762. Reprint, Charleston, SC: Biblio Bazaar, 2011.

Dyson, Freeman. "How We Know." Review of James Gleick, *The Information: A History, a Theory, a Flood*. In *The New York Review of Books*, March 10, 2011. mast.queensu.ca/~math474/How-We-Know-Freeman -Dyson-NYREV-march11.pdf.

"The Enteric Nervous System: The Brain in the Gut." 1996. https://web projects.oit.ncsu.edu/project/bio181de/Black/endocrine2/endocrine2 _news/id36.htm.

Erickson, Kristen, and Heather Doyle. "What Is a Gravitational Wave?" NASA Space Place website, June 4, 2020. https://spaceplace.nasa.gov /about-us/en.

Erker, Paul, Mark T. Mitchison, Ralph Silva, Mischa P. Woods, Nicolas Brunner, and Marcus Huber. "Autonomous Quantum Clocks: Does Thermodynamics Limit Our Ability to Measure Time?" In *Physics Review* 10, no. 7 (July–September 2017). https://arxiv.org/abs /1609.06704.

Falk, Dan. "A Debate over the Physics of Time." *Quanta Magazine*, July 19, 2019. https://www.quantamagazine.org/a-debate-over-the -physics-of-time-20160719.

Firth, John. *Constantine the Great*. Self-published, 2017.

Flynn, Charles. *After the Beyond: Human Transformation and the Near-Death Experience*. Englewood Cliffs, NJ: Prentice-Hall, 1986.

Fröböse, Rolf. "Scientists Find Hints for the Immortality of the Soul." *Huff-Post UK*, August 16, 2014. https://www.huffingtonpost.co.uk /rolf-froboese/scientists-find-hints-for-the-immortality-of-the-soul _b_5499969.html.

Gallup, George. *Adventures in Immortality*. London: Souvenir, 1982.

Gershon, Michael. *The Second Brain: The Scientific Basis of Gut Instinct and a Groundbreaking New Understanding of Nervous Disorders of the Stomach and Intestines*. New York: Harper Collins, 1998.

Gill, N.S. "The Myth of Er from the Republic of Plato: English Translation by Jowett of Plato's Myth of Er." ThoughtCo.com. Accessed May 13, 2021. https://www.thoughtco.com/the-myth-of-er-120332.

Gohd, Chelsea. "Ancient Quasars Provide Incredible Evidence for Quantum Entanglement." Space.com, August 21, 2018. https://www.space.com/41569-ancient-quasars-evidence-quantum-entanglement.html.

Gordon, Dan. "Understanding the Constant Dialogue That Goes On between Our Gut and Our Brain." UCLA Newsroom website, July 25, 2017. https://newsroom.ucla.edu/stories/understanding-the-constant-dialogue-that-goes-on-between-our-gut-and-our-brain.

Grey, Margot. *Return from Death: An Exploration of the Near-Death Experience*. London: Arkana, 1985.

Greyson, Bruce. "A Typology of Near-Death Experiences." *American Journal of Psychiatry* 142 (1985): 967–69.

———. "The Incidence of Near-Death Experiences." *Medicine and Psychiatry*, December 1998. https://www.newdualism.org/nde-papers/Greyson/Greyson-_1998-1-92-99.pdf.

Greyson, Bruce, and Nancy Evans Bush. "Distressing Near-Death Experiences." *Psychiatry* 55, no. 1 (February 1992): 95–110.

Hagan, John C. III, ed. *The Science of Near-Death Experiences*. Columbia, MO: University of Missouri Press, 2017.

Hattersley, Laurence. *A Second Opinion: An Insight into Good Health, Disease, and Our Relationships with Them*. Self-published, 2015.

Hawking, S.W., and Thomas Hertog. "A Smooth Exit from Eternal Inflation?" *Journal of High Energy Physics* 27 (2018). https://doi.org/10.1007/JHEP04(2018)147; https://arxiv.org/pdf/1707.07702.pdf.

Holden, J.M., B. Greyson, and D. James, eds. *The Handbook of Near-Death Experiences: Thirty Years of Investigation*. Santa Barbara, CA: Praeger/ABC-CLIO, 2009.

Hollander, Bernard. *In Search of the Soul and the Mechanism of Thought, Emotion, and Conduct*. London: Palala Press, 2018.

Janiak, Andrew. "Newton's Philosophy." The Stanford Encyclopedia of Philosophy website, May 6, 2014. https://plato.stanford.edu/entries/newton-philosophy.

Joye, Shelli. *The Electromagnetic Brain: EM Field Theories on the Nature of Consciousness*. Rochester, VT: Inner Traditions, 2018.

Kaku, Michio. *Einstein's Cosmos: How Albert Einstein's Vision Transformed Our Understanding of Space and Time*. New York: Norton, 2005.

————. *The Future of Humanity: Terraforming Mars, Interstellar Travel, Immortality, and Our Destiny Beyond Earth*. New York: Doubleday, 2018.

Kellehear, Allan. *Experiences near Death: Beyond Medicine and Religion*. Oxford: Oxford University Press, 1996.

KHOU *Great Day Houston* Psychic Readings. YouTube, 2016. https://www.youtube.com/watch?v=n4FEd-rxp9M&t=7s.

Kuhn, Robert Lawrence. "The Illusion of Time: What's Real?" Space.com, July 6, 2015. https://www.space.com/29859-the-illusion-of-time.html.

Küng, Hans. *Eternal Life?* London: Collins, 1984.

Lanza, Robert, and Bob Berman. *Biocentrism: How Life and Consciousness Are the Keys to Understanding the True Nature of the Universe*. Dallas: BenBella Books, 2009.

Long, Jeffrey. "How Many NDEs Occur in the United States Every Day?" NDERF.org. https://www.nderf.org/NDERF/Research/number_nde_usa.htm.

Long, Jeffrey, and Paul Perry. *Evidence of the Afterlife*. Reprint, San Francisco: HarperOne, 2010.

————. *God and the Afterlife: The Groundbreaking New Evidence for God and Near-Death Experiences*. San Francisco: HarperOne, 2016.

Lorimer, David. *Whole in One: The Near-Death Experience and the Ethic of Interconnectedness*. London: Penguin, 1990.

Lucas, George. *Star Wars Episode IV: A New Hope*. Twentieth Century Fox, 1977. Film.

Maxwell, James Clerk. *A Dynamical Theory of the Electromagnetic Field*. London: Royal Society, 1865.

McFadden, Johnjoe. "The CEMI Field Theory: Seven Clues to the Nature of Consciousness." In Jack A. Tuszynski, ed., *The Emerging Physics of Consciousness*. Berlin: Springer, 2006: 387–406. https://www.researchgate.net/publication/226078423_The_CEMI_Field_Theory_Seven_Clues_to_the_Nature_of_Consciousness.

Mendoza, Marilyn A. "Why Some People Rally for One Last Goodbye Before Death." *Psychology Today*, October 2018. https://www.psychologytoday.com/us/blog/understanding-grief/201810/why-some-people-rally-one-last-goodbye-death.

————. "Terminal Lucidity Revisited: The Mystery Continued." *Psychology Today*, September 30, 2019. https://www.psychologytoday.com/us/blog/understanding-grief/201909/terminal-lucidity-revisited.

Merrick, Richard. "The Physics of Consciousness." Token Rock website,

August 22, 2009. https://www.tokenrock.com/blogs/the-physics-of
-consciousness-378.

Mersini-Houghton, Laura, and Rudy Vaas, eds. *The Arrows of Time: A Debate in Cosmology*. New York: Springer Heidelberg Dordrecht, 2012.

Miller, Steve. "Jet Airliner." Capitol Records, 1977. Accessed August 17, 2020. https://www.discogs.com/The-Steve-Miller-Band-Book-Of -Dreams/release/774273.

MIT Technology Review. "Biophoton Communication: Can Cells Talk Using Light?" May 22, 2012. https://www.technologyreview.com /2012/05/22/185994/biophoton-communication-can-cells-talk-using -light.

Moffic, Evan. "Do Jews Believe in an Afterlife?" ReformJudaism.org, 2020. https://reformjudaism.org/practice/lifecycle-and-rituals/death -mourning/do-jews-believe-afterlife.

Molnar, Michael. *The Star of Bethlehem: The Legacy of the Magi*. New Brunswick, NJ: Rutgers University Press, 2013.

Moody, Raymond. *Life after Life*. New York: Bantam, 1975.

———. *The Last Laugh: A New Philosophy of Near-Death Experiences, Apparitions, and the Paranormal*. Charlottesville, VA: Hampton Roads, 1999.

———. "Getting Comfortable with Death and Near-Death Experiences: An Essay in Medicine and Philosophy." *Missouri Medicine* 110, no. 5 (2013): 368–71. https://www.ncbi.nlm.nih.gov/pmc/articles /PMC6179873.

Moody, Raymond, and Paul Perry. *Glimpses of Eternity: Sharing a Loved One's Passage from This Life to the Next*. Paradise Valley, AZ: SAKKARA, 2010.

Morse, Melvin. *Closer to the Light: Learning from Children's Near-Death Experiences*. New York: Villard, 1990.

Moskowitz, Clara. "Star Trek's Deflector Shield Envisioned for Mars Mission." Space.com, November 19, 2008. https://pdfpiw.uspto.gov /.piw?docid=08981261.

Nahm, Michael. "Reflections on the Context of Near-Death Experiences." *Journal of Scientific Exploration* 25 (2011): 470–71.

Nahm, M., and B. Greyson. "Terminal Lucidity in People with Mental Illness and Other Mental Disability: An Overview and Implications for Possible Explanatory Models." *Journal of Near-Death Studies* 28, no. 2 (Winter 2009): 87–106.

Nahm, Michael, Bruce Greyson, Emily Kelly, and Erlendur Haraldsson. "Terminal Lucidity: A Review and a Case Collection." *Archives of*

Gerontology and Geriatrics 55, no. 1 (July 2011): 138–42. www.research
gate.net/publication/51497433_Terminal_lucidity_A_review_and_a
_case_collection.

NASA, The Imagine Team, Goddard Space Flight Center. "The Electromagnetic Spectrum." Imagine the Universe, March 2013. imagine.gsfc
.nasa.gov/science/toolbox/emspectrum1.html.

NASA Science. "What Is a Gravitational Wave?" NASA Science Space
Place website, June 4, 2020. https://spaceplace.nasa.gov/gravitational
-waves/en.

National Institute of Neurological Disorders and Stroke. Accessed September 7, 2018. https://www.ninds.nih.gov/Disorders/All-Disorders
/Coma-Information-Page.

Norwich, John Julius. *Byzantium: The Early Centuries*. New York: Knopf,
1988.

———. *Byzantium: Decline and Fall*. New York: Knopf, 1995.

Oaklander, Mandy. "The Science of Crying." Time.com, March 16, 2016.
https://time.com/4254089/science-crying.

O'Connell, Cathal. "Universe Shouldn't Exist, Say CERN Physicists." *Cosmos*, October 22, 2017. https://cosmosmagazine.com/physics/universe
-shouldn-t-exist-cern-physicists-conclude.

Oman, Charles. *The Dark Ages: 476–918 AD*. N.p.: Augustine Books, 2017.

Orwig, Jessica. "Neil deGrasse Tyson's Best Quotes May Make You Fall in
Love with Science All Over Again." *Business Insider*, November 22,
2015. https://www.businessinsider.com/15-inspirationl-quotes-from
-neil-degrasse-tyson-2015-11.

O'Shaughnessy, Brendan. "Royal Beauty Bright: Notre Dame Astrophysicist
Researches the Christmas Star." University of Notre Dame Stories.
Office of Public Affairs and Communications, November 30, 2018.
https://www.nd.edu/stories/royal-beauty-bright.

Pitstick, Mark R. *Toward Heaven on Earth: Remembering Your Soul*.
Self-published, 1997.

Pitstick, Mark, and Gary Schwartz. *Greater Reality Living: Integrating
the Evidence for Eternal Consciousness into Your Daily Life*. N.p.:
CreateSpace, 2018.

Popova, Maria. "George Lucas on the Meaning of Life." BrainPickings,
March 17, 2014. https://www.brainpickings.org/2014/03/17/george
-lucas-meaning-of-life.

Popp, Fritz-Albert. "About the Coherence of Biophotons." Abstract. *Macroscopic Quantum Coherence: Proceedings of the International Conference*.

Singapore: World Scientific, 1998. 130–50. https://inis.iaea.org
/search/search.aspx?orig_q=RN:31042082.

Potts, Michael. "Does N,N-Dimethyltryptamine (DMT) Adequately Explain Near-Death Experiences?" *Journal of Near-Death Studies* 31, no. 1 (2012): 3–23. digital.library.unt.edu/ark:/67531/metadc937961.

Raichle, Marcus E., and Debra A. Gusnard. "Appraising the Brain's Energy Budget." *Proceedings of the National Academy of Sciences of the United States of America* 99, no. 16 (2002): 10237–39. doi:10.1073/pnas.172399499.

Rawlings, Maurice. *Before Death Comes*. London: Sheldon, 1980.

Ring, Kenneth. *Life at Death: A Scientific Investigation of the Near-Death Experience*. New York: Coward, McCann, and Geoghegan, 1980.

Ring, Kenneth, and Sharon Cooper. *Mindsight: Near-Death and Out-of-Body Experiences in the Blind*. Palo Alto, CA: William James Center for Consciousness Studies, 1999.

Rivas, Titus, Anny Dirven, and Rudolf H. Smit. *The Self Does Not Die*. Durham, NC: IANDS, 2016.

Roney-Dougal, S.M., and G. Vogl. "Some Speculations on the Effect of Geomagnetism on the Pineal Gland." *Journal of the Society for Psychical Research* 59, no. 830 (1993): 1–15.

Rumi, Mevlana Jalaluddin. *The Rumi Collection*. Edited by Kabir Helminski. Translated by Andrew Harvey. Boston: Shambhala, 1998.

Sainadh, U. Satya. "We Did a Breakthrough 'Speed Test' in Quantum Tunneling, and Here's Why That's Exciting." TheConversation.com, March 19, 2019. https://theconversation.com/we-did-a-break through-speed-test-in-quantum-tunnelling-and-heres-why-thats-exciting-113761.

Savić, Dobrica, ed. *Tesla in His Own Words: Wisdom from One of the World's Greatest Inventors*. Vienna: self-published, 2019.

Solomon, Brian. "Donating Star Wars Billions Will Make George Lucas One of the Biggest Givers Ever." *Forbes*, November 4, 2012. https://www.forbes.com/sites/briansolomon/2012/11/04/donating-star-wars-billions-will-make-george-lucas-one-of-the-biggest-givers-ever.

Staff writers of Space Daily. "Armor Could Form 'Force Field.'" Space Daily website, March 20, 2009. https://www.spacedaily.com/reports/Armor_could_form_force_field_999.html.

Stein, James. "Planck's Constant: The Number That Rules Technology, Reality, and Life." *Nova*, October 24, 2011. https://www.pbs.org/wgbh/nova/article/plancks-constant.

Strabo. *Geography.* Translated by H. C. Hamilton and W. Falconer, 1903. Accessed June 8, 2021. http://www.perseus.tufts.edu/hopper/text?doc =Perseus:text:1999.01.0198:book=13:chapter=4.

Sutherland, Cherie. *Transformed by the Light: Life after Near-Death Experiences.* New York: Bantam, 1992.

Tablang, Kristin. "Thomas Edison, B.C. Forbes, and the Mystery of the Spirit Phone." *Forbes*, October 25, 2019. https://www.forbes.com/sites /kristintablang/2019/10/25/thomas-edison-bc-forbes-mystery-spirit -phone.

Tillotson, Brian. Method and system for shockwave attenuation via electromagnetic arc. US Patent 8,981,261 B1, filed May 30, 2012, and issued March 17, 2015. https://pdfpiw.uspto.gov/.piw?docid=08981261.

Van Lommel, P. "Near-Death Experiences: The Experience of the Self as Real and Not as an Illusion." *Annals of the New York Academy of the Sciences*, October 2011. 10.1111/j.1749-6632.2011.06080.x.

Vashisth, S. "A Beautifully Refreshing Perspective of Quantum Consciousness." *International Journal of Science and Consciousness*, October 2017. http://ijsc.net/docs/issue10/beautifully-refreshing-perspective-quantum -consciousness.pdf.

Walker, Evan Harris. *The Physics of Consciousness: The Quantum Mind and the Meaning of Life.* New York: Basic Books, 2000.

Williams, Kevin. "A Group of Firefighters Near-Death Experience." Near-Death.com. September 20, 2019. http://near-death.com/firefighters -nde.

Wilson, Andrew. *World Scripture: A Comparative Anthology of Sacred Texts.* Vadnais Heights, MN: Paragon House, 1998.

Wootton, D. "History: Science and the Reformation." *Nature* 550 (2017): 454–55. https://doi.org/10.1038/550454a.

Zaleski, Carol. *Otherworld Journeys.* New York: Oxford University Press, 1989.

Zarrelli, Natalie. "Dial-a-Ghost on Thomas Edison's Least Successful Invention: The Spirit Phone." Atlas Obscura website, October 18, 2016. https://www.atlasobscura.com/articles/dial-a-ghost-on-thomas-edisons -least-successful-invention-the-spirit-phone.

ABOUT THE AUTHOR

MARK ANTHONY, JD, PSYCHIC EXPLORER (aka the Psychic Lawyer), is the author of the spiritual bestsellers *Never Letting Go* and *Evidence of Eternity*.

Mark's credentials are unparalleled in the paranormal world. He's a world-renowned fourth-generation psychic medium who communicates with spirits. He is also an Oxford-educated trial lawyer who has tried hundreds of cases. He is licensed to practice law in Florida, in the District of Columbia, and before the United States Supreme Court.

As the Psychic Explorer, Mark travels the world examining supernatural phenomena at spiritual and mystical destinations. He is an expert in spirit communication, survival of consciousness, near-death experiences, ancient mysteries, and the paranormal. He has an extensive background in quantum physics, history, archaeology, philosophy, and theology. Plus, he's got a great sense of humor.

When the legal system and the paranormal collide, Mark is the media's "go-to guy." As a nationally recognized paranormal expert and legal analyst, he's commented on a wide range of legal-paranormal topics, such as solving cold cases, the use of DNA to identify Jack the Ripper, alleged demonic possession as a defense to murder, and how a haunted reputation in real estate affects property values.

Mark is regularly featured on ABC, NBC, CBS, FOX affiliates, Gaia TV, the Shift Network, and major talk radio shows, including *Coast to Coast AM* and *Darkness Radio*, as well as in print media worldwide.

Because of his credibility and accuracy as a psychic medium, Mark is featured by Gary E. Schwartz of the University of Arizona in his book *Human Interaction with the Divine, the Sacred, and the Deceased: Psychological, Scientific, and Theological Perspectives.*

Mark is the cohost of the livestream TV show *The Psychic & The Doc* on the Transformation Network and is a regular columnist for *Best Holistic Life* magazine. He is a headline speaker at conventions, expos, and spiritual organizations such as IANDS, Association for Research and Enlightenment (Edgar Cayce's ARE), Afterlife Research and Education Institute (AREI), Vail Symposium, Sedona Spirit Symposium, Osher Lifelong Learning Institute, and universities including Brown, Columbia, Harvard, and Yale.

Visit Mark online at www.AfterlifeFrequency.com.